D1480514

La Belle Dame sans Merci
& the Aesthetics of Romanticism

The Return of Tannhäuser to the Venusberg

La Belle Dame sans Merci
& the Aesthetics of Romanticism

by Barbara Fass

QUEENS COLLEGE
CITY UNIVERSITY OF NEW YORK

Wayne State University Press, Detroit 1974

Library of Congress Cataloging in Publication Data

Fass, Barbara, 1936–
   La belle dame sans merci and the aesthetics of romanticism.

   Bibliography: p.
   1. Literature, Modern—19th century—History and criticism.   2. Romanticism.   3. Literature, Comparative—Themes, motives.   I. Title.
PN751.F3   809'.933'75   73-8365
ISBN 0-8143-1509-7

To Linda & Steven

Contents

Contents

 *Preface*

In this book I have used the word *romantic* in a rather broad fashion. I do so with full awareness that the word is susceptible to many definitions, some of which are contradictory, and that there is some controversy over whether there exists continuity of thought in the nineteenth century, or whether one should distinguish among the ideas of clearly differentiated periods. Since change itself was one of the few constants in the nineteenth century, differences as well as similarities would have to be accounted for.

Whatever these differences are, one phenomenon came into being with romanticism (I make no attempt to date its beginning), and from it others followed. I refer to the emphasis on the individual, and with that the stress on imagination over reason; the subjective and relative over the objective; and the spontaneous over the ordered. The resultant inwardness experienced by the individual often placed him in conflict with the world in which he lived, and when the century experienced reactions against these premises, the ideas were nonetheless there to be reckoned with. Even as this book is being prepared for publication, the United States, together with a large part of the world, is witnessing a resurgence of romanticism as well as a backlash against the forces that undermine what the new romantics speak of as the "establishment." Many of the writers I will discuss in the following pages were both fascinated and repelled by romanticism, were drawn to what was beautiful in its productions and distrustful of its irrationalism, and were at one and the same time romantic and anti-romantic.

In any event, when I speak of *romantic*, these are the ideas with which I am primarily concerned. One outcome of romanticism became apparent very early and has persisted to this day: the writer began to question his very existence as artist as well as his responsibility to a world in which he was not comfortable. Such an artist, whether he wrote in 1800 or 1974, I would call the romantic artist.

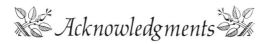Acknowledgments

For my understanding of the patterns inherent in the fairy mistress stories, I am particularly indebted to Charles R. Dahlberg, who first pointed out to me the *double entendre* in the words *sans merci*, and to Robert P. Miller, who has for years shared with me his knowledge of "loathly ladies." Joseph Raben first focused my attention on the social consciousness of the great romantic poets, and William E. Buckler taught me to realize the significance for my study of the Victorian dichotomy between Hebraism and Hellenism. Harry Levin read the manuscript when it included only English and German writers; I owe to his advice the later inclusions of French writers. Others who provided more invaluable aid than I can here describe when they read all or part of the manuscript are Mario D'Avanzo, Robert A. Greenberg, the late E. L. McAdam, Jr., Burton Pike, Murray Prosky, M. L. Rosenthal, Donald Stone, and Michael Timko.

Michael Kowal has my gratitude for the extreme care with which he compared translations from the German and French with their original texts. Hugo Kaufmann also helped me with German: once a classicist, now an economist, he seemed glad to deal once more with literature. I am particularly grateful to Peter B. Leavy for his extensive editorial assistance.

My father, Joel Widom, typed and proofread the manuscript in several of its stages. The help of my mother, Marion Widom, goes back a long time, when she taught me to read and introduced me to the fairyland that has held me in thrall these many years.

I wish also to acknowledge permission of the following to use copyrighted material:

W. W. Norton & Company, Inc., and Sidgwick & Jackson, Ltd., for Anthony Burgess, *The Eve of St. Venus* (1970).

Oxford University Press, for Jean Giraudoux, *Plays*, trans. Roger Gellert (1967), and Prosper Mérimée, *The Venus of Ille*, trans. Jean Kimber (1966).

Angel Flores, ed., *An Anthology of French Poetry from Nerval to Valery*, trans. Steven Stepanchev, Doubleday Publishing Co. (1962), for Charles Baudelaire, "La Beatrice."

Random House, Inc., Alfred A. Knopf, Inc., for Thomas Mann, *Royal Highness*, trans. A. Cecil Curtis (1939), and *Doctor Faustus* (1963) and *The Magic Mountain*, trans. H. T. Lowe-Porter (1964).

Geoffrey Wagner, ed., for *Selected Writings of Gérard de Nerval*, Grove Press, Inc. (1957).

T. Fisher Unwin and A. P. Watt & Son, for W. B. Yeats, *Poems* (1895), by permission of The Yeats Estate.

Macmillan Publishing Company, Inc., Mr. M. B. Yeats, the Macmillan Company of London & Basingstoke and the Macmillan Company of Canada Ltd. for lines from "Crazy Jane Talks with the Bishop," *Collected Poems*, © 1933 by Macmillan Publishing Co., Inc., renewed 1961 by Bertha Georgie Yeats; lines from "To the Rose upon the Rood of Time," and "The Stolen Child," *Collected Poems*, © 1906 by Macmillan Publishing Co., Inc., renewed 1934 by William Butler Yeats; lines from "The Two Kings," © 1916 by Macmillan Publishing Co., Inc., renewed 1944 by Bertha Georgie Yeats; lines from "All Souls' Night" and "Sailing to Byzantium," © 1928 by Macmillan Publishing Company, Inc., renewed 1956 by Georgie Yeats; selections from *Mythologies*, © Mrs. W. B. Yeats, 1959; *Essays and Introductions*, © Mrs. W. B. Yeats, 1961; *Explorations*, © Mrs. W. B. Yeats, 1962.

The Victorian Newsletter, New York University, for Barbara Fass, "William Morris and the Tannhäuser Legend: A Gloss on the Earthly Paradise Motif," Fall 1971.

Comparative Literature Studies, University of Illinois, for Barbara Fass, "The Little Mermaid and the Artist's Quest for a Soul," Sept. 1972.

Code for Citations in Text

Where a translation is cited, the original is indicated by italicized numbers. When italicized numbers appear alone, it means that the translation or paraphrase is my own. Only the primary authors treated in this book will have their original texts cited.

DF   Thomas Mann. *Doctor Faustus*. Trans. H. T. Lowe-Porter. New York: Alfred A. Knopf, 1963. *Gesammelte Werke*, vol. 6. Frankfurt: S. Fischer, 1960.

EW   Joseph von Eichendorff. "The Marble Statue." Trans. F. E. Pierce. *Fiction and Fantasy of German Romance: Selections from German Romantic Authors, 1790–1830*. Ed. F. E. Pierce and Carl F. Schreiber. New York: Oxford Univ. Press, 1927. *Werke und Schriften in vier Bänden*. Ed. Gerhart Baumann and Siegfried Grosse. Stuttgart: Cotta, 1957.

GN   *Selected Writings of Gérard de Nerval*. Trans. and ed. Geoffrey Wagner. New York: Grove Press, 1957. *Oeuvres*. Ed. Albert Béguin and Jean Richer. 2 vols. Paris: Pléiade, 1960–61.

HW   *The Works of Heinrich Heine*. Trans. and ed. Charles G. Leland. 20 vols. New York: Croscup and Sterling, ca. 1900. *Heinrich Heines Sämtliche Werke*. Ed. Ernst Elster. 7 vols. Leipzig: Bibliographisches Institut, 1890.

JG   Jean Giraudoux. *Plays: Amphitryon, Intermezzo, Ondine*. Trans. Roger Gellert. New York: Oxford Univ. Press, 1967. *Théatre*. 2 vols. Paris: Grasset, 1954.

KL   *The Letters of John Keats*. Ed. Hyder E. Rollins. 2 vols. Cambridge, Mass.: Harvard Univ. Press, 1958.

KP   *The Poetical Works of John Keats*. Ed. H. W. Garrod. 2d ed. Oxford: The Clarendon Press, 1958. *Lamia* will be cited according to part and line numbers.

LT   Ludwig Tieck. "The Runenberg." Trans. Thomas Carlyle. *Fiction and Fantasy of German Romance* (see EW). *Die Märchen aus dem Phantasus; Dramen*. Ed. Marianne Thalmann. Munich: Winkler, 1964.

MM   Thomas Mann. *The Magic Mountain*. Trans. H. T. Lowe-Porter. New York: Alfred A. Knopf, 1964. *Gesammelte Werke*, vol. 3 (see DF).

NB   John Davidson. *New Ballads*. London: John Lane, 1897.

SB   E. T. A. Hoffmann. "The Mines of Falun." Trans. Leonard J. Kent and Elizabeth C. Knight. *Selected Writings of E. T. A. Hoffmann*. Chicago: Univ. of Chicago Press, 1969. *Die Serapions-Brüder*. Munich: Winkler, 1963.

SP   *The Complete Works of Algernon Charles Swinburne*. Ed. Edmund Gosse and Thomas J. Wise. 20 vols. London: William Heinemann, 1925–27.

T   Richard Wagner. *Tannhäuser and the Tournament of Song at Wartburg: Romantic Opera in Three Acts*. Trans. and ed. Natalia Macfarren. New York: G. Schirmer, n.d. German and English texts on same page.

TLP   *The Works of Thomas Love Peacock*. Ed. H. F. Brett-Smith and C. E. Jones. 10 vols. London: Constable, 1924–34.

U   Friedrich de la Motte Fouqué, *Undine and Other Stories*. Trans. and ed. Edmund Gosse. London: Oxford World's Classics, n.d. *Undine*. Ed. W. Walker Chambers. London: Thomas Nelson, 1961.

VI   Prosper Mérimée, *The Venus of Ille and Other Stories*. Trans. Jean Kimber. London: Oxford Univ. Press, 1966. *Romans et Nouvelles*. Ed. Henri Martineau. Paris: Pléiade, ca. 1951.

VT   Aubrey Beardsley. *The Story of Venus and Tannhäuser*. London: Privately printed, 1907.

WM   William Morris. *Collected Works*. 24 vols. London: Longmans, Green, 1910–15.

WP   Richard Wagner. *Prose Works*. Trans. and ed. William Ashton Ellis. 8 vols.

London: Kegan Paul, Trench, Trübner, 1893–99. *Gesammelte Schriften und Dichtungen.* 10 vols. Leipzig: E. W. Fritzsch, 1888.

YCP   *The Collected Poems of W. B. Yeats.* New York: Macmillan, 1963.

YP   W. B. Yeats. *Poems.* London: T. Fisher Unwin, 1895.

Introduction

Ah, would that I had never been
The lover of the Fairy Queen!
Or would that through the sleepy town,
The grey old place of Ercildoune,
And all along the little street,
The soft fall of the white deer's feet
Came, with the mystical command
That I must back to Fairy Land! [1]

Many writers told a similar tale during the nineteenth
century. Keats called his *Lamia*, Yeats entitled his *The Wanderings
of Oisin*; in Germany their contemporaries E. T. A. Hoffman and
Hugo von Hofmannsthal each wrote on the legend of the mines at
Falun. The story of Tannhäuser was frequently recounted in both
England and Germany: William Morris's *The Hill of Venus* was the
concluding tale of *The Earthly Paradise*; Swinburne's *Laus Veneris*
was one of the most famous poems in the infamous *Poems and
Ballads* (first series). Thomas Mann, in the early twentieth century,
worked the Tannhäuser legend into *The Magic Mountain*, and in so
doing summarized virtually all of the ways it had been used in the
previous hundred years or so. Not long after, in France, Jean
Giraudoux dramatized Friedrich de la Motte Fouqué's *Undine
[Ondine]*, proving that even in the modern world these ancient stories
of humans in love with unearthly creatures have maintained their hold
on the imagination. How popular these tales have been is also evident
in the extensive scholarship devoted to their sources in folklore.

When Philip S. Barto published his study on the origins of the Tannhäuser legend, he noted that "so attractive a theme as the story of Tannhäuser and the Mountain of Venus has not failed, ever since its revival by the Romanticists, to arouse the attention of modern literary investigation, and numerous indeed have been the efforts made to explain its origin and its significance." [2] In the more than fifty years that have passed since Barto made this point, there has been no lessening of interest in the story. [3] But neither Barto nor other scholars have explained why a centuries-old motif suddenly acquired renewed significance for the romantic writer. Not only did individuals adapt the motif for frequently similar purposes but the variations in their treatment also make it possible to trace through these stories the major developments in nineteenth-century aesthetics.

One characteristic frequently associated with romanticism, especially by its unfriendly critics, is its "escapism," which can take many forms: the worship of pristine nature; a yearning for the Middle Ages; or a hedonistic indulgence in pleasure. A more encompassing generalization concerning romantic escapism is that the romantic artist seeks refuge in an imaginary world he has himself created, refuge from the pain or tedium of a mundane existence. Such imaginative flight is hardly peculiar to the romantics, and the earthly paradise motif can be traced back to very old sources. But in the nineteenth century two earlier trends were accelerated and provided ideological justification for escapism. First, a split occurred between ethics and aesthetics, resulting in an increasingly vehement proclamation of art's autonomy from rhetorical ends. Artistic technique itself eventually supplied a means of escape, a retreat into formalism popularly known as art for art's sake, whose background has been traced to Immanuel Kant's conception of artistic "purposiveness without purpose." [4] Second, a new theory of the artistic imagination grew out of German idealism, one which removed the barriers between the dream world of the artist and the so-called real world. In his study of Hoffmann, Harvey Hewett-Thayer notes that a

> philosophy that denies objective reality, that allows the individual to create his world, or rather maintains that he does and must create it, is obviously a boon to the dreamer. The world of dreams is just as real as the world of his sense perceptions, since he creates them both. Without hesitation

16

he can choose the world in which he prefers to live. To many of the Romanticists these philosophical theories provided a sanction for their dreaming, for their otherworldliness. But not to all.[5]

"But not to all." Here is a vital key to understanding much romantic literature as well as a means of refuting some of the criticism directed against it. The best romantic writers never forgot the distinction between the real and their dream world, and would agree with Keats's claim in the *Ode to a Nightingale* that "the fancy cannot cheat so well / As she is fam'd to do, deceiving elf" (KP 260). They worried about their escapist tendencies and theorized about art's role in society. Baudelaire argued in his essay on Wagner's *Tannhäuser* that "all great poets naturally and fatally become critics." [6] The artistic dilemmas of the romantics became the subject of their work, and they wrote not escapist poems so much as poems and stories *about* what it means to try to escape this world.

For such a self-conscious artist there existed a mythical figure whose story allowed him both to indulge his fancies and to express his conflicts. Borrowing from a French courtly love poem, Keats gave this figure what I will consider her generic name, La Belle Dame sans Merci. What she is actually called, however, is less important than the story in which she appears. For the moment I will supply a convenient example, *Tannhäuser*, which can be read as the myth of the romantic artist, telling as it does of a poet who leaves his own world for a supernatural abode whose splendors and pleasures reflect the outermost limits of the human imagination's capacity for sensuous description. But the story also depicts Tannhäuser's final dreariness in his dreamworld-come-true, and his longing to return to the earth and be absolved of guilt. For the Middle Ages, the legend's concern with the sins of the flesh and eternal damnation made its lesson applicable to all men (although the fact that Tannhäuser, like his legendary brothers, Thomas of Erceldoune and Oisin, is a poet suggests that the peculiar significance of the adventure for the writer was not lost on earlier ages). The romantic, looking back at an age when his position in relation to society was defined by the Horatian ideal of an art that taught as well as pleased, while in his own time many artists seemed to abandon social responsibility, found that the legend and its variants could suggest a special meaning. La Belle Dame sans Merci for him was not only the captivating figure of romance and folklore but also his own, highly ambiguous muse.

Lest the title of this book set up expectations that remain unfulfilled, Keats's place in it should be clarified. He is but one of many writers to be discussed, and the chapter on *Lamia* is in itself no more important than others, even those concerned with less renowned figures. Keats's genius, however, lies not only in the beauty of his verse but also in a vision and insight so profound that from the very beginning of romanticism he comprehended its peculiar dangers. And because his use of the Belle Dame sans Merci theme encompasses most of the crucial issues, and because he saw perhaps more clearly than any other author save Thomas Mann the potentialities of the motif, he will often be referred to. But his influence on other authors will be discussed only in some instances, whereas obvious connections may sometimes receive no notice. William Morris said that Keats's *La Belle Dame sans Merci* was a germinal poem for his own circle of Victorian poets.[7] This statement provides one source for a temptation to trace echoes of Keats's poem wherever such echoes can be found. But then I am equally tempted to follow a myriad of echoes and influences among the writers whose tales I will be analyzing, even at the risk of digression. I will resist such enticements, however, for this book is not primarily a study in sources. What has finally determined the cross-references is two-fold: either the influence of one writer on another aids my analysis of the latter's work, or the comparison has an interest and freshness that makes it worth noting. There is little new in claiming that Keats affected Morris's verse.[8] Less commonplace is a comparison of Keats to Thomas Mann, with whom he shares many themes. In any event, it will never be my intention to prove influence for its own sake, especially since any emphasis on sources would detract from my thesis: that the romantic writer could independently perceive in the Belle Dame sans Merci story an ideal expression of his plight regarding the dichotomy between art and life.

That Keats borrowed from Alain Chartier the title of his ballad suggests a French tradition that may appear slighted by my discussion of only three French writers. The explanation is both simple and complicated. A complex problem would arise from an attempt to explain how French romanticism differs from English and German. Even if such a feat could be accomplished briefly, and it cannot be, my intention would remain highly speculative: to prove that this difference accounts for what is actually a simple answer to the apparent underrepresentation of French writers. Where the major English and German writers of the nineteenth century eagerly took up the Belle Dame sans Merci story, their French contemporaries seemed relatively uninterested in the tale. The examples to choose from are few, and it is noteworthy that both Gérard de Nerval and Jean Giraudoux were strongly influenced by German culture.[9] When Giraudoux wrote his dramatic adaptation of *Undine*, he was treating a popular German story whose source is the medieval French legend of Mélusine.[10] And while Mélusine was not neglected by French scholars in the nineteenth century, she was hardly a favorite subject among poets or novelists. Gérard de Nerval's oblique reference to "Lusignan" as well as his reference to a "fée" in *Los Desdichados* (GN 1:3) are rare allusions to her story in the literature of nineteenth-century France. It is known, furthermore, that the fairy he had in mind is Mélusine only because of a note he made in a manuscript; the poem itself by no means makes it clear, and, in addition, it is believed that Nerval was indebted to Heine for his conception of Mélusine.[11] The German writer not only treated her legend but expressed his contempt for women by congratulating Lusignan for having a mistress who was only half serpent. Nerval, however, wrote nothing so memorable about the fairy, and Mélusine remains a minor if not insignificant figure in his writing. Far more central to his fantasy world is Jenny Colon, the *femme fatale* more readily comparable to Alain Chartier's Belle Dame sans merci[12] than she is to the serpentine enchantress of French legend.

The distinction between La Belle Dame sans Merci and the *femme fatale* is a crucial one obscured by those who use the terms as though they were synonymous. Mario Praz is an important influence in his *Romantic Agony*, where he quotes Keats's ballad but then discusses literary figures who may be more accurately deemed perverse descendants of Chartier's heroine.[13] How the latter differs from Keats's fairy is a matter that needs to be established.

Although the French romantics paid scant attention to the type of fairy endowed by Keats with the name of Chartier's Belle Dame sans merci, the fairy has a well-established lineage in French medieval literature. She appears in the *Lais* of Marie de France, where Guigemar and Lanval (similar to the hero of the anonymous Breton

19

Lai de Graëlent) meet and dwell with supernatural mistresses who seem, if strange, nevertheless benign.[14] More cruel is the woman Chrétien de Troyes calls a "pucele sanz merci," Orguelleuse de Logres,[15] who, in the *Contes del Graal*, mistreats Gawain and is the subject of a warning to the knight in a scene comparable to the dream sequence in Keats's ballad. Like Laudine in *Yvain*, Orguelleuse is mortal, but her origins have been traced to the fairy mistresses of Celtic myth, and she thus remains in that tradition,[16] of which the most renowned fairy is Morgain la Fée, whose many guises are described by Roger Sherman Loomis. He points to "the gross inconsistency between the legends which painted the fay as a lustful, treacherous woman and those which portrayed her as charming and faithful." [17] She can be either "the faery mistress or the tender foster mother or the malevolent sorceress or the efficient leach or the great queen." [18] Whether or not she is evil, is "sans merci," thus depends on the particular tale in which she appears. Much will be made of this ambiguity by romantic writers not certain whether their muse is a demon or an agent of divine inspiration.

During the Renaissance the fairy is best recognized not in French but in Italian literature, appearing as Armida in Tasso's *Jerusalem Delivered* and Alcina in Ariosto's *Orlando Furioso*. The influence of both as well as that of other enchantresses from Celtic and classical mythology produced Acrasia, the temptress of Spenser's Bower of Bliss.[19] After the Renaissance, however, La Belle Dame sans Merci virtually disappeared from major literature where she had heretofore made her home, to return, as Barto noted, in the romantic age. How she traveled from France to Italy to England is not the concern of this book. Nor, indeed, will I attempt to trace an accurate itinerary or even an ancestry for this fairy who also lent herself to Homer's characterization of Calypso, Circe, and the Sirens, and who took mortal form to appear in *The Aeneid* as Dido. For now the two points being stressed are: first, that Keats's fairy does have a distinguished past in French medieval literature; second, that once she left France, she apparently surrendered her substantial hold on the French imagination, which preferred to concentrate on one of her distant relatives, the *femme fatale*.

None of the enchantresses mentioned above bears strict resemblance to Alain Chartier's Belle Dame sans merci, the subject of a typical courtly love poem. In love with a mortal and not a supernatural lady, her would-be lover pines as does Keats's knight, not because of his strange experience but because the object of his passion will not be his. Chartier's Belle Dame sans merci differs from other such ladies of medieval literature only to the degree of her independence and forthrightness. Indeed, she is hardly a *femme fatale* at all and can only be called such because of her suitor's anguish. But his distress, the reader is led to suspect, is a romantic agony largely self-induced.[20]

The typical beloved of the medieval courtly knight, like the Celtic fairy with whom she shares certain qualities,[21] enthralls him by a combination of beauty and imperiousness, inflaming his passions without granting him ease. Chaucer, influenced by the French tradition, may have described this commonplace situation in *Merciles Beaute*, a short lyric poem whose very title is a noteworthy variation of La Belle Dame sans Merci:

> Allas! that Nature hath in you compassed
> So great beautee, that no man may atteyne
> To mercy, though he sterve for the peyne.
> So hath your beautee fro your herte chaced
> Pitee, that me ne availeth not to pleyne.[22]

Sometimes the lady submits, only to prove unfaithful. In *Against Women Unconstant* her lover is pictured as the victim of her wiles:

> Madame, for your newefangelnesse,
> Many a servaunt have ye put out of grace.[23]

To such a lady may the *femmes fatales* of French fiction, the Manon Lescauts and Carmens, owe their ancestry.[24] More overtly sensual and cruel than her medieval models, one of these perverse descendants appears in Baudelaire's ironic *La Béatrice* as both the parody and counterpart of idealized woman (another strain in the courtly tradition). In this poem the speaker finds his Beatrice not in paradise but in an inferno where he envisions himself mocked by demons. He could have resisted them had his "lady" not taken part in his torture:

I would have turned my sovereign head aside
(My pride could dominate, as from a mountaintop,
That cloud of demons and their disturbing cries)
Had I not seen among that obscene troop—
Ah, crime that strangely did not stagger the sun!—
The empress of my heart, with crystal eyes,
Who, laughing with them, mocked my black distress
And pitched them, now and then, a lewd caress.[25]

Baudelaire's conception of the *femme fatale* evokes another motif popular in France during the nineteenth century, the demon mistress (for example, the vampire). But the gothic tale belongs to another tradition, one with which this book is not concerned.[26]

La Belle Dame sans Merci of ancient lore developed, then, into differentiable types. In her original form she remains the fairy who exercises an uncanny power over the mortal who succumbs to her charms. In mortal form, she becomes the *femme fatale*, the unattainable temptress who keeps her admirer in a perpetual state of longing, or the frequently faithless partner of a destructive love affair. La Belle Dame sans Merci and the *femme fatale* have much in common, especially when judged by their influence over their lovers, and the stories in which they appear often follow similar patterns (compare, for example, *Jerusalem Delivered* and the *Histoire du Chevalier des Grieux et de Manon Lescaut*, both of which involve men who risk or surrender their integrity because of deep infatuations for eventually repentant mistresses). But the two kinds of temptresses must be distinguished, for there is a fundamental difference in what each offers. The *femme fatale* promises pleasure, specifically sexual in nature; La Belle Dame sans Merci, while offering the same pleasure, also dwells in a land that embodies human dreams of physical perfection and immortality. For the romantic writer it was often the elfin grotto itself that endowed La Belle Dame sans Merci with her compelling attractiveness.

What a book omits is almost as significant a part of its conception as what it includes. In the folklore of the world, La Belle Dame sans Merci is ubiquitous, and it is impossible to afford her comprehensive treatment in a single book. It would be particularly impossible in light of my thesis that the Belle Dame sans Merci story is an allegory for the romantic writer. For example, the Japanese *Legend of Urashima* tells of a fisherman who dwells in the otherworld, tires of it, and returns to a world that no longer has a place for him. Can this oriental Tannhäuser in any way symbolize the modern Japanese writer, and does he take some form in his work? [27] I cannot begin to speculate. But there are some areas about which I can be expected to have knowledge and in which possibly glaring omissions warrant explanation.

The writer whose absence may be most significant is Tennyson. Clyde de L. Ryals has convincingly demonstrated the influence of Keats's *La Belle Dame sans Merci* on Tennyson's early verse.[28] That I did not wish merely to repeat what he had written is not my only reason for Tennyson's exclusion. I have long been convinced that the symbol in his poetry that comes closest to what La Belle Dame sans Merci represents to Keats, for example, is the Grail. For Tennyson, the ascetic could easily stand in for the aesthete; and King Arthur's lament in *The Idylls of the King* may without difficulty be read as a reproach to the artist who dwells in a Palace of Art:

> Was I too dark a prophet when I said
> To those who went upon the Holy Quest,
> That most of them would follow wandering fires,
> Lost in the quagmire?—lost to me and gone,
> And left me gazing at a barren board,
> And a lean Order—scarce return'd a tithe—
> And out of those to whom the vision came
> My greatest hardly will believe he saw;
> Another hath beheld it afar off,
> And leaving human wrongs to right themselves,
> Cares but to pass into the silent life.[29]

About the time I began to think of the Merlin and Vivien episode in the *Idylls* and the relationship it might have to my reading of the Grail material, I discovered that Fred Kaplan, who was as concerned as I with the theme of Merlin as artist,[30] had already treated this episode. After reading his exposition, I was satisfied that I could refer my own reader to it and have since felt less need to readjust my thinking about Tennyson, who, again, I associate more with the Grail than La Belle Dame sans Merci.

The omission of American writers perhaps needs a more detailed explanation. Although La Belle Dame sans Merci has not lacked for attention in the United States by such literary figures as Hawthorne and Poe, influenced by English and continental sources, yet their stories either relate to themes outside of my study or depart significantly from their European sources. Poe's *Ligeia* could be profitably analyzed in the light of his review of Fouqué's *Undine*; but I have already noted that the gothic tradition to which Poe's tale belongs is only tangentially associated with the Belle Dame sans Merci story. Similarly, when a critic suggested that the Mélusine legend provided the source for Oliver Wendell Holmes's *Elsie Venner*, Holmes replied that he knew nothing of this fairy when he wrote his novel, although he was familiar with Keats's *Lamia*. His intention was to test the doctrine of original sin, and thus his "poor heroine found her origin, not in fable or romance, but in a physiological conception fertilized by a theological dogma." [31] The same theological issue seems to apply to *Rappaccini's Daughter*, because Hawthorne's tale, according to Hyatt H. Waggoner, "concerns the origin, the nature, and the cure of man's radically mixed, his good-and-evil being." [32] It is this Puritan context that characterizes and sets apart American versions of the Belle Dame sans Merci theme. Not that Puritanism is unrelated to my study; indeed, a section of it will treat Philistinism as an offshoot of what is popularly known as the Protestant ethic. But the American themes of sin, guilt, and repression lead in another direction from mine, although I would welcome a modern study of the connection between Puritanism and romanticism.[33]

Hawthorne would supply important material for such a work. *Rappaccini's Daughter* is prefaced by remarks in which the author claims to be translating the works of one M. de Aubepine. This invented personage is described as holding an "unfortunate position between the Transcendentalists" (which according to Hawthorne's ensuing description seems to be his term for aesthetes) and those who command a popular audience. Hawthorne distinguishes among three forms of Aubepine's writings, classifying them as historical, contemporary, and entirely remote from the concerns of the world.[34] Thus, *Rappaccini's Daughter* is provided with a frame that points to

Hawthorne's particular awareness of the artist's uncertain role in society. In addition, the famous introductory essay to *The Old Manse* describes the dwelling in terms that qualify it as a Palace of Art: "Certainly it had little in common with those ordinary abodes which stand so imminent upon the road that every passer-by can thrust his head, as it were, into the domestic circle." [35] But its previous inhabitants were clergymen, not writers, and the moral purpose of their work only arouses the author's guilt: "I took shame to myself for having been so long a writer of idle stories, and ventured to hope that wisdom would descend upon me. . . . Profound treatises of morality . . . these were the works that might fitly have flowed from such a retirement." [36] Was Rappaccini's poisonous garden the realm of art, and the "Belle Empoisonneuse," Beatrice, to be understood in terms of aesthetics as well as theology? If so, aesthetics in this instance would have to be studied against the specific background of American Puritanism. Rather than make a feeble beginning or hopelessly tangle my own themes, I reluctantly chose to omit the material altogether.

One American writer whose treatment of La Belle Dame sans Merci seems to demand comparison to the European tradition is James Branch Cabell. A strange writer with an uncertain reputation,[37] he did not seem important enough to warrant a study of the eighteen volumes he considered part of a single work,[38] although their recent publication as paperbacks may eventually lead to a revival of interest in his fiction. For Henry James, I cannot make similar claims about the obscurity of the author. *The Last of the Valerii* is a notable version of a story related by Burton in his *Anatomy of Melancholy* and told or adapted by William Morris, Thomas Hardy, Anthony Burgess, Joseph von Eichendorff, and Prosper Mérimée, among others. Because James is concerned with European culture and the aesthetic theme predominates in *The Last of the Valerii*, his short story seems to belong with its European analogues. But a full understanding of the story hinges on a contrast between two worlds, Europe and America. Having chosen to exclude the latter from my book, I can only afford James's work passing mention, hoping, nevertheless, that I have provided the background necessary for a study of La Belle Dame sans Merci in American literature.

To the earlier comments about the method and how I arrived at decisions concerning cross-references, I should add a brief statement about my use of translations from French and German texts.

One of the great advantages of myth, with which I am here dealing, is that it speaks a language of its own, largely independent of the particular tongue through which it is expressed. Attention will be focused on the manipulation of basic patterns, whether by John Keats, Gérard de Nerval, or Thomas Mann. This is not to say that I consider words themselves unimportant, for it would be preposterous to believe that great writers failed to employ language to treat uniquely the motifs they handled in common with others. But rarely will I be concerned with a close textual matter, and therefore I think it unnecessary to quote the original. I can, however, assure the reader that no translator's turn of phrase has been responsible for an interpretation not borne out by the text itself. English translations were chosen because they were either the latest or the most accessible, and not because of aesthetic distinctions, for the same reason that translations were deemed adequate in the first place. For those fluent only in English, I am pleased that translators have made these beautiful stories of La Belle Dame sans Merci available. For those who read the original, I will feel gratified if my study provides an understanding that makes more fully realizable the artist's range of connotation and innuendo as he relates tales that have proved as enthralling to the audience as the ambiguous fairy did to her artist-lover.

1
SEDUCTRESS or PENITENT:
The Symbolic Otherworld

There are two basic strands in the Belle Dame sans Merci story, and they are significantly different. Although rarely combined, when they are, a noteworthy ambiguity is revealed, which is obscured when only one side of the story is developed. An example will focus attention on their subsequent divergence.

In the fifteenth century, Antoine de la Sale told a story about a German knight's travels in Italy and his visit to the Sibyl's mountain, where there exists a magnificent habitat with beautiful women devoted to the pleasures of their male companions.[1] The knight joins their company but is alarmed by a mysterious weekly event during which the ladies seclude themselves and assume the forms of serpents and other monsters. The transformation alerts the knight to their evil nature, and, his piety aroused, he leaves the mountain for Rome, where he can receive absolution for his sins.

The two strands lead, on one side, to the hero, who leaves the world to experience sensuous and sensual joy in a magic realm, and, on the other, to a mysterious power exercised over the women of this realm, as if they were undergoing some punishment. This duality points to a significant double entendre in the very words *belle dame sans merci*, which can signify the fairy's lack of pity for the mortal she lures from the world, or her own deprivation, since she exists without the hope of divine grace. The demonic creature who is excluded from God's mercy is herself to be pitied. Whether or not Keats was aware of this linguistic ambiguity, he makes use of the concept involved—when he asks whether his Lamia is the demon's self or some penanced lady elf—by the very fact of providing alternatives (KP 1:55–56). The matter is left up in the air, making *Lamia* difficult to interpret. Keats did know, however, about two distinct groups of tales, one depicting the fatal seduction of a mortal, the other portraying the suffering of the enchantress. More important, he recognized the difference between the thematic strands and how they could be merged to produce ambiguity. His insight makes it possible to recognize the crucial elements of stories in which La Belle Dame sans Merci appears.

Antoine de la Sale's story is clearly an analogue to the Tannhäuser legend.[2] According to the version included by L. Achim von Arnim and Clemens Brentano in *Des Knaben Wunderhorn*,[3] Tannhäuser has lived with Venus for a year when he is seized with a desire to return to earth. A dialogue with the goddess depicts her futile attempts to hold her lover (in other versions of the legend, the knight invokes the name of the Virgin Mary, making Venus powerless to restrain him). He seeks forgiveness in Rome, but the Pope is appalled to learn of his sojourn in the Venusberg. Instead of offering absolution, he holds out his wooden staff, announcing to Tannhäuser that his sins will be remitted only when the staff bears flowers. Sad and hopeless, Tannhäuser returns to a joyfully receptive Venus. When, three days later, the Pope's staff miraculously blooms, messengers sent out to find the knight can discover no trace of him, for Tannhäuser must remain with Venus until Judgment Day.[4]

The flowering of the staff may take its significance from a historical context, being read as a sign of German Protestant anticlericalism, an assertion that the Roman priesthood is working contrary to the will of God. But it can also be read symbolically as the triumph of the Dionysian element in paganism over Christian austerity—in short, as a sanction of erotic passion. For this reason the Tannhäuser legend would be useful for a condemnation of institutional restraints and is so interpreted by recent critics of Swinburne's *Laus Veneris*. A similar opposition to established religion can be found in the Irish story of Connla the Fair, son of a high king of Ireland. He is approached one day by a woman from Mag Mell, the Land of the Living, where there is "neither death nor want nor sin," but only "perpetual feast" and "peace . . . without strife." [5] Connla's father summons a Druid to banish this creature who would steal his son, and she is constrained to leave. As she does, she gives Connla an apple, which, however much he eats, is never consumed. (Traditionally, he who eats the food of the fairies must dwell with them.) And when she returns, the Druids are helpless to restrain Connla, although he does not leave without a sorrowful backward glance: "It is not easy for me. Although I love my people, longing for the woman has seized me."[6] The story has an interesting touch in the fairy's prophecy that the Druids will be forced to surrender their power to St. Patrick.

The saint himself is found in the story of Oisin's travels in the Land of the Living. In its earliest extant version, written by the eighteenth-century Gaelic poet Michael Comyn, St. Patrick is merely a structural device for eliciting from Oisin the narrative of his sojourn with the fairy Niamh.[7] But when Yeats adapted Comyn's material for his *Wanderings of Oisin*, he made St. Patrick an ideological opponent of the fairy, thus giving him a role similar to the Pope's in *Tannhäuser*.[8] In both the Irish and German stories, the heroes spend some time in fairyland, tire of it, and return to a world where they cannot be reconciled to hostile Christian forces.

In the three stories, *Tannhäuser*, *Connla*, and *Oisin*, the common factor is a triad consisting of the hero, a supernatural woman, and a religious figure intent on combating her power. The story of the Greek student seduced by Lamia has a philosopher, Apollonius Tyanaeus, assuming the third role. Robert Burton included this tale in the *Anatomy of Melancholy* (where Keats found it), telling how Lycius lived with a phantasm in her home in Corinth, and how he at last married her. To her wedding

> amongst other guests, came Apollonius; who, by some probable conjectures, found her out to be a serpent, a lamia; and that all her furniture was, like Tantalus' gold, described by Homer, no substance but mere illusions. When she saw herself descried, she wept, and desired Apollonius to be silent, but he would not be moved, and thereupon she, plate, house, and all that was in it, vanished in an instant.[9]

Lamia has no recourse against the penetrating intellect of Apollonius. That philosophers have this ability to exorcise demonic power is also revealed in the *Gesta Romanorum*, where it is told how the Queen of the North "nourished her daughter from the cradle upon a certain kind of deadly poison" so that when she grew up, she could wed and destroy Alexander. Aristotle, recognizing his pupil's dangerous infatuation for the beautiful girl, warns that Alexander will perish if he touches her. His contention is proved when a condemned prisoner is forced to kiss the girl, who is then sent posthaste back to her mother.[10] When Nathaniel Hawthorne related a similar event in *Rappaccini's Daughter*, he obviously saw its relation to the Lamia myth, for he drew on Keats's poem and endowed his poison-transmitting heroine with ambiguously pathetic characteristics.[11]

In another analogue to *Lamia*, about the ring given to Venus, the figure who exorcises the power of the temptress pays for his meddling by being torn to pieces. The hero of the Venusring story unwittingly pledges himself to the goddess when he places his wedding ring on her statue during the athletic games played to celebrate his marriage. Later he cannot retrieve the ring from the statue; still worse, Venus comes between him and his bride at night, claiming him for herself and preventing the consummation of his union. In desperation he seeks the help of a magician and priest who is skilled in combating the older, demonic pagan forces.[12] This story is frequently compared to *Tannhäuser* because each involves the goddess Venus. Early Christian proselytizers did not try to prove that pagan deities were mere fictions; instead they relegated the local gods to the rank of demons and banished them to appropriate realms. The Venusberg is commonly associated with hell.

A crucial fourth figure makes an appearance in the Venusring story, the mortal wife of the hero enthralled by La Belle Dame sans Merci. Playing a minor role in this tale, in others she assumes a more important function.

The fourteenth-century Middle High German romance of *Peter von Staufenberg* hints at this significant conflict between the mortal woman and the fairy. The tale concerns a distinguished knight, who, on his way to church one day, meets a beautiful woman sitting by the roadside. Immediately struck by her beauty, he falls in love with her and gains her for his mistress. But she warns him that if he ever marries, he will die on the third day after the wedding.[13] Staufenberg remains faithful until he succumbs to the pressures of family and priests and weds a mortal. The fairy's prophecy is fulfilled.[14]

When a fairy is the rival of a mortal wife or sweetheart, she almost invariably loses the contest. Even Staufenberg's fairy mistress enjoys a dubious triumph, since his death proves not only his wife's loss but hers as well. An interesting twist to this struggle can be found in the French romance, *Ogier the Dane*.[15] At birth, Ogier receives gifts from a succession of fairies; the last one, Morgain la Fée, promises that one day he shall dwell at her side in Avalon. Ogier lives a full, heroic life, during which he marries and has a family; in old age, his youth and vigor are restored by Morgain, who comes for him as pledged. Later, when the world again needs his prowess in battle, she returns him to fight against the pagans, using her magic powers to make him forget Avalon. But as he is about to wed a mortal queen, Morgain comes to reclaim Ogier, who gladly returns with her to the otherworld. The significance of this tale, in contrast to others, is that Ogier fulfills his duty to the mortal world not just once but twice; his abode in Avalon may be looked upon, then, as his reward and not the place to which he escapes from worldly care. It is perhaps for this reason that Morgain la Fée can tempt him away from his intended bride without his experiencing the doubts of a Connla, who casts a longing eye at those he leaves behind.

The stories summarized above reveal a triadic structure, consisting of the hero, the fairy, and a third figure, either a cleric, a philosopher, or a mortal woman. Occasionally, however, the action is confined to the hero and the fairy, as in the folk ballad *Thomas Rhymer*.[16] Thomas dwells with the Queen of Elfland for seven years (a common number for such a sojourn). Why or how he is released is not explained, nor is his stay in the otherworld described. But the one detail in the story which deserves special notice is that when Thomas first beholds the Elf Queen, he hails her as the Virgin Mary, to which she replies,

> O no, O no, Thomas, she said,
>   That name does not belang to me;
> I am but the queen of fair Elfland,
>   That am hither come to visit thee.[17]

In some versions of *Tannhäuser*, the German knight is released from the Venusberg only after he invokes the Virgin's name. Since Elfland was likened to hell by the medieval mind, its queen was an evil counterpart to the Virgin Mary, Queen of Heaven. The hero's error lies in confusing the two.

This perceptual error receives different but perhaps related treatment in the romance of *Thomas of Erceldoune*.[18] After sexual intercourse with Thomas, his fairy mistress is transformed into an ugly hag. The metamorphosis clearly allies La Belle Dame sans Merci to the loathly ladies of such works as Chaucer's *The Wife of Bath's Tale*.[19] In both the ballad and romance, Thomas's perception of reality remains in question. Similarly, in Keats's *La Belle Dame sans Merci*, the knight's attraction to the fairy is undermined by figures in a dream who might be her past victims or merely a projection of his own doubts. The relationship of beauty to truth is at issue in these works, where the hero either mistakes the identity of the fairy or watches her metamorphosis into a loathsome, evil creature. Indeed, the pattern of the story which confines the action to the hero and his seductress more easily lends itself to psychological analysis than do those patterns in which a third figure reflects part of the internalized concerns of the mortal seduced by La Belle Dame sans Merci. In one case the focus is on his interior struggle and not, as in the other, on a battle waged over him. Such a battle, of course, may dramatize the inner conflict, but its expressive form will differ.

The loathly lady motif in these stories links the Tannhäuser legend and its analogues to the other group of tales about La Belle Dame sans Merci, those emphasizing an enchantment, perhaps as punishment, inflicted on the fairy herself. For such loathly creatures are obviously related to the beautiful women transformed into serpents in Antoine de la Sale's tale. And just as one side of his work points to the German Tannhäuser story, so does the other lead to the famous French legend of Mélusine. As punishment for a transgression against her father, Mélusine's fairy mother enchants her daughter, who must assume one day each week the partial shape of a serpent (in illustrations she usually appears to be a mermaid). If she weds a man who will agree not to spy on her during her weekly seclusion, who will, in short, never learn her secret, she can gain an immortal soul. Mélusine does marry a human, but the children born to them are so monstrous or deformed that his suspicions are aroused and he breaks his promise. Brokenhearted by this betrayal, Mélusine flies out of her home in the form of a fifteen-foot serpent, shrieking horribly.[20]

Paracelsus, in his treatise on nature spirits, compares Mélusine to the mistress of Peter von Staufenberg, because both fairies were betrayed by their men. Paracelsus's defense of Staufenberg's fairy and his condemnation of Mélusine, who he claims was (despite her supernatural origins and weekly transformations) a Catholic are amusing. Her lot, he says, was to be victimized by her church's superstitions, and he warns others who belong to her faith that they too will end as serpents.[21] Although generally unmoved by Mélusine's quest for an immortal soul, Paracelsus nevertheless provides a crucial interpretation of those enchantresses who are themselves "sans merci." Describing the spirits believed to inhabit nature, he explains their desire for human lovers:

> You must understand this in the following way: God has created them so much like man and so resembling him, that nothing could be more alike, and a wonder happened in that they had no soul. But when they enter into a union with man, then the union gives the soul. It is the same as with the union that man has with God and God with man, a union established by God, which makes it possible for us to enter the kingdom of God. If there were no such union, of what use would the soul be to us? Of none. But now there is that union with man, and therefore the soul is of use to man, who otherwise would have no purpose. This is demonstrated by them also: they have no soul, unless they enter into a union with men, and now they have the soul. . . . From this it follows that they woo man, and that they seek him assiduously and in secret. A heathen begs for baptism and woos it in order to acquire his soul and to become alive in Christ. In the same way, they seek love with man, so as to be in union with men.[22]

Among the spirits seeking such a union is the undine, or water spirit.[23]

Combining the stories of Mélusine and Peter von Staufenberg, and adopting the ideas and generic name he found in Paracelsus's treatise, the nineteenth-century writer Friedrich de la Motte Fouqué created *Undine*.[24] In it a German knight, Huldbrand, setting out on perilous adventures in order to impress the lady Bertalda, finds himself stranded at a fisherman's home on a lonely strip of land attached to a mysterious forest. The fisherman has a beautiful, capricious daughter named Undine, and Huldbrand, falling in love with her, marries her despite his suspicions concerning her essence—suspicions that turn to revulsion when she admits her supernatural origin. Her father, the King of the Sea, sent her to land to wed a mortal and thus win a soul. The water spirits live very long, happy lives; but when they die, they merely combine with their natural element, water. Her marriage to Huldbrand will shorten her earthly existence, but she will gain everlasting salvation. If her husband, however, reproaches her for any misdeed while they are near water, she will have to return to the sea.

So long as they dwell in the fisherman's cottage, Undine and Huldbrand are happy; but when they return to his home, his instinctive revulsion and renewed attraction to Bertalda combine to thwart Undine's quest. She and Bertalda become engaged in a conflict that Undine inevitably loses when her husband breaks his promise and Undine must return to the sea. Huldbrand prepares to marry Bertalda, but on his wedding day the sorrowful Undine appears before him, and as she enfolds him in a loving embrace, he dies. Like Mélusine, Undine is betrayed by her husband; like the fairy mistress of Peter von Staufenberg, she kills the man who faithlessly prepares to marry a mortal.[25]

Hans Christian Andersen's *The Little Mermaid*, based on Fouqué's novella, relates a similar quest for an immortal soul, but with a significantly new note added to the story. For Undine, marriage to a mortal was the means to an end, the gaining of a soul; in contrast, the Little Mermaid has fallen in love with human beings and their world, and in her underseas garden she lovingly tends the statue of a boy salvaged from a wrecked ship. When, on her fifteenth birthday, she is allowed to surface above the water, she rescues the drowning prince of a nearby land. Yearning after him, she sells her beautiful voice to a sea witch in order to obtain a pair of legs. Despite the physical agony that each step causes her, she seeks her prince, marriage to whom will also mean her gaining a soul. But if he should marry another, she will turn to foam on the crest of a wave. When the Prince betrays her, the Little Mermaid denies herself a final chance to save her own life by taking his. Unable to follow in the footsteps of Undine, she throws herself into the sea. As a reward for this self-sacrifice, she is allowed to exist in a kind of purgatory, with the ultimate promise of a soul. This sentimental ending should not deceive the reader into underestimating the Little Mermaid's appeal. Andersen's tale was one of Thomas Mann's favorites, and it plays a significant role in *Doctor Faustus*.

The mermaid's failure to achieve salvation through union with a mortal[26] is also experienced by the Lady of the Land, whose story is related in Mandeville's *Travels*. A young man is wrecked upon strange shores where he finds a captive woman awaiting rescue. Each night she is transformed into a horrible monster with a serpentine tail and menaces the countryside. If the young man will kiss her three times during her metamorphosis, she will be disenchanted and they will live happily together. He manages the kiss twice, but with each she becomes more ferocious, and he cannot summon the courage for the third. Without gaining the promised happiness, he leaves her realm, and she must retain her beastly shape until a braver man appears.[27] In this story, less popular than the mermaid's, the attention has been shifted from La Belle Dame sans Merci to the hero who disappoints her. The Lady of the Land thus points up another significant difference between the Tannhäuser and Mélusine legends. In the first, the mortal is victimized by an enchantress who has destroyed his ties to the world without herself being able to fulfill his needs. In the latter, it is he who has failed and denied her the salvation she seeks through union with him. How this distinction between the motifs can be associated with the romantic's perplexing relation to the world he lives in will be clearer if the various components of the Belle Dame sans Merci stories are viewed in the context of his quest for symbols that might express his deeply felt ambivalence toward art.

Of primary importance is the nature of the otherworld itself, a land of dreams-come-true, where man is forever young and pleasures forever available. It is a static realm, lacking the earthly cycles of birth and death, a point worth stressing, for if the otherworld is, as the Irish put it, the Land of the Living, that is, a world in which no one dies, it also appears that it is a world in which no one is born. In literary (as compared with folk) treatments of the fairies La Belle Dame sans Merci rarely has children; she is ultimately sterile. Yeats altered his source for *The Wanderings of Oisin* and made no mention of the children born to Niamh and her mortal lover. In the rare case of Mélusine, who is a mother, it is her children's deformity that leads to her betrayal by her husband. The point is that La Belle Dame sans Merci and the land in which she dwells are not creative. What they supply instead is perpetual bliss, and bliss, when it is its own end, inevitably palls.

35

In the ancient stories, the fairy's domain could be found in a cave under the earth, in the heart of a mountain, under the sea, or on an island. Although its specific locus is of interest chiefly to folklorists, location can frequently provide symbolic meaning to the writer. H. R. Patch, studying the allegorical use of the otherworld in medieval literature, claims that the "underground realms of fairy lore do not explain the mountain foundations of Otherworld scenes," which "seem to be the product of a different sort of fancy or vision." [28] He notes that the figure of the mountain "is employed to express the meaning of inaccessibility—whether to love or to fortune—the difficulties of approach, and the perils of success." [29] For the romantic, this inaccessibility could define what the Germans call *Sehnsucht*, the vague longing for pure spirit.[30] The mountain's height itself points to remoteness from the world and hence a place of escape. Both Ludwig Tieck and Thomas Mann distinguish between the mountain and the flatlands, using this differentiation to contrast fantasy and reality, escape from the world and commitment to duty. Then there is the cave, which, whatever other implications it may have for Freudians, can symbolize man's descent into his own consciousness, the exploration of his own imagination. Such inwardness can of course represent as much a source of retreat as does a longing for inaccessible regions. Indeed, as Coleridge's "caverns measureless to man" suggest, the cave and mountain have analogous associations.

Whereas the physical location of the otherworld may have symbolic value, more important than geography is the supernatural realm's potentiality for sensuous description, limited only by the artist's abilities. For the otherworld is not only the object of the poetic imagination but the very symbol for that imagination as well. As Heine says in his *Elementary Spirits*,

> in the fairy land, Avalon, the unfortunate knights find their ladyloves once more, and there Count Lanval and Gruelan may gossip about them to their heart's content. Here, too, Ogier the Dane rests happily from his heroic deeds in the arms of his Morgana. Ye French know all these stories. Ye know Avalon, but the Persians know it too, and call it Djinnistan. It is the land of poetry. [HW 11:129; 4:388]

"Es ist das Land der Poesie." Does Heine mean that fairyland is the place where poetry is born or that it is the place about which poetry is written? Probably he means both.

For Paracelsus, the supernatural realm was the proper subject of literature.

> There is more bliss in describing the nymphs than in describing medals. There is more bliss in describing the origin of the giants than in describing court etiquettes. There is more bliss in describing Melusine than in describing cavalry and artillery. There is more bliss in describing the mountain people underground than in describing fencing and service to ladies. For in these things the spirit is used to move in divine works, while in the other things the spirit is used to seek the world's manner and applause, in vanity and dishonesty.[31]

Paracelsus's novel variety of the *contemptus mundi* theme almost foreshadows the later romantic reaction against the triviality of contemporary life. His revulsion against the emptiness of court life points to the romantic's hatred of Philistinism, a hatred that later writers would use to rationalize an ivory tower existence.

If for the romantics, then, fairyland was both the imagination itself and the object of the imagination, both a symbol for the poet's private world and the place about which he wrote, for the artist who felt the pull of the world and was unable to ignore his responsibility to it, this circle was unsatisfactory. Thus, of equal importance to him was the theme that the hero rarely remains content with La Belle Dame sans Merci.

The religious import of the hero's desire to return to the world, sometimes to gain absolution for his sins, was crucial for the medieval storyteller, since it gave his tale a didactic purpose. Most romantic writers (Eichendorff is a notable exception) found the religious and didactic element was not significant, and thus the motive for the return to earth took on differing meanings. Sabine Baring-Gould's brief account of the Tannhäuser legend combines both the traditional and the newer romantic (particularly Wagnerian) strains, so that there is some confusion about why the knight leaves the Venusberg.

Seven years of revelry and debauch were passed, and the minstrel's heart began to feel a strange void. The beauty, the magnificence, the variety of the scenes in the pagan goddess's home, and all its heathenish pleasures, palled upon him, and he yearned for the pure fresh breezes of earth, one look up at the dark night sky spangled with stars, one glimpse of simple mountain flowers, one tinkle of sheep-bells. At the same time his conscience began to reproach him, and he longed to make his peace with God.[32]

The first motive is of distinct importance for the romantic writer, although such an attachment to the earth is not confined to the nineteenth century. John A. MacCulloch, in relating the traditional story of Oisin, notes:

These stories illustrate what is found in all Celtic tales of divine or fairy mistresses—they are the wooers, and mortals tire of them and their divine land sooner than they weary of their lovers. Mortals were apt to find that land tedious, for, as one of them said, "I had rather lead the life of the Féinn than that which I lead in the *síd*"—it is the plaint of Achilles, who would liefer serve for hire on earth than rule the dead in Hades.[33]

But if neither romantic escapism nor a more healthy human attachment to reality is new, the confusion likely to result from an attempt to distinguish the real from the imagined world was more characteristic of the nineteenth century. Consequently, romantic fairy tales, like the German *Kunstmärchen*, differ from folk tales because of their deliberate psychological complexity.[34] Harvey Hewett-Thayer notes that in such stories "the boundaries between the natural and supernatural are vague and shifting; the characters are never certain where these boundaries lie,"[35] and Edwin Zeydel, addressing the same point in his book on Ludwig Tieck, describes three main categories of romantic fairy tales, one in which supernatural characters have dealings with ordinary men, one in which the atmosphere and characters are exclusively supernatural, and one in which the supernatural is a mere hallucination of the hero.[36] This last category is reflected in Keats's *Ode to a Nightingale* when the poet asks, "Do I wake or sleep?" (KP 260). In *La Belle Dame sans Merci* the distinction between dreams and what the knight really experi nces is deliberately blurred.

Keats's ballad raises still another point about the "return" motif. Just as it is true that the hero usually wearies of his supernatural abode, it is also true that he cannot readjust to the world: Keats's knight sojourns disconsolately about the cold hillside; Tannhäuser's rejection by the Pope virtually forces him to return to Venus; Yeats's Oisin, who finds his heroic friends dead and a new, hostile religion in place of the old, defiantly tells St. Patrick that he will join his companions even if they be in hell. This cycle of escape, return, and disillusionment could symbolize for the romantic artist his alienation from a world from which subjectivist theories of art and an increasingly Philistine reading public helped sever his ties, forcing him to live an imaginative if sometimes guilt-ridden existence.

These stories of fairy mistresses, indeed, involve conflict, for the hero is almost never without guilt or, while living in the otherworld, experiences a desire to return home. The true aesthete, therefore, would have to find another tale to express his uncomplicated allegiance to a world of pure art. Hence, to read works like Morris's *The Earthly Paradise* and Yeats's *The Wanderings of Oisin* as examples of their authors' aestheticism is an error, if only because the pattern of these tales forced the authors to consider the question of the hero's return to the world where they in turn then had to direct their own attention.

The return motif in the Tannhäuser pattern of the Belle Dame sans Merci story can be linked with the quest motif in the Mélusine pattern, because both involve a yearning for the human realm. But the relevance of the "penanced elf" theme for the artist leading an ivory tower existence is less obvious than the theme of his seduction by a fairy. How the Mélusine pattern is related to his dilemma can perhaps be made clearer by looking at the major onslaught against aestheticism that took place in the 1930s, when the political and social events of the time, as well as the flourishing of Marxist criticism, made theories of art for art's sake appear particularly dangerous. Among the several books written on the subject of escapist art was H. W. Garrod's *Poetry and the Criticism of Life.* A metaphor that Garrod develops to expound his thesis brings to mind

39

the story of the fairy who hopes to win a soul through union with a mortal.

Aesthetes are likely to emphasize the connection between poetry and music, since music is the least representational of the arts and thus the least "mundane." In actuality, states Garrod, poetry is closest to prose, a precarious location in which it holds a "station always on the edge of that precipice, to have only this hair-breadth remove from the very negation of itself." Poetry, he claims, chooses this position because it affords opportunities for discourse: "It has deliberately elected to *say* things." [37] To reinforce his point, he personifies the art:

> Here in truth is what staggers the aestheticians—the immensity of the sacrifice made by poetry; who, when she might have been music, or some imagined ecstasy, elected to occupy a middle station, a station somewhere between prose and (may I say it?) the divine Logos. *Alone of the arts she has put on humanity.* [38]

Here is an arresting parallel between poetry, which for the sake of mankind denies itself an ideal existence, and those stories in which the fairy is anxious to unite with a mortal, taking on the sufferings of humanity to win her soul.

That the parallel clearly occurred to Thomas Mann is shown in *Doctor Faustus* when he used Andersen's Little Mermaid to symbolize the plight of his hero, the composer Adrian Leverkühn. Both the mermaid and the artist are frustrated in their yearnings to establish close ties to the world, although the narrator of the book, Zeitblom, shrinks from what he considers to be the yearning of genius for Philistinism. "If only," he mourns, "there had not been that trembling in his voice when he spoke of the need of art to be redeemed, of art being *per du* with humanity" (DF 322–23; 6:430). In a most unusual fashion, the translation provides a meaningful ambiguity absent in the original "dem du," but in accord with the novel's theme. By being *per du*, that is, on a familiar basis with humanity, art is also likely to be *perdu*, surrendering its essence and aesthetic autonomy. To be redeemed, to gain legs and hopefully a soul, the Little Mermaid yields her beautiful voice.

In *Doctor Faustus* the tormented Leverkühn identifies himself with the pathetic mermaid.

> He talked . . . about the little sea-maid in Andersen's fairy-tale, which he uncommonly loved and admired; not least the really capital picture of the horrid kingdom of the sea-witch, behind the raging whirlpools, in the wood of polyps, whither the yearning child ventured in order to gain human legs instead of her fish's tail . . . perhaps to win, like human beings, an immortal soul. He played with the comparison between the knife-sharp pains which the beautiful dumb one found herself ready to bear every step she took on her lovely new white pins and what he himself had ceaselessly to endure. He called her his sister in affliction and made intimate, humorous, and objective comments on her behavior, her wilfulness, and her sentimental infatuation for the two-legged world of men. [DF 343–44; 6:457]

The little Mermaid also makes her appearance in *Royal Highness*, a novel which Mann says "analyzes the life led by royalty as a formal, unreal existence, lifted above actualities; in a word, the existence of the artist." [39] The hero's sister, the Princess Ditlinde, has married a commoner and thus joined the "real" world.

> And when people say that I am a bad Princess, because I have in a way abdicated, and fled here where it is rather warmer and more friendly, and when they say that I lack dignity or consciousness of Highness, or whatever they call it, they are stupid and ignorant. . . . I seem to myself like the little mermaid in the fairy-tale which the Swiss governess read to us, if you remember—who married a mortal and got legs instead of her fish's tail. [40]

The princess, however, has mistaken the details of Andersen's story, endowing it with a happy ending consistent with the outcome of her own marriage. In reality, the Little Mermaid's infatuation with the world of men led her out of her own element into a hostile environment that rejected her.

Whereas Mann gives the mermaid's willingness to put on

humanity—as Garrod expresses it—its most explicit mythical value for the artist who yearns to leave his ivory tower without, however, surrendering the integrity of his art, Keats also seems to have been aware of these implications in the motif. "Poetry must work out its salvation in a man," he wrote in one of his letters (KL 1:374), almost foreshadowing Mann's writing about the "need of art to be redeemed." Both Mann and Keats were acutely aware of the interdependence of art and life, as well as the frustration inherent in an attempt to make them entirely compatible.

If La Belle Dame sans Merci were a penanced elf, then she could be redeemed by her faithful lover and any failure was his. But if she were a demon, then his love for her was the result of a deception and he could only occasionally glimpse beneath her surface beauty the hidden, hideous truth. In the former instance, beauty longs to be wed to truth, and the artist can be the means through which they are united in the world. In the latter instance, beauty and truth can only be reconciled in the private, illusionary world of the artist's imagination, and, tragically, all poets seem by necessity to be *mere* dreamers.

But the ambiguity perceived by Mann and Keats to exist in the character of La Belle Dame sans Merci is a subtle one, and a pattern much easier to identify involves the fairy's conflict with a mortal woman. It is therefore not surprising that more artists employ this pattern to express their conflicts between illusion and reality, art and life. But a struggle between supernatural and mortal women can become complicated in those instances when the otherworld itself is seen from a Christian point of view.

If a major feature of romanticism lies in a desire to escape from the mortal world of suffering to some paradise, the promise of Christianity as revealed in the New Testament is an extraordinarily romantic one. Ascetic withdrawal from this world, encouraged by Christians ("He who finds his life will lose it, and he who loses his life for my sake will find it," says Jesus [Matt. 10:40]), is rewarded by everlasting joy in the next. Thus the world itself is a Venusberg, and the otherworld, the unearthly paradise, is man's true home. This principle has been applied by Ernst Elster to the Tannhäuser legend, which, he notes, is always influenced by the spirit of the time in which it originated.

> It stands and falls with a dualistic perception of life, with the view that two hostile principles govern this world: one evil,

that aims at sensual enjoyment and worldly pleasure, and one good, that celebrates its highest triumph in ascetic mortification and flight from the world. This opposition, which was unknown to the civilized nations of antiquity and which through the modern way of perceiving again was repressed and adjusted, was given during the Christian Middle Ages its most pronounced expression.[41]

For the romantics, the dilemma was exactly the reverse. The artist who denied the world was forced to choose, as Yeats put it in *The Choice*, between perfection of life or of work (YCP 242). But for the religious romantic, Eichendorff for example, man's ethical relationship to this world was closely associated with his religious views and hence the otherworld. The writer, depending on the position taken, could assign different roles to La Belle Dame sans Merci and to mortal woman. The enchantress could represent either an evil fantasy world that lured the hero away from his duties to the real world, where he left behind a betrayed mortal sweetheart or wife; or, paradoxically, she could represent *this* world, the sinful materialism that kept the hero away from the path to his real home, heaven, and in this instance, it would be the pious mortal woman who was aligned with the otherworld. In short, while La Belle Dame sans Merci usually stands for illusion or the amoral and ephemeral realm of aesthetics, and the mortal for mundane reality, still we must be aware that in a religious context it is this world and not a supernatural one that is illusory. Such a reversal in the story is important to its treatment by Eichendorff and Wagner.

When the internal struggle of the artist is reflected in a struggle between two women, there is at least some hope for his hero, who, even if he must give up one precious half of his existence, can survive because he has the other. This is not the case when the conflict takes place between La Belle Dame sans Merci and the priest or philosopher who challenges her power. Here the ensuing battle will almost invariably destroy her lover, since his direct confrontation with a world hostile to the values of his fairy mistress is involved.

The priest or philospher may or may not represent forces internalized by the hero. There is a clear enmity between Oisin and St. Patrick in Yeats's poem; whereas in *Lamia*, Lycius is Apollonius's student and had once looked up to the sage as a "trusty guide"

(KP 1:375). Thus, unlike the mortal woman, whose struggle with the fairy seems to dramatize what Arnold called the dialogue of the mind with itself, the philosopher or priest is likely to represent the artist's conflicts with the outside world. The pattern of the story which pits Venus against the Pope became increasingly popular during the middle and end of the nineteenth century, when artists felt not so much a longing *for* the social realm (which is represented by the attractive mortal woman) as a rejection *by* it.

One last important element in the Belle Dame sans Merci story is that a commonly recognized distinction exists between the Celtic and Teutonic fairy, the former dominating and even wooing the hero, the latter existing as his submissive devotee[42]—a difference noteworthy because the theme of domination has to do with the conflict between reason and imagination. The issues involved are perhaps best summarized in the seventeenth-century poem by Samuel Daniel, *Ulysses and the Siren*. The Siren fails to tempt Ulysses, who cannot be trapped by her subtle arguments, and thus she is forced to capitulate:

> Well, well, Ulysses, then I see
> I shall not have thee here,
> And therefore I will come to thee,
> And take my fortunes there.
> I must be won that cannot win,
> Yet lost were I not won:
> For beauty hath created been,
> T'undo, or be undone.[43]

For aesthetics, Daniel's poem reflects a classical tradition in which form and rule control the artist, who will not surrender to spontaneous impulses. It is precisely this that Robert Graves considers the defect of the mode: "The Classical poet, however gifted and industrious, fails to pass the test [of the 'true' poet] because he claims to be the Goddess's master—she is his mistress only in the derogatory sense of one who lives in coquettish ease under his protection." [44] For the romantic this control by the poet of his muse, whom Graves calls the White Goddess, must be relinquished. Thus Daniel's paradox, "I must be won that cannot win" is significantly reversed in Yeats's description of the Gaelic muse:

> The *Leanhaun Shee* [fairy mistress] seeks the love of mortals. If they refuse, she must be their slave; if they consent, they are hers, and can only escape by finding another to take their place. The fairy lives on their life, and they waste away. Death is no escape from her. She is the Gaelic muse, for she gives inspiration to those she persecutes. The Gaelic poets die young, for she is restless, and will not let them remain long on earth—this malignant phantom. [45]

This is the extreme romantic position: to be an artist one must lose the struggle to dominate La Belle Dame sans Merci, even if to do so results in total isolation and, ultimately, death.

The nineteenth-century writers who turned their attention to the fairy stories did so with a conscious realization that such tales could be personal myths. They found a symbolic correspondence between the world's relation to fairyland and their own to art. The popular stories of La Belle Dame sans Merci reveal how easily elements in them could be adapted to the concerns of romanticism. Each writer who related the tales, however, achieved a remarkable degree of individuality in his handling of common motifs.

THE ARTIST'S QUEST for a SOUL

In October 1818 Keats wrote to his friend Richard Wood-house about the quality of life he wished to achieve: "I am ambitious of doing the world some good: if I should be spared that may be the work of maturer years—in the interval I will assay to reach to as high a summit in Poetry as the nerve bestowed upon me will suffer. The faint conceptions I have of Poems to come brings the blood frequently into my forehead—All I hope is that I may not lose all interest in human affairs" (KL 1:387–88). This concern could also be found in the recently published *Endymion*, a poem that concerns "the tie of mortals each to each" (KP 177), and a poem in which the moral, "There never liv'd a mortal man, who bent / His appetite beyond his natural sphere, / But starv'd and died" (KP 177–78), is somewhat belied by the ending, in which the real and ideal are miraculously united. But this denouement is pure wish-fulfillment. For the most part the poem reflects the conflicts that were to trouble Keats throughout his poetic career, that "He ne'er is crown'd / With immortality, who fears to follow / Where airy voices lead" (KP 101–02), although he felt more and more that airy voices lead to

> A mad-pursuing of the fog-born elf,
> Whose flitting lantern, through rude nettle-briar,
> Cheats us into a swamp, into a fire,
> Into the bosom of a hated thing.
>
> [KP 104]

In Germany in April 1818, the very month Keats's poem appeared, Ludwig Tieck wrote to his brother about that "vacuous ideal which draws many friends of art after it like a will-o'-the-wisp, so that they believe they can hover and live without time, creed and peculiarity in a region of beauty, a veritable Beyond, cutting off behind them all ties and threads, memories and feelings which bind them to their world and age." [1] It is not that Keats and Tieck in this context at almost the same time and in identical imagery should express the same apprehension about the loosening ties between art and the world that is surprising, but that there was no direct connection between them. Keats never knew Tieck's several versions of the Belle Dame sans Merci story,[2] although each would use the motif to similar ends.

Thomas Carlyle in 1828 published his own translations of some German tales, including Tieck's *The Runenberg* and Hoffmann's *The Golden Pot*. After that the English and German traditions were closely related. May Morris says about her father's version of the Tannhäuser story, for example, that it was influenced by Tieck's, a treatment she considered superior to Wagner's (WM 6:xxvi). But in the period 1811 to 1819 the English and German works that are so strikingly analogous are for the most part not influenced by each other. Only the translation of *Undine*, which Keats read some time in 1818, provides a link between him and German writers whose works were analogues to his own.

Today *Undine* is readily available in translation as a children's book in an edition that is lovely but confesses to having shortened most of the "philosophical meditations." [3] Perhaps this is just, for readers have been drawn to the tale less for philosophy than for beauty. It was admired by, among others, Goethe, Keats, Poe, Rossetti, and Morris. Hoffmann composed an opera based on *Undine*, and Wagner is said to have been re-reading it on the day of his death. The story's appeal is not easy to define, however, although Heine's poetic praise may aptly express feelings evoked by it:

> The genius of poetry kissed Spring while she slept, and she awoke smiling, and all the roses gave forth perfume, and all the nightingales sang, and what was sung and breathed Fouqué put into words and called it "Undine." [HW 11:57; 5:337]

Friedrich de la Motte Fouqué's novella, despite the praise it has received, is nevertheless an anomaly: nothing else in the author's enormous canon can compare with it, and were it not for *Undine*, Fouqué might be consigned to oblivion even in his own country.[4] Edmund Gosse, who translated the tale, called its author "somewhat stupid" (U vii). But, of course, the quality of this one work belies the charge.

There is actually very little criticism directed toward *Undine* outside of that inspired by the folklore and the nature philosophy that lie behind it.[5] The discussions that do exist never suggest that *Undine* expresses Fouqué's own aesthetic conflicts.[6] Yet this story about a knight torn between a supernatural and a real woman was written by a man about whom there is some controversy as to whether he represented the epitome of romantic escapism or was truly interested in the events of his time.

W. W. Chambers insists that Fouqué was involved in the problems of Germany and wished to influence events through his writings. If anything, claims Chambers, he may have been too concerned with contemporary problems and for this reason is little read today. Even more important, Fouqué sought popularity because "he was deeply aware of the gulf which separated literature from the mass of the people" (U *viii*). He hoped not only to entertain a wide public but to awaken in them a profound sense of nationalism, believing that by this awakening many of Germany's problems could be solved. Noting Fouqué's anxiety about destructive foreign influences, Chambers interprets in this context Huldbrand's revulsion at discovering that his beautiful Undine is an alien, unearthly creature.

Then there is the view that Fouqué's writings point to his attachment to a feudal, chivalric age, idealistically conceived and forever lost. Ralph Tymms claims in his book on German romanticism that Fouqué's interest in literary medievalism was a means by which "he tried to rescue himself from the vulgarity and coarseness of everyday life . . . one of the most blatant . . . instances of romantic escapism in German literature." [7] This was also Heine's view:

> Undine may be regarded as the muse of Fouqué. But though she is infinitely beautiful, and suffers like us, and is so tormented with earthly sorrows, she is still a supernatural

being. This our age rejects all such aerial and watery forms, however beautiful they may be; it demands actually living beings; least of all does it care for nixies, who are in love with noble knights. That was the case. The going back to the past, the endless praise of noble birth, the incessant exaltation of old feudal forms, the never-ceasing knight-errantry, at last became repulsive to the middle class of the German people, and they turned away from the poet behind his time. In fact this everlasting sing-song of harness, steeds in tournaments, chatelaines, fair damosels, monks, love-worship and religion, or whatever the mediaeval properties were called, became at last tiresome; and as the ingenious hidalgo, Friedrich de la Motte Fouqué, buried himself more and more in his books of chivalry, and lost, in dreams of the past, all comprehension of the present time, even his best friends turned away from him, shaking their heads. [HW 11:57–58; 5:337]

The polarity between romantic escapism and social consciousness is itself more than an incidental motif in Fouqué's writings. About the time that *Undine* appeared in 1811, he also wrote *The Magic Ring*, a novel in which the hero, Otto, is torn between his envy of a pilgrim, who could "travel across kingdoms, seas, and rivers, to distant unknown lands," and his attachment to the woods and meadows of his home, which hold him, he says, like a "Zauberring." [8] *Zauberring*, also the title of the book, is significantly ambiguous. Otto does leave the magic circle of his family in search of adventure concerning a magic ring. The "Zauberring" is therefore both the source of the adventure and the magical appeal of the home to which the hero eventually returns.

Undine reflects these contrasting facets in the personalities of the water nymph and her mortal rival, Bertalda, and shares with *The Magic Ring* the conflict between the home, with its secure circle of family and duty, and the exciting world of the imagination and adventure which beckons to the hero. It can be argued that, before those later writings in which Fouqué retreated further and further into the imaginative world of romance, stories like *Undine* depict a struggle against his own romantic impulses.

A double focus of interest in *Undine* can be accounted for by the essential difference between its two major sources, *Peter von*

Staufenberg and *Mélusine*.[9] The first depicts the seduction of the hero by a fairy who causes his death when he weds a mortal; the second portrays a fairy who hopes to win a soul for herself. Whether Fouqué recognized the possibilities to be realized by intertwining these two points of view, or created what might be looked upon as a structural accident by adapting two sources with conflicting emphases, there is no doubt that one reason for the power of *Undine* is the impasse created as each protagonist longs to live in the world of the other although able to survive only in his or her own.

The otherworld of *Undine* is a lonely strip of land bordering on a lake with a dark forest behind it that is rarely traversed by human beings, for it was "so full of weird creatures and strange apparitions, that most folks must be driven by great necessity before they would adventure within it" (U 3; 3). The supernatural elements in this realm are closely associated with nature itself, for they are the *Elementargeister* (sylphs, gnomes, salamanders, undines) who are themselves harmless, although they occasionally give birth to monsters (giants, dwarfs, will-o'-the-wisps, sirens) who play malicious tricks on human beings. One of the sorrows of the nature spirits is that they are confused with the mutations they sometimes produce. That her husband makes such an error will be the tragic undoing of Undine.

The setting of *Undine* provides an ambiguous ethical dimension to the tale. Undine's foster parents, an elderly fisherman and his wife, seem like characters in a Wordsworth poem. They live a secluded life, for "save the fisherman and his family . . . few or no human beings were ever to be met with in this lovely place" (U 3; 3). The pious fisherman can pass without harm through the dark forest behind his home, and he is so attached to his solitary environment that he only reluctantly contemplates moving away for the sake of his daughter. He tells how, as he "passed through the roar and rattle of the city, and thought of this tongue of land that was so dear to me, I kept repeating, 'This is the riot in the midst of which my next home will have to be made, or, at least, in some place not much less noisy' " (U 12; 11). But this fondness for isolation is not to be taken as evidence of the fisherman's antisocial behavior. He is hospitable to those rare individuals who chance upon his home; and Undine's foster mother, who has seen no one but her family for years, thinks that it "would be a terrible thing to realize that one was cut off from all other people for ever, even though one does never know them or see them" (U 36; 33).

The balance struck by the couple between an evasion of civilization and an ethical commitment to humanity is one whose very precariousness serves to emphasize the theme of escape and guilt in *Undine*. Fouqué has essentially begged the question in his depiction of the natural-supernatural setting where Huldbrand finds his fairy wife. In their simple piety and concern for their fellow human beings, Undine's foster parents might represent a moral ideal, except that there remains in the book a primitivistic belief that this morality is preserved because it is uncorrupted by modern life. Beauty and truth are still unreconciled, or reconciled only at the cost of excluding the real world beyond that inhabited by nature spirits and humans who find seclusion more congenial than social interaction. Fouqué's story demonstrates the ease with which a Wordsworthian pastoral setting can be transformed into a Venusberg.

Huldbrand's experience in this lonely place is indeed that of a Tannhäuser. Only his guilt ties him to his homeland, now cut off from the fisherman's abode by flood waters:

> He had the illusion that no world existed on the other side of the encircling torrent, and that it was quite vain to imagine that he should ever mix any more with his fellow-men; and if now and again he heard his grazing horse neigh to him, as if rousing him and calling him to knightly deeds, or if his scutcheon flashed out upon him from the midst of the embroidery of the saddle and the caparison, or if his beautiful sword all unawares fell from the nail from which it dangled in the cottage, gliding with a shock out of the scabbard, he quieted his dubious thoughts. [U 29; 26]

Huldbrand is a romantic figure, not only in the sense that he is a hero familiar from chivalric literature (in Tasso's *Jerusalem Delivered*, Rinaldo is similarly diverted from the charms of Armida) but also in that his desire to evade the duties of the world marks in him that pattern of behavior associated with romanticism:

> [He was lost] in his own strange fancies. The world beyond the forest torrent seemed . . . to have been receding farther

and farther from him; but the blossoming island, on which he was living, grew greener, and smiled on him with redoubled sweetness. [U 36–37; 33]

Huldbrand also shares with the romantics the ultimate manifestation of his escapism, a pronounced death wish. The knight who stands on a piece of land encircled by flooding waters and imagines himself cut off forever from other mortal beings is ironically found at the end in a grave similarly encircled by water: this time it is the small stream whose form Undine has taken to hold her lover in her arms forever. Huldbrand's death becomes the fulfillment of his yearning to escape from a world that makes its claims on him primarily through his sense of guilt. He, too, has been half in love with easeful death, and when Undine steps toward him to enfold him in her deathly embrace, he sighs, "Oh! if it might be so . . . if I might only die upon a kiss of thine!" (U 99; 89). But from the point of view of the narrator, such a death is less fulfillment than punishment for having surrendered to the power of his own illusions. On this matter Fouqué is explicitly didactic, for Huldbrand deceives himself not only by falling in love with the unearthly Undine but also in thinking he can reconcile her to his world. Within this moral context *Undine*, while a charming work, remains, however, unxceptional. Fouqué transcended the obvious message of his tale in his portrayal of the water sprite herself.

In contrast to Huldbrand, who abandons the real world, and whose marriage to a sprite is a symbolic expression of his alienation, Undine moves from isolation to social commitment as she gains a soul through marriage to a mortal. She learns in this conversion to humanity both how to love and how to suffer, experiencing that mixture of fulfillment and grief which accompanies the transition from innocence to experience.

As a sprite Undine is a capricious though captivating creature, who torments her foster parents with her waywardness and disobedience. This propensity toward mischief reveals her to have only superficial affection for the fisherman and his wife, although she lavishes caresses on them as readily as she provokes them to anger: not that she is bad, but that, lacking a soul, she also lacks true sympathy for human feelings. When a cask of beer is found in the flood-besieged forest and worry is expressed over its owner, she scornfully insists that "everybody is bound to take care of himself; and what do other people matter?" (U 32; 29).

Undine's "conversion" brings up two matters: a possible loss the tale itself suffers, and the philosophical profundity it acquires. After her marriage to Huldbrand, Undine becomes almost a typical, dutiful German *hausfrau:*

> She was like that all through the day—quiet, kind, and attentive, a little housemother, and at the same time a little tenderly bashful and maidenly being. The three, who had known her for so long a time, expected every moment to see a transformation back into her capricious mood. [U 44; 39]

This change has bothered Ralph Tymms, who sees in Undine's new personality the death of any charm in the work,[10] and the meaning of Venus's similar transformation in Heine's *Tannhäuser* has puzzled critics. The best gloss may have been provided by the narrator, Zeitblom, in Mann's *Doctor Faustus*, who could not conceive of the artist going to the masses without a considerable loss to art itself. That Tymms finds Fouqué's work much duller after Undine's domestication gives ironic sustenance to Zeitblom's fears.

But what Undine loses in the amoral beauty that characterized her earlier in the work, she makes up for by a profound insight into the nature of reality. She comprehends as her husband cannot that both joy and pain are inherent in human love, and that if before her marriage she was spared human suffering, so was she denied true happiness: "The pains and the pleasures of love are so closely intermingled, and depend so much on one another that to divide them is impossible. Smiles break forth out of the heart of tears, and tears out of eyes that are in the very act of smiling" (U 72; 64). Perhaps this passage inspired Keats's image of Joy's hand forever at his mouth bidding adieu. The theme of the *Ode on Melancholy* is identical to Undine's speech, and Keats may have read more deeply into Fouqué's tale than most of its admirers.

By recognizing the intrinsic suffering that comes with all human happiness, Undine accepts that human condition which romantic artists seek to evade. Indeed, she urges the resistant

Huldbrand to return with her to his homeland. Nevertheless, Undine acquires a soul with great apprehension:

> To have a soul must be a delightful thing, but a most fearful thing too. Would it not be better . . . in God's name— would it not be better to have nothing to do with it? . . . Heavy must be the burden of a soul . . . heavy indeed. The very idea of its approach overshadows me with sorrow and anguish. And ah! a little while ago I was so happy, so light-hearted! [U 40–41; 36]

But the previous happiness of Undine was the happiness of innocence, of dreams, and she lacked the self-knowledge and insight that come with human experience. The implications of her plight may go beyond anything that Fouqué consciously intended, but *Undine* should still be read within the context of a major theme in romantic literature.

Underlying Fouqué's novella is another theme, one that points to his longing for a world in which beauty and love are immutable. In the real world they are not; Fouqué knows this, so he feels bound to give his work a realistic consistency once his lovers have returned to Huldbrand's domain. What ensues is inevitable, and behind the sentimentality of his writing can be glimpsed his genuine, romantic regret over the process that takes place:

> He who writes down this story, because it stirs his heart, and because he hopes that it may do the same to others, prays you, dear reader, for a favour. Forgive him, if now he is content briefly and in general terms to tell you what happened during a somewhat long period. [He relates the manner in which Huldbrand's love for Undine fades as he is increasingly drawn to her mortal rival.] The writer knows that all these matters could, and perhaps should, be dwelt upon at length. But it would be far too painful to him to do so, for he has experienced such things in life, and is too full of their memory not to shrink from them. No doubt you have just the same feeling, dear reader, since such is the common fate of mortal man . . . and perhaps a gentle tear slips down your cheek at the thought of that withered garden-plot which was once so deeply your delight. [U 67–68; 60–61]

This nostalgia is where Undine and her husband differ. Huldbrand evinces the romantic desire to escape the mutable world to which he feels dutifully bound, but the strangeness of his bride frightens and repulses him, even more so after they return to his home. He is unable to reconcile his conflicting feelings, partly because he does not understand the meaning of what the priest says when he marries him to Undine: "There is no great difference between wedding and weeping, and he who does not wilfully blind himself, has to recognize that" (U 95; 85). Huldbrand's emotions remain divided between two worlds that he cannot unite, while Undine, in accepting the human condition, resolves the conflict by realizing that the real world is also the source of true joy, and that one escapes the perils of this life only by surrendering the warm relations that bind human beings to each other.

Undine's tragic situation after she is married and her attempts to be human are rejected is basically the fault of Fouqué, who cannot himself resolve the contradictions in his work. Just as he presented the lonely islet as both a positive retreat from the modern world and a Venusberg in which Huldbrand neglects his duties, so is he unable to come to terms with Undine's basic nature. Once she accepts the human lot, achieves a soul, becomes a housewife, and returns to Huldbrand's realm, the only reason they should not live happily ever after is the hero's distrust of her. The moral of the story is that the real and the supernatural cannot be reconciled, but the reason is not explained although the cause for the failure seems not to be rooted in the nature of reality per se so much as in the mind of one for whom reality is reduced to the unambiguous terms of a mundane existence.

The dramatic tension is provided by Huldbrand's betrayal of his wife, because throughout there is an ironic disparity between what Undine is and what Huldbrand perceives her to be. She knows herself that "she was a being created for the glory and joy of God, that indeed she knew . . . and she was ready to let [her family] do with her whatever should be for the glory and joy of God" (U 14; 13). The priest who presides at her marriage decides that there is "nothing that is evil about her, although much that is strange" (U 41; 37), and Fouqué gives the reader no cause to think otherwise. His characterization provides a clear contrast to the Lamia or Mélusine stories, where the serpentine shape of the fairies has evil associations beyond the perceptions of their lovers.

But for Huldbrand, it is precisely Undine's strangeness that endows her with an aura of wickedness. On his wedding night he is "disturbed by strange and horrible dreams of phantoms, who endeavoured with horrid grins to disguise themselves as fair women, or else of fair women whose faces suddenly became the masks of dragons" (U 42; 38).

Huldbrand's nightmare is comparable to the experience of Keats's knight in *La Belle Dame sans Merci*. But where Keats leaves unresolved whether or not his fairy is an evil being who had victimized many, Fouqué seems to have taken care to dispel in the reader any such notions. Undine is clearly *not* a Duessa whose beauty masks a hideous reality. Thus Huldbrand is mistaken in his aversion to his wife, but this error obviates the moral of Fouqué's comments that one must suffer for giving in to tempting illusions (U 27–28; 25). If Undine is not an illusion, for what is Huldbrand being punished?

The difficulty is that Undine is both a nature spirit longing for a soul in the manner described by Paracelsus, and in this sense is to be pitied and helped, and, at the same time, a symbol of the hero's longing for the exotic and unreal, for which he must suffer because such longing draws him away from his duties to the world. In a sense, Fouqué's combination of *Peter von Staufenberg* and *Mélusine* was bound to make this difficulty, for unless he handled the ambiguities in such a way that they were clearly ambiguities, the tale was inevitably bound to create confusion. He mixed in *Undine* both Christian values and Paracelsus's treatise on the nature spirits, a work undertaken to defend such spirits from Christians, who considered them inherently evil.

Undine might have better reflected Fouqué's ambivalence toward his romantic tendencies had he endowed his fairy heroine with both aspects of La Belle Dame sans Merci instead of presenting her as an obviously benign creature. As it is, Undine's profound and stoic acceptance of the mixed joys and sorrows that come with the human soul make her worthy of her husband's love. The hostility of the world that thwarts her would later become a prominent feature in the works of such writers as Hoffmann and Heine, for whom Huldbrand would be a recognizable Philistine. Yet, both Undine's tragic end and her potentially successful transformation from a capricious sprite without attachment to human beings into a docile and even dull housewife contain their own warning for the nineteenth-century artist. From one, he receives despairing confirmation of his fears that the worlds of imagination and reality cannot be reconciled. From the other he sees, what is tantamount to the same thing, that if any reconciliation is achieved, it is on the world's terms, and these are ultimately destructive of aesthetic values. A happy ending to *Undine* would have provided no solution to his predicament, while its pitiful conclusion foreshadowed the form taken by the literature that followed and that was influenced by it.

THE SAGE and the TEMPTRESS

The same year that *Undine* made its first appearance in English, 1818, *Rhododaphne* was published anonymously. Its author, Thomas Love Peacock, was keenly aware of the artist's difficult position in a world hostile to the development of art, and his sometimes satirical views on literature were expressed in the *Four Ages of Poetry* and *An Essay on Fashionable Literature*, where he reveals an essentially classical attitude. But so convinced was Peacock that he was living in a decadent era that his classicism is ironically transformed into romantic nostalgia for the Golden Age, and thus his attachment to the ancient world is no less "escapist" than Fouqué's to the Middle Ages.

Peacock's theories of literature not only thread their way through the narrative of *Rhododaphne* but also point to what is perhaps most striking about the poem: his unawareness that his story proper could be adapted to express his concerns. And yet the ease with which the narrative could have absorbed ideas that seem merely appended to the poem demonstrates, once again, the intrinsic suitability of the Belle Dame sans Merci story for what Peacock wanted to say.

For Peacock the function of poetry was to combine ethics with aesthetics. He speaks disparagingly of the literature of his contemporaries, "which aims only to amuse and must be very careful not to instruct" (TLP 8:263), and says in his essay on *Moore's Epicurean* that even if the novel he is disparaging "had merits of any kind, poetical, descriptive, narrative, or dramatic, much higher than any which it, in our judgment possesses, they would scarcely reconcile us to the total absence of any moral purpose in a work of so much pretension" (TLP 9:67). But what kind of teaching literature should conduct is not entirely clear. Peacock agrees with Sidney that the function of poetry is to aid morality, and writes in the *Essay on Fashionable Literature* that "poetry precedes philosophy, but true poetry prepares its path" (TLP 8:274–75). Apparently, however, the philosophy that will follow poetry is of a rather simple kind, for in the *Four Ages of Poetry* he states,

> It is only the more tangible points of morality, those which command assent at once, those which have a mirror in every mind, and in which the severity of reason is warmed and rendered palatable by being mixed up with feeling and imagination, that are applicable even to what is called moral poetry: and as the sciences of morals and of mind advance towards perfection, as they become more enlarged and comprehensive in their views, as reason gains the ascendancy in them over imagination and feeling, poetry can no longer accompany them in their progress, but drops into the background, and leaves them to advance alone. [TLP 8:11]

There is a matter-of-factness about this statement, lacking the emotional charge of Keats's indictment of philosophy because it has clipped the angels' wings and unwoven the rainbow. Nor is Peacock ostensibly trying to protect poetry from the inroads of science and reason, for by promoting the moral function of art, he clearly rejects the idea of pure poetry. His contradictions reach an impasse in the *Essay on Fashionable Literature*:

> Fancy indeed treads on dangerous ground when she trespasses on the land of opinion—the soil is too slippery for her glass slippers, and the atmosphere too heavy for her filmy wings. But she is a degenerate spirit if she be contented within the limits of her own empire, and keep the mind continually gazing upon phantasms without pointing to more important realities. [TLP 8:274–75]

The impasse, however, causes him no agony. Advocating the dual function of literature to teach and delight as well as its subservience to philosophy, Peacock feels no need to involve himself in the conflict between life and art. Thus he does not fear that fancy may *be* a phantasm, a Belle Dame sans Merci who will seduce artists and destroy their moral purpose.

If poetry in an advanced scientific and intellectual age cannot keep pace yet is not to travel alone, what happens to the poet? If he is sensible, says Peacock in the *Four Ages of Poetry,* he will devote himself to other pursuits:

> But in whatever degree poetry is cultivated, it must necessarily be to the neglect of some branch of useful study: and it is a lamentable spectacle to see minds, capable of better things, running to seed in the specious indolence of these empty aimless mockeries of intellectual exertion. [TLP 8:22]

This passage should be approached with caution since its very tone points to Peacock's satirical bent. Did he really want all poets to become civil servants and the like? Moreover, in his view of poetry as a useless branch of study, essentially no different from any other study save in its lack of utility, there is revealed a Philistinism he actually abhorred. But even if satiric exaggeration be granted, the romantic artist who devoted himself to art for art's sake could find beneath the possible irony a sting to his conscience. Keats said that the sickness that afflicted mankind affected him more than acclaim as a poet ever would, and fretted throughout his career about the utility of art.

Behind Peacock's mockery there is also concern for a problem that would become increasingly serious as the century progressed: the poet's audience was diminishing. He wrote to Shelley that he was "convinced . . . that there is no longer a poetical audience among the higher class of minds; that moral, political, and physical science have entirely withdrawn from poetry the attention of all whose attention is worth having" (TLP 8:219). The rest of the public insists on being amused without being instructed; hence his reference in the *Four Ages of Poetry* to "the promiscuous rubbish of the present time" (TLP 8:22). Poetry, then, was degenerating for two reasons: because the intellectual advancement of the age deprived her of her best readers; and because the remaining audience refused to be taught by her, depriving her of her true function.

For Peacock the answer was a devotion to the literature of the Golden Age, when poetry "attained its perfection," reaching the "point which it cannot pass," so that now "genius . . . seeks new forms for the treatment of the same subjects" (TLP 8:9). Since in the *Four Ages of Poetry* imitation is itself not recommended, Peacock is in a sense forced to recommend that would-be poets turn their energies in other directions, jestingly or seriously negating the poetic impulse at its expressive source. As for the cultivated reader, "There are more good poems already existing [that] are sufficient to employ that portion of life which any mere reader and recipient of poetical impressions should devote to them, and these having been produced in poetical times, are far superior in all the characteristics of poetry to the artificial reconstructions of a few morbid ascetics in unpoetical times" (TLP 8:22). Yet, in his own devotion to the Golden Age of classical literature, Peacock is no less ascetic. He makes no claims for the social value of the ancient works, admitting as a basic premise that in his own time, "intellectual power and intellectual acquisition have turned themselves into other and better channels" (TLP 8:24). Logically, then, even the literature of the ancients loses its primary function to teach and delight and exists for its own sake as a source of pleasure.

The aestheticism inherent in Peacock's views about the Golden Age is unapologetically set forth in the sonnet that prefaces *Rhododaphne*:

The bards and sages of departed Greece
Yet live, for mind survives material doom;
Still, as of yore, beneath the myrtle bloom
They strike their golden lyres, in sylvan peace.
Wisdom and Liberty may never cease,
Once having been, to be: but from the tomb
Their mighty radiance streams along the gloom
Of ages evermore without decrease.
Among those gifted bards and sages old,
Shunning the living world, I dwell, and hear,
Reverent, the creeds they held, the tales they told:
And from the songs that charmed their latest ear,
A yet ungathered wreath, with fingers bold,
I weave, of bleeding love and magic mysteries drear.
[TLP 7:8; my italics]

The story he weaves is about a youth who dwells with an enchantress outside of the "living world," but he makes no implicit analogy between his hero and the ascetic. A sequential analysis of *Rhododaphne* will reveal the extent to which Peacock's failure to make the connection adversely affects his poem.

The first of *Rhododaphne*'s seven cantos opens at the temple of Thespian Love, where Anthemion, whose sweetheart Calliroë is dying of some unknown illness, hopes that his offering of flowers will save her life. Among the blossoms is the amaranth,

> That no decay nor fading knows,
> Like true love's holiest, rarest light.
> [TLP 7:12]

Anthemion's love for Calliroë is of this holy nature, but as he makes his offering, he experiences a strange vision in which

> It seemed the brazen statue frowned—
> The marble statue smiled.
> [TLP 7:12]

The brazen statue is of heavenly love, the marble of earthly love. And, indeed, Anthemion's pure love seems doomed as his wreath withers at the altar.

In the midst of his despair, Anthemion encounters Rhododaphne, who cannot understand his distress:

> —What ails thee, stranger? Leaves are sear,
> And flowers are dead, and fields are drear,
> And streams are wild, and skies are bleak,
> And white with snow each mountain's peak,
> When winter rules the year;
> And children grieve, as if for aye
> Leaves, flowers, and birds were past away:
> But buds and blooms again are seen,
> And fields are gay, and hills are green,

And streams are bright, and sweet birds sing;
And where is the infant's sorrowing? [1]
[TLP 7:13]

Her exposition of nature's cyclical process (whose relevance to the story is never clarified, making the passage seem inflated beyond any possible meaning it provides) is only dimly heard and ill understood by Anthemion. Neither now nor at any other time in the poem will his fidelity to Calliroë be shaken by promises of another love to succeed hers. His unresponsiveness characterizes his essentially passive role in the tale. He accepts Rhododaphne's offer of some more flowers, which do not wither on Love's altar, and when she offers him a flower for himself, bidding him to remember her until it fades, he takes it unconsciously, awed by this beautiful maiden who "on his fancy wrought / Her mystic moralisings" (TLP 7:16). The canto ends with his staring at her until she passes out of sight. He seems about to become enthralled, but unfortunately (for the sake of the story) never does.

Canto II opens with a question: Is the spell of love so strong that

only one fair form may dwell
In dear remembrance, and in vain
May other beauty seek to gain
A place that idol form beside
In feelings all pre-occupied?
[TLP 7:19]

The question is answered almost immediately. Having met his Belle Dame sans Merci, Anthemion is unmoved:

Yet not a passing thought of change
He knew, nor once his fancy strayed
From his long-loved Arcadian maid.
[TLP 7:19]

63

That the question is so quickly answered robs the work of suspense and hence interest; Rhododaphne's intrigue and not Anthemion's conflicts occupy what action ensues. Most untypically, Calliroë and Rhododaphne are not conceived in terms of a battle waging inside Anthemion, for Rhododaphne makes no strong claim on his attention until she resorts to magic. Anthemion wears her flowers as unconsciously as he took them; the warning about their evil power comes entirely from an outside source, an elderly man who asks him why he profanes Love by wearing the laurel-rose whose name Rhododaphne bears. He tells Anthemion that these flowers belong to Thessalian witches who control the elements and whose powers are so mighty that

> little may all aid avail
> To him, whose hapless steps around
> Thessalian spells their chains have bound.
>   [TLP 7:24]

And it is clear throughout the poem that what Anthemion needs is protection from external demonic powers, not from his own fancy.

So far the poem is almost exclusively narrative in form. Canto III, however, opens on a different note:

> By living streams, in sylvan shades,
> Where winds and waves symphonious make
> Sweet melody, the youths and maids
> No more with choral music wake
> Lone Echo from her tangled brake,
> On Pan, or Sylvan Genius, calling,
> Naiad or Nymph, in suppliant song
>
> . . . .
> In ocean's caves no Nereid dwells:
> No Oread walks the mountain-dells:
> The streams no sedge-crowned Genii roll
> From bounteous urn: great Pan is dead:
> The life, the intellectual soul
> Of vale, and grove, and stream, has fled

For ever with the creed sublime
That nursed the Muse of earlier time.
[TLP 7:29–30]

Here is Peacock's lament for the Golden Age. And gone is the dispassionate, ironic tone of the *Four Ages of Poetry*, where it is acknowledged that "there are no Dryads in Hydepark nor Naiads in the Regent's-canal" (TLP 8:19). But there is nothing in the story of Anthemion, Calliroë, and Rhododaphne to serve as a gloss on the "Pan is dead" motif that sounded throughout the nineteenth century.[2] Keats, whose treatment of the fairy mistress was profoundly influenced by *Rhododaphne*,[3] began *Lamia* with a similar lament, but his story itself works out this conflict between imagination and its enemies. Lament and story exist side by side in *Rhododaphne*; they are never integrated.

After what must be considered Peacock's aside about the loss of the age in which his story is set and whose literature he is ostensibly imitating, he continues his narrative. Anthemion again meets Rhododaphne and she asks him why he is not wearing her flowers. When he repeats the elderly stranger's warning, she replies:

—The world, oh youth! deems many wise,
Who dream at noon with waking eyes,
While spectral fancy round them flings
Phantoms of unexisting things;
Whose truth is lies, whose paths are error,
Whose gods are fiends, whose heaven is terror;
And such a slave has been with thee,
And thou, in thy simplicity,
Hast deemed his idle sayings truth.
[TLP 7:34–35]

The passage, out of context, is fraught with potentiality. The evocation of those who "dream at noon with waking eyes" suggests the confusion of illusion with reality basic to so many stories of La Belle Dame sans Merci. When Keats's Lamia asks her lover who Apollonius is, he replies, expressing his confusion,

'Tis Apollonius sage, my trusty guide
And good instructor; but to-night he seems
The ghost of folly haunting my sweet dreams.
[KP 1:375–77]

In *Rhododaphne,* however, there is no confusion, and the speech is
nothing more than a revelation of the temptress's duplicity. For who
is the dreamer in Peacock's poem? The old stranger is correct about
the unambiguously wicked Thessalian witch. Anthemion, himself,
although a poet—"the Muses' gentlest son, / The shepherd-bard of
Helicon" (TLP 7:31)—is no dreamer. Conceived of along classical
lines, he sings songs to peace and wisdom, and his control of himself is
the very reason that his Belle Dame sans Merci is unable to enthrall
him. Rhododaphne's reproach is therefore void of any true significance, for no one in the poem dreams at noon with waking eyes.

Rhododaphne manages to kiss Anthemion, despite his resistance, and after she does so, she tells him that now his lips will be
poison to anyone but her. Canto IV of the poem is an inflated
account of how Anthemion is subsequently the cause of Calliroë's
death. Again, it is the opening of this canto that demands attention—
more so than the action it introduces.

Magic and mystery, spells Circean,
The Siren voice . . . .
. . . .
Have passed away: for vestal Truth
Young Fancy's foe, and *Reason chill,*
Have *chased* the dreams that *charmed* the youth
Of nature and the world, which still,
Amid that vestal light severe,
Our colder spirits leap to hear
Like echoes from a fairy hill.
Yet deem not so. The Power of Spells
Still lingers on the earth, but dwells
In deeper folds of close disguise,
That baffle Reason's searching eyes:
Nor shall that mystic Power resign
To Truth's cold sway his webs of guile,

Till woman's eyes have ceased to shine,
And woman's lips have ceased to smile,
And woman's voice has ceased to be
The earthly soul of melody.
[TLP 7:41–42; my italics]

This passage is almost certainly the source of Keats's famous and oft-quoted question: "Do not all charms fly / At the mere touch of cold philosophy?" (KP 2:229–30), although it is, ironically, *Lamia* and not *Rhododaphne* that could serve as a poetic companion to Peacock's *Four Ages of Poetry*. In that essay, "Young Fancy" and "Reason chill" are presented as potential enemies. But Anthemion's reasoning is never seriously threatened by Rhododaphne, who in any event hardly qualifies as "the dream that charmed the youth." Nor can it even be said that she is the woman whose eyes, lips, and voice reflect the "earthly soul of melody." Neither can the beautiful and innocent Calliroë be such a woman, for there is nothing in the poem to suggest that she stands opposed to "vestal Truth," which is Fancy's "foe." It is true that Rhododaphne is associated with "spells Circean" and "Siren voice," but one can hardly, given her portrayal, lament her demise; it is she, not Truth, who spreads "webs of guile." In terms of Peacock's narrative, this passage does nothing but create confusion.

The resolution of Peacock's narrative points to the significance this passage might have had in *Rhododaphne*. After Calliroë's death, Anthemion, drugged by Rhododaphne, spends many sensual hours with her in a palace where they are entertained by bacchic revels. Finally a *deus ex machina* appears as Uranian Love, invades the pleasure palace, and kills Rhododaphne with a bow and arrow. Her death signals the resurrection of Calliroë, who, reunited with Anthemion, helps him build a tomb for his seductress. This surprising and sentimental ending no doubt proves the generosity associated with true love.

My intention has not been to attack Peacock's *Rhododaphne*, but to demonstrate the ease with which the narrative in the poem could have accommodated other thematic elements. The conflict between beauty and truth, art and science, fancy and reason—all concerns of Peacock—could have been expressed through a rivalry between Rhododaphne and Calliroë, Rhododaphne and the elderly sage of Canto II, or even Rhododaphne and Uranian Love. How this could have been done can be seen by comparing one brief section of *Rhododaphne* with its parallel in *Lamia*. The basis for the comparison hinges on Peacock's image of "Reason's searching eyes."

When Uranian Love prepares to shoot Rhododaphne, he fixes upon her an intense gaze:

> Lo! there, as in the Thespian fane,
> Uranian Love! His bow was bent:
> The arrow to its head was drawn:
> His frowning brow was fixed intent
> On Rhododaphne.
> [TLP 7:84]

But there is no link between this scene and Peacock's earlier reference to "Reason's searching eyes," since Uranian Love does not symbolize reason. Keats was able to make better use of the scene when he presented the confrontation between Lamia and Apollonius:

> The bald-head philosopher
> Had fix'd his eye, without a twinkle or stir
> Full on the alarmed beauty of the bride,
> Brow-beating her fair form.
> [KP 2:245–48]

Apollonius actually embodies the murdering intellect, and Lycius begs his teacher to "shut, shut those juggling eyes, thou ruthless man!" (KP 2:277). Seeing how easily the philosopher destroys dreams, he cries out to the wedding guests:

> "Corinthians! look upon that gray-beard wretch!
> Mark how, possess'd, his lashless eyelids stretch
> Around his demon eyes! Corinthians, see!
> My sweet bride withers at their potency."
> [KP 2:287–90]

Keats had been able to perceive how the Belle Dame sans Merci story could itself be related to Peacock's important diatribe against destructive rationality.

Both *Rhododaphne* and *Lamia* express lament for a time which existed before the cold eyes of reason had banished satyrs, fauns, and nymphs—that is, imagination or romance—from the world. That Keats was able to combine into an organic whole what remained merely juxtaposed elements in Peacock's poem bears an ironic relation to Peacock's poetic theories. His classicism led to aestheticism as he shunned the living world to dwell in antiquity. But whereas a similar temptation to escape made Keats feel immensely guilty, Peacock apparently experienced no such conflict. First, tradition upheld his tenacious support of the classics; their study carried intellectual and social sanction. Second, in his own life he combined successfully literary pursuits and his job in the East India Company. A man of the world, he was an able satirist; he was not a great poet, and, more important, he was apparently not a poet who felt the need to question on a deeply personal level the poet's relation to society. Peacock was not without conflicts, but they were not those suffered by romantics who knew themselves to be seduced by La Belle Dame sans Merci. In *Rhododaphne* he merely wanted to tell the story, although a lament over the age he was depicting worked its way into the poem. But this lament was kept a subordinate theme, and if he did not recognize that his tale was perfectly suited to express his concerns, it was probably because they were not so pressing. Two years after *Rhododaphne* appeared, when he wrote the *Four Ages of Poetry*, he did so without the gravity that would mark Shelley's reply in the *Defense of Poetry*.

Rhododaphne, because it exists for its own sake, does not fulfill what Peacock considers to be the essential function of literature: to teach and delight. With its depiction of the conflict between isolated beauty and the real world, it teaches less than *Lamia*. Not that *Lamia* is didactic—Keats hated art that he felt had a design upon the audience—but in exploring the implications of escapism, Keats transcends it; his work becomes purposive. And he became, as Baudelaire said every great poet ultimately became, a critic. Keats thus affirms his ties to that "living world" Peacock occasionally abandoned to dwell in the Golden Age.

It is easy to deprecate Peacock by comparing him to Keats,

and so perhaps unfair to make the comparison. In his recent study of Peacock, Carl Dawson frankly admits that the satirist lacked Keats's insight into mythology, and this kind of frankness is probably the best way to deal with the matter. Dawson's discussion of *Rhododaphne*, however, concludes on a note that is particularly ironic given the fact that Peacock refused to read *Lamia* when Shelley urged him to look at this last volume of Keats's poems (TLP 8:219; Peacock was generally contemptuous of Keats's handling of classical myths). Dawson's final defense in favor of *Rhododaphne* is that Keats found it worth drawing upon for his own poems.[4]

Although *Lamia* is a more profound poem than *Rhododaphne*, its interpretation remains unclear. Keats endowed his serpentine heroine with an ambiguous nature, making her both demon and penanced elf, and the ensuing difficulty in coming to terms with her has provided a challenge for many critics.[5] The very attempt to resolve the ambiguity may be an error, however, and perhaps a search for an unresolved conflict within Keats to see whether or not *Lamia* may reflect it will be more fruitful. One of Keats's dilemmas would in fact go far to explain this puzzling poem, although it may be difficult to grasp from the perspective of his exalted reputation among English poets. Could Keats have predicted this, his doubts might have vanished, and *Lamia* might not have been written at all; but, in fact, he had little reason to anticipate such repute and his attitude toward poetry was marked alternately by rejection and passionate commitment.

Long after his death, Keats was mistakenly considered an aesthete, although now it is well understood that he himself made the crucial distinction between the asocial dreamer and the poet who could be "physician to all men" (KP 514). What is less of a critical commonplace, however, concerns Keats's deeply felt conflict between poetry and some other pursuit—often philosophy and, more significantly, medicine.[6] After he left surgery to write, an anxiety that he might prove useless to a suffering world disturbed him. He frequently suspected that poetry had seduced him from his profession, and in the fairy mistresses of folklore and romance he could find his tantalizing muse.

The failure of *Endymion*, published in April 1818, elicited from one critic the advice that Keats should return to his apothecary, a jibe whose impact the critic could hardly have suspected.[7] Keats's life between this time and the spring of 1819, when most of his great poems were written, provided little basis for confidence that in becoming a poet he had made the right decision. The problem was not merely the unfavorable reviews and persistent financial difficulties, but his engagement to Fanny Brawne, which was overshadowed by three concerns: that his ill health made their marriage unlikely; that he would not be able to support her so long as he was a poet; and that, even worse, for her sake he might have to give up writing. His friend, John Hamilton Reynolds, had done so to pursue a law career that would provide for wife and children.

Keats's letters convey his ambivalence toward poetry, which sometimes absorbs him completely and at other times provokes his contempt. In April 1817, he wrote to Reynolds that "I find that I cannot exist without poetry—without eternal poetry—half the day will not do—the whole of it—I began with a little, but habit has made me a Leviathan—I had become all in a Tremble from not having written any thing of late" (KL 1:133). A year later, more conscious of a world of troubles, he wrote to another friend, Benjamin Bailey, about his misfortunes, affirming, however, that "life must be undergone, and I certainly derive a consolation from the thought of writing one or two more Poems before it ceases" (KL 1:293). Shortly thereafter Keats went on a walking tour of Scotland, writing his brother Tom that he should "learn poetry here and . . . henceforth write more than ever, for the abstract endeavor of being able to add a mite to that mass of beauty which is harvested from these grand materials, by the finest spirits, and put into ethereal existence for the relish of one's fellows" (KL 1:301).

One reason that Keats absorbed himself in his art to the frequent exclusion of life was an essentially negative attitude toward women. His persistent sore throat has been interpreted by Aileen Ward as a symptom of venereal disease,[8] and this may account for the shame and disgust in a letter to Bailey in which he says, "When I am among Women I have evil thoughts, malice spleen . . . I am full of Suspicions." He admits that he does not have a "right feeling towards Women" (KL 1:341). As a result, it is to poetry and not to women that Keats will pay court. In September 1818, he again wrote on the subject of love and poetry, this time to Reynolds: "I never was in love—Yet the voice and shape of a woman has haunted me these two days—at such a time when the relief, the feverous relief of Poetry

71

seems a much less crime—This morning Poetry has conquered—I have relapsed into those abstractions which are my only life—I feel escaped from a new strange and threatening sorrow—and I am thankful for it" (KL 1:370). In another, and later letter to Reynolds, he writes, "Poetry—that is all I care for, all I live for" (KL 2:147).

What Keats means when he talks of the relief of poetry being "a much less crime" can perhaps be understood by the fact that all along these affirmations about his writing were qualified by strong reservations concerning the abstractness of art—that is, its remoteness from life. First, there is his persistent belief that he has some responsibility to ease the sufferings of men. A telling letter to Bailey finds him writing that "were it my choice I would reject a petrarchal coronation—on account of my dying day, and because women have Cancers" (KL 1:292). Later he asserts his ambition to be of service to the world, aiming in the meantime for the highest degree of poetic success that his talents will allow. He hopes, however, that while composing he "may not lose all interest in human affairs" (KL 1:387–88). In addition to his social consciousness is the recognition that domestic life is not without redeeming virtues. He assures Reynolds, shortly before the latter's wedding, that "one of the first pleasures I look to is your happy Marriage—the more, since I have felt the pleasure of loving a sister in Law. . . . Things like these, and they are real, have made me resolve to have a care of my health" (KL 1:325). One could not be far wrong in imagining that what was less real to him was the ethereal existence of the poet.

The tension between poetry and a more real existence did not decrease as he began to work on his great poems, perhaps because he was genuinely unaware of their worth, and so could not assuage his guilt and justify his profession. To Benjamin Haydon he expresses a sense of total failure: "I am three and twenty with little knowledge and middling intellect. It is true that in the height of enthusiasm I have been cheated into some fine passages, but that is nothing" (KL 2:43). It was very important for him to believe in his work, but the reviews of *Endymion* had already shaken his confidence and he had written to the Keatses in America that the "only thing that can ever affect me personally for more than one short passing day, is any doubt about my powers for poetry—I seldom have any, and I look with hope to the nighing time when I shall have none" (KL 1:404). But he apparently had more doubts than he was willing to admit.

72

He certainly did not seem to recognize the merit of *La Belle Dame sans Merci,* perhaps the most beautiful literary ballad in English, for he did not include it in the 1820 volume of his poems. Written in April 1819, when Keats was at the height of his powers, the poem seems to reflect depression, his fear of the overpowering seduction of poetry, and his frustrated efforts at success. *La Belle Dame sans Merci* is a series of paradoxes: the fairy is lovely and seems harmless, but she has presumably lured many to their doom; she feeds her lover manna dew and honey, wild, exotic fare but not suited to mortal needs; her song is sweet, but it commands too exclusive a commitment to its melody; the love she offers is ecstatic, but the ensuing sleep brings nightmares; the knight has perhaps escaped great danger, but his loss of her portends his death. Almost all of these paradoxes also apply to the effect of poetry on Keats. If he were not genuinely talented, poetry would prove only a phantasm, the pursuit of which had caused many to waste their lives. From a practical viewpoint, poetry, like manna dew, provided no sustenance; he was always worried about money. In addition, the music of poetry had lured him away from medicine, and his recurrent fear that in the end he would prove useless to the world was tantamount to a nightmare. Finally, Keats knew that whatever its dangers, for him to abandon poetry would be to live a life hardly preferable to death.

His engagement heightened his conflicts. Although he had written the odes that alone would secure his reputation he again seemed unaware of their worth. In June he expressed scorn for his poetic gifts, concluding, "I hope I am a little more of a Philosopher than I was, consequently a little less of a versifying Pet-lamb" (KL 2:116). But the idea of marriage aroused fears that he might have to give up writing, and he complains to Fanny herself that "you absorb me in spite of myself—you alone: for I look not forward with any pleasure to what is call'd being settled in the world; I tremble at domestic cares—yet for you I would meet them" (KL 2:133). The next month, August, finds him writing that "I equally dislike the favour of the public with love of a woman—they are both a cloying treacle to the wings of independence" (KL 2:144)—to the wings of Pegasus, he might have added—and the very next day he wrote to Reynolds, who had been grounded by family obligations: "I am convinced more and more day by day that fine writing is next to fine doing the top thing in the world" (KL 2:146). Here he affirms the claims of life over art, but in the same letter he confesses that all he really lives for is his writing.

In September 1819, a month after this almost defiant letter to Reynolds, Keats finished *Lamia*. The letters about poetry reveal two main themes. They indicate, first, his oscillation between love for and rejection of poetry; second, his art is frequently viewed in the context of his relations with women. While his feelings of inferiority (he does not believe women "care whether Mister John Keats five feet high likes them or not" [KL 1:342]) intensify his devotion to his muse, success with a woman and the prospect of marriage make him fearful that he will have to abandon the muse. The two themes are related and in *Lamia* are rendered through two main patterns: the combination of sources to create the basic ambiguity that defines the character of his temptress; and the subtle contrast between fairies and real women.

Basically *Lamia*, like *Rhododaphne*, is an analogue to the Tannhäuser story. Lamia entices Lycius to her enchanted palace in Corinth, where he lives in a sensuous delight until, aware of noises from the city, he is drawn back to reality. Lamia knows that "but a moment's thought is passion's passing bell" (KP 2:39), and the loss of her lover seems inevitable. But at this point the influence of *Undine* on Keats's poem produces a meeker and fearful Lamia, who begs Lycius not to invite Apollonius to their wedding. Her plea is comparable to Undine's plea that Huldbrand should not reproach her near water, where her relatives would be able to reclaim her for the sea. In both cases a tabu has been imposed; in both cases the heroes fail to heed the warnings of their fairy mistresses.[9]

Because of the double strain, the Tannhäuser and Mélusine patterns (or Rhododaphne and Undine, to keep Keats's immediate sources as a context), Lamia is a veritable split personality. At times she is the characteristically pitiless fairy mistress intent on dominating her prey:

> The cruel lady, without any show
> Of sorrow for her tender favourite's woe,
> But rather, if her eyes could brighter be,
> With brighter eyes and slow amenity,

Put her new lips to his, and gave afresh
The life she had so tangled in her mesh.
[KP 1:290–95]

This "demon" offers the illusion of lasting joy, cutting off her lover's contact with the world that threatens their relationship. But she herself is dependent on her victim and, fearing what marriage will do to them,

Trembled; she nothing said, but, pale and meek,
Arose and knelt before him, wept a rain
Of sorrows at his words; at last with pain
Beseeching him, the while his hand she wrung,
To change his purpose.
[KP 2:65–69]

But her Undine-like meekness is to no avail. Pointing to her desire to survive in Lycius's world, it makes his tragedy her own as well.

This split in Lamia between the demon and penitent is largely a substitute for that pattern in which the conflict between the real and supernatural worlds is expressed through the hero's attraction to two women, one mortal and the other supernatural. Nevertheless, the "real woman" does make herself felt in *Lamia*, in lines that have drawn much negative attention from critics:

Let the mad poets say whate'er they please
Of the sweets of Faeries, Peris, Goddesses,
There is not such a treat among them all,
Hunters of cavern, lake, and waterfall,
As a real woman.
[KP 1:328–32]

The passage has been used as a reminder that even in his later poems Keats was capable of the bad verse that frequently marred *Endymion*.[10] And, admittedly, the lines are not graceful, tinged with a

75

vulgarity emphasized in the Rodgers and Hammerstein song, "There is nothing like a dame." Nevertheless, the idea Keats expresses in these lines is central not only to *Lamia* but also to much of his verse. And perhaps *earthy* is a better word than *vulgar* to describe Keats's sentiment concerning the treat supplied by real women. For that is the issue: by preferring the real to the supernatural, the poet literally comes down to earth.

It is impossible to describe here all of the stories that Keats knew in which the struggle between a real and a supernatural woman revealed that in the end men really do prefer mortals,[11] but the critical attention the passage has received warrants a brief survey to demonstrate how prevalent the theme was and how it must have impressed itself on him.

Undine provides such an example when the narrator expresses sadness at being forced to tell

> how step by step the affections of Huldbrand began to be diverted from Undine to Bertalda, how Bertalda ever with more growing passion came forward to meet the young man, and how he and she seemed rather to dread the poor wife as if she were a stranger to their affections than to pity her, how Undine wept. [U 67–68; 60–61]

Keats, when reading *Rhododaphne*, saw that although Anthemion was momentarily excited by the enchantress, whose "soft touch thrilled like liquid flame," he remembered his mortal sweetheart, Calliroë,

> All pale and sad, her sweet eyes dim
> With tears which for herself and him
> Fell: by that modest image mild
> Recalled, inspired, Anthemion strove
> Against the charm that now beguiled
> His sense, and cried, in accents wild,
> —"Oh maid! I have another love!"
> [TLP 7:37]

Similar defeats are common to the False Florimell and Almanseris, enchantresses of *The Faerie Queene* and *Oberon*.[12] Spenser shows how the False Florimell, placed by the side of the True Florimell, disappeared.

> The glorious picture vanisheth away,
> Ne any token doth thereof abide:
> So did this Ladies goodly forme decay,
> And into nothing goe, ere one could it bewray.[13]

Almanseris meets an almost identical fate when the man she would enthrall compares her to his wife, Amanda.

> He seems contrasted beauties to compare;
> While artful graces opening like a snare
> With livelier colors picture in his mind
> Amanda's loveliness of angel kind.
> Before her modest charms the wanton melts in air.[14]

A close analysis of Keats's markings in his edition of *Antony and Cleopatra* reveals what may be the strongest evidence that he was particularly conscious of the bitter rivalry between mortal and enchantress.[15] Since Shakespeare's play is in the Belle Dame sans Merci tradition, many of the passages that Keats chose are predictable: for example, Cleopatra's imagining herself fishing and pretending that each fish is an Antony so that she could say, "Ah, ha! you're caught" (2.5.14), or her being likened to a serpent of the Nile (1.5.25). Other passages noted by Keats need not be explained; the sheer beauty of Shakespeare's verse is sufficient motive. But a marked passage especially noteworthy, because seemingly unexceptional, is the rather prosaic one in which Cleopatra bids her servant to learn something of Octavia, Antony's new wife:

> Go to the fellow, good Alexis; bid him
> Report the feature of Octavia: her years,

Her inclination, let him not leave out
The colour of her hair; bring me word quickly.
[2.5.114–17][16]

Keats's underlining here cannot be merely the result of his awareness of the aging Cleopatra's vulnerability, although mutability is a constant theme in his poems. Shakespeare had compared the Egyptian Queen to Venus, and Egypt can be likened to a Venusberg in which Antony, enthralled, neglects his duties in Rome. Thus, the passage in *Lamia* about the "real woman," as well as Keats's own conflict between his muse and social responsibility, make it likely that *Antony and Cleopatra* reflected back to Keats his own dilemma. Hence the fragile link that ties the mortal lover to his temptress would have been emphasized by those claims of reality symbolized by the wife or mortal beloved.

There is a generally recognized and persistent dichotomy in Keats's poetry between the impulse to escape from earthly ties and a commitment to the world. It is, he tells Apollo in a minor, untitled poem, a ghastly thing to be so torn, for although his soul aspires to the God of Poetry, his

> body is earthward press'd.
> It is an awful mission,
> A terrible division;
> And leaves a gulph austere
> To be fill'd with worldly fear.
> [KP 482]

It is such a "worldly fear," an anxiety aroused by a consciousness that the fancy is a deceitful elf who does not cheat so well as she is famed to do, that had brought him to conclude in *Endymion* that the aspiration of mortals beyond their earthly limits severs the very bonds of human brotherhood and sours the pleasures to be found on earth. In *Endymion*, however, the romantic impulse is so strong that, despite the maturing intellect, wish-fulfillment has its way. Once Endymion settles for mortal love, his sweetheart turns out to be the ideal Cynthia, whom he had been mistakenly pursuing. The conflict between the real and supernatural woman is resolved by making them one. By the time he wrote *Lamia*, Keats could no longer sustain such tenuous fantasies.

An important link between *Endymion* and *Lamia* helps make clear the role played by the real woman in the latter poem. When Endymion realizes that there "never liv'd a mortal man, who bent / His appetite beyond his natural sphere, / But starv'd and died," he thanks the human maid for redeeming his life "from too thin breathing" (KP 177–78). In *Lamia*, the enchantress tells Lycius

> That finer spirits cannot breathe below
> In human climes, and live: Alas! poor youth,
> What taste of purer air hast thou to soothe
> My essence?
> [KP 1:280–83]

Lamia understands better than Lycius the disparity between her essence and his. Mortals could not breathe in her world and she could not in theirs. She also knew from the accumulated experience of past fairies who had lost their lovers to real women that sooner or later reality draws men back to their proper domain and the wives or sweethearts who wait there. Thus she did the only thing she could think of to hold Lycius, and

> threw the goddess off, and won his heart
> More pleasantly by playing woman's part.
> [KP 1:336–37]

Like Undine, Lamia is willing to surrender her immortal being for the love of mortal man. Yet her quest also is doomed. Lamia is only *playing* woman's part, however sincerely, and Lycius is never really deceived, having always believed that she was "not mortal, but of heavenly progeny" (KP 2:86). As soon as his "spirit pass'd beyond" the "golden bourn" of her palace and went into "the noisy world almost forsworn" (KP 2:32–33), he is as uneasy as Huldbrand after Undine is brought to his own home. Neither hero can live content in the supernatural world; neither can keep his Belle Dame sans Merci alive in his own.

By playing the role of mortal woman, Lamia is attempting to bridge that gap between the real and unreal worlds that romantic poets could not leave intact. Therefore, she cannot be dismissed as the mere poetry of dreams, for she is willing to abandon if possible her own domain. Lamia understands the essentially classical strain in the great romantic poet, one that ties him to the world, and if she assumes reality as but another ploy to bind him even more closely to his delusions, the submissive quality she takes on with her mortal role renders her failure pathetic. There is probably no blame implied in *Lamia*. Like Keats, who embraced poetry partly because of his frustration with real women and then feared himself lost in a realm of abstractions, Lycius cannot "breathe" in the rarefied atmosphere of Lamia's enchanted dwelling. Apollonius is but the instrument which points to the irreconcilability of their worlds by exposing the harsh truth beneath the part Lamia is playing and destroying the weak link she had forged between illusion and reality. It is not that she is evil, but that she is attempting the impossible. Reality itself must be defined in terms of a gap that cannot be bridged.

Lamia begins and ends with a dream; it begins with the "real dream" of Hermes and ends with the "foul dream" of Lycius:

> Real are the dreams of Gods, and smoothly pass
> Their pleasures in a long immortal dream.
> [KP 1:127–28]

Only the gods can have their beauty and their truth at the same time, experiencing dreams that are real. But the god-poet, like Apollo, could redeem poetry by reconciling the sensuous with the ideal, the world with fantasy, Apollonius with Lamia. To be such an Apollo was Keats's most passionate desire, because it would justify his choosing poetry over medicine, his following the troops of fairies that floated with the sunbeam into the hall where he was listening to lectures on anatomy.[17] Had Keats been sure of his own work, had his relationship with women not made poetry a too frequent substitute for more healthy relations between human beings, he might not have felt obliged to expose Lamia as the "foul dream" (KP 2:271) he sometimes thought she was. His penanced elf might have found her salvation in a man, as Keats had said poetry must (KL 1:374).[18]

4
DEMONIC GEMS

The dichotomy in Keats between the imaginative life and one devoted to a more down-to-earth existence also characterizes Ludwig Tieck, whose "entire career," says his biographer, Edwin Zeydel, "may be described as an attempt to flee from his subjectiveness and strong self-consciousness." [1] Tieck resolved the conflict between art and reality by turning from the *Kunstmärchen*, or literary fairy tale, whose landscape is frequently a projection of the artist's interior consciousness and hence encourages his inwardness, to realistic fiction.[2] As Heine put it in *The Romantic School*, the man "who only loved art in naïve outpourings of the heart, now appeared as the foe of what was visionary, as a depicter of modern middle-class life" (HW 10:351; 5:288).

Tieck's conflicts had apparently reached a crisis around the time he wrote *The Runenberg*. It concerns a man whose life is ruined because he is torn between attraction to the goddess of the strange and lonely Runenberg and love for his wife. That such a story could depict Tieck's own state of mind is suggested by a letter he wrote to Friedrich Schlegel in December 1803, a year after he finished the haunting tale.[3]

He begins by apologizing for his failure to write sooner. The year-long silence is not to be understood as a lessening of his friendship; indeed, he believes that every dead and distant friend is like an organ torn from our insides. But now his desire for communication has been awakened by the mode of life he has been leading. He has been dwelling in Zeibingen in the greatest loneliness, "cut off from all men and the diversions of the city," with the result that he withdraws more and more into his own thoughts and studies. The outside world, despite his seeming lament at being cut off from it, has become a matter of indifference: "Therefore I can pass on to you no news or novelty, since I really do not know what is going on; it may be that nothing is taking place, at least that what I nevertheless occasionally experience appears to me as almost nothing, and for this reason I have also lost interest in things." But this indifference has a beneficial effect on that which he most loves, his study of past literature: "It is absolutely necessary to limit myself much more externally in order to further expand my inner love." He compares himself to Don Quixote, since they both dwell imaginatively in an idealized past, and describes himself as living in a "timeless region, in which only the rising and setting of the sun, the waning and waxing of the moon, spring and winter give me pleasure, so that in my limited surroundings I almost live in the beautiful loneliness of a cloister." In light of what we will see is Tieck's general preoccupation with the mutability of the natural world, it is remarkable that he paradoxically describes this timeless region in cyclical terms.

In contrast to his own delight in this "beautiful loneliness," Tieck has an anxiety to make Schlegel understand him, and he wants to feel that the outpourings of his soul in this very long letter will fall on sympathetic, comprehending ears. This ambivalent attitude can also be found in the hero of *The Runenberg*, who is extremely lonely, after he achieves his goal of escaping to remote mountains, and longs for someone to talk to. Tieck even suggests that he would like to work with a collaborator, and regrets that Schlegel lives so far away. More important still is his revelation that this devotion to his work is a renewed one, for he had recently passed out of a period in which it had seemed a genuine evil. He had been unable to speak of this before, but now that the crisis has passed, he would like to describe it to his friend.

He recalls a past letter in which Schlegel had noted that while for him life was beginning to appear more and more like a wild joke, Tieck seemed to be increasingly earnest. Actually, says Tieck, he had been a melancholy child and what Schlegel observed was characteristic: "It was . . . natural for me, without pain, without misfortune, without external cause, to view life itself as a heavy burden and to be sorry for everything which must be consumed in this conflagration of life that wants to burn up all beauty, innocence, youth, fineness, longing, love, in its perpetual flame." His romantic sensibilities were repelled by the eventual decay of all that was beautiful in the world, since he would prefer to see life itself in poetic terms. Thus when reality came, it did so with such "intensified and frightful confusion" that it seemed as if it seized him "like a dark night."

Tieck's feeling at that time was such that he, suffering a recoil from his tendency to turn life into poetry, rejected poetry itself as some infernal power that was destroying him.

> Primarily I was frightened of everything that until now had been most loved: my love for poetry, my talent appeared to me as essentially evil, something which was destroying me; all long since annihilated doubts surged up newly confirmed and active in me, and emanated from that which I could not help but take for truth itself. Once before I had been sensible of the painful birth of a new epoch in me, but it was light in comparison to this sad time, in which all youth, all joy in life, and all beauty seemed on the point of collapse. My anxiety was so intense that I would have been happy if I could have lived entirely alone or in a cloister under instruction, separated from everything.

Tieck's rejection of poetry is particularly noteworthy in the metaphor he chooses to describe the situation: everything appeared "as if a disastrous, evil magic was exercising on me its devastating and hellish power." It would not be difficult to translate this "struggle with myself and all that is evil and fantastic" to the realm of the fairy tale, where a confrontation with the uncanny powers of the Runenberg may very well depict Tieck's own anguish.

The Runenberg concerns Christian, a gardener's son, who yearns for a life more challenging than his father's. When the story opens, Christian, intrigued by what he has read about the mountains, is living in them the solitary life of a hunter. Overcome by a desire for companionship and the familiar world he has left behind, Christian is only too glad to relate his personal history to the stranger who suddenly and unaccountably appears before him and who, before disappearing again into a mine shaft, describes the Runenberg. Its legendary wonders now beckon to the young man. Upon reaching the mountain, Christian chances upon a strange and splendid dwelling in which he beholds a beautiful giantess, who, presumably unaware of his admiring eyes, appears naked before him. As it turns out, she does know he is there and presents him, before she and her habitat suddenly vanish, with a jeweled tablet as a memento of his strange experience.

Christian returns to the plains, where he takes work with a gardener, later marrying the daughter, Elizabeth. Although acutely aware of how she differs from the goddess whose image still fascinates him, he remains content for several years, during which time a daughter is born. One day a stranger comes to visit the family and remains for several months. Christian is disturbed by an element of familiarity he cannot identify in the visitor, who entrusts to his host a pile of gold coins when he leaves. They will be Christian's if the guest does not return within a year. The gold reawakens the lust for the mountains, and Christian leaves his family in search of more treasure, to reappear after several years as an old, strange looking, wild creature, who insists that his worthless pebbles are precious jewels. At the approach of Elizabeth's new husband, he kisses his terrified daughter, who does not remember him, and disappears, this time forever.

Christian's conflict is symbolized by the contrast between the mountains and flatland that runs throughout *The Runenberg.* Significantly, however, the story begins not with Christian's obsessive longing for the mountains but rather with his desire for contact with others after his dreams have been realized. From the beginning, then, Tieck's hero provides a negative critique of his own *Sehnsucht,* although the opening lines of the story are essentially ambiguous and delay any final judgment:

> A young hunter was sitting in the heart of the Mountains, in a thoughtful mood, beside his fowling-floor, while the noise of the waters and the woods were sounding through the solitude. He was musing on his destiny; how he was so young, and had forsaken his father and mother, and accustomed home, and all his comrades in his native village, to seek out new acquaintances, to escape from the circle of returning habitude; and he looked up with a sort of surprise that he was here, that he found himself in this valley, in this employment. [LT 37; 61]

In contrast to the solitude and strangeness of the mountains, the home is encircled by secure familiarity. This very circle, however, is limiting in that the ordinary routine of daily life is devoid of wonder. Thus the "returning habitude" of ordinary life finds its antithesis in the changing melody of the water that flows through the mountains. This melody, whose meaning Christian now realizes is eternally hidden from him, had lured him away from his family to unknown regions that now seem so frightening in their solitude.

If Christian in the mountains feels as cut off as the great clouds that, symbolically "[lose themselves] behind the mountain" (LT 37; 61), in the flatlands he is "like a bird which is taken in a net, and struggles to no purpose" to be free (LT 40; 63). This is the world of his father, a gardener, whose "little hampered garden, with its trimmed flower-beds" (LT 40–41; 64), is odious to the son, who feels keenly the limitations of his environment. Tieck depicts, then, the internal ambivalence of his hero and its external manifestation in the conflict between the father, who can almost speak to the flowers upon which he tenders great care, and the son, who yearns beyond the confines of this life and finds in the wildness of the mountains the focal point of his rebellion. By extension, the fundamental conflict between classicism and romanticism into which the father-son confrontation easily fits can be seen.[4] The orderly flowerbeds reflect a classical concern for form and limits, while Christian evidences the romantic impulse to break away from all that is regulated. His decision to leave the parental home transforms him into the archetypal wanderer so many romantics found embodied their artistic spirit.[5] But his ultimate loneliness and revulsion at his isolated state indicate the magnetic pull of reality that prevents the romantic artist from dwelling contentedly in his dreamworld.

In short, nature, tamed and confined to neat, orderly gardens, represents the familiar world of Christian, while the wild nature of the unexplored mountains becomes the object of his romantic desires.[6] In contrast to both is the enchantress's dwelling on the Runenberg. Hers is a world of precious stones and crystal that, although having their source in nature, are inorganic and suggest the immutable beauty of art. To Christian the fairy of the Runenberg seems of a "different race from mortals" (LT 43; 67); her body is described as gleaming "like marble" (LT 44; 68). He forgets both himself and the world in contemplation of her "more than earthly" beauty (LT 44; 68). The tablet she gives him glitters with gems which almost blind him by their splendor. But their primary effect is to direct him inward toward his own imagination, whose powers have released sad and joyful melodies evoking figures of hope and despair, desire and voluptuousness. This inner world is strange to him, however, and as it usurps the place of external reality, he "no longer knew himself" (LT 45; 68).

What symbolism inheres in Tieck's conception of inorganic matter in *The Runenberg*? The matter has provoked controversy among critics unable to find a strong link between the inner world of Christian and the precious stones of the mountain.[7] Traditionally, the metals of the earth after which man lusts were held to exercise a pernicious spell over him, often leading him to insanity. Ralph Tymms equates man's desire for gold with his sensual appetite which pulls him down to the level of animals; he notes that under the enchantment of the Runenberg goddess, Christian "loses his living, healthy relationship with organic nature, with the plants and fruitfulness of the natural world, and gravitates instead towards the elemental magic of gold; his very heart seems to turn into something cold and hard, a lump of metal."[8] But this argument is inconsistent, for even if man's lusts reduce him to bestiality, he still maintains his relation to organic nature as one of the animals. In contrast to Tymms, H. A. Korff altogether denies the sexual element, and finds a decided difference between the Runenberg and the Venusberg. For him, the metals of the mountain represent that which lies beneath the sensuous life: elemental inorganic nature, dead matter, which was first organized through life yet nevertheless rebelled secretly against organized form.[9] But in emphasizing the psychic meaning of inorganic matter for the rebellious, romantic spirit, Korff fails to account for Christian's erotic response to the naked figure of the Runenberg.

The critical dilemma may be overcome by recognizing the significance of the fairy's gift to Christian. It is not a piece of jewelry that she gives him, but a tablet, which infers a symbol for literature. When this symbolism is placed in the context of Christian's marriage and subsequent dissatisfaction, the tension in *The Runenberg* points to Tieck's own conflict between life and art. The erotic impulse is itself neutral; the issue is how to channel it.

When Christian awakens from a deep sleep after his experience on the Runenberg, he is anxious to rejoin society. He visits a church in the flatlands, where his attraction to a lovely girl convinces him of "the necessities of poor human nature; of man's dependence on the friendly Earth, to whose benignity he must commit himself"

(LT 46; 69). This is then the outcome of his profound encounter on the mountain, at least for the time being: the desires which have been aroused in him can only be satisfied in the natural world. For "poor human nature" the ideal beauty of the Runenberg is inaccessible and hence unsatisfying. Although his wife will always suffer in comparison to the vision on the mountain, and he will lament on their wedding night, "No, thou art not that form which once charmed me in a dream, and which I can never entirely forget; but I am happy beside thee" (LT 48; 71), it is Elizabeth's relationship to the natural world that provides for Christian a bulwark against the demonic pull of his otherworldly yearnings. Attracted by the mountains at one point during their marriage, he cries out, "Elizabeth is no vain dream" (LT 49; 72). But Christian's humble realization that only in nature can man fulfill himself is undermined by a sensibility repelled by the changes that occur in the natural world.

The "new life" (LT 47; 71) that Christian joyfully anticipates with Elizabeth is reflected in their spring wedding, just when the birds commence their song and flowers bloom. For organic nature this is the hopeful beginning of a cycle which must end with winter and death. Christian focuses on the latter part of this cycle, after the gold left by the mysterious stranger reawakens his old feelings about the mountains. His gloom over the mutable world increases until illusion and reality are completely inverted:

> He set himself on the height, and again looked over upon the smoking cottages; he heard the music of the psalm and organ coming from the little church; children, in holiday dresses, were dancing and sporting on the green. "How have I lost my life as in a dream!" said he to himself: "years have passed away since I went down this hill to the merry children; they who were then sportful on the green, are now serious in the church; I also once went into it, but Elizabeth is now no more a blooming childlike maiden; her youth is gone; I cannot seek for the glance of her eyes with the longing of those days; I have wilfully neglected a high eternal happiness, to win one which is finite and transitory." [LT 54; 77–78]

For Christian the earthly realm is no longer real; the one that is eternal and unchanging is the one he had found on the Runenberg.

The wife who had been a "blühende" maiden is now withered. Yet for her and for the world of process implied in this progressive form of "to bloom," he had sacrificed a higher existence. His erotic feelings, awakened on the mountains, had been satisfied in the only way he knew, through marriage, and now he regrets his choice.

Some interpretation of the naked Runenberg fairy that will take into account the relationship between Eros and aesthetics can now be formulated. Since Freudian critics have had much to say in this area, it is perhaps appropriate to invoke their aid. Herbert Marcuse, for example, writes that one view of the aesthetic realm is that it is "essentially 'unrealistic,' " that "it has retained its freedom from the reality principle at the price of being ineffective in the reality. Aesthetic values may function in life for cultural adornment and elevation or as private hobbies, but to *live* with these values is the privilege of geniuses or the mark of decadent Bohemians." [10] For the "normal" person, or one who longs to be normal, the aesthetic realm is limited in its potential for human fulfillment. Thus Christian recognizes his dependence on the "benign earth" in the same way that Keats's Endymion gave up his ideal love, concluding that the mortal man whose appetite went "beyond his natural sphere / But starv'd and died" (KP 178).

The return to the reality principle means, however, a repression of the erotic impulse, and this, according to Marcuse, separates art from life: "Art challenges the prevailing principle of reason: in representing the order of sensuousness, it invokes a tabooed logic—the logic of gratification as against that of repression. Behind the sublimated aesthetic form, the unsublimated content shows forth; the commitment of art to the pleasure principle." [11] Art, he claims, "is perhaps the most visible 'return of the repressed,' " for it "aims at an 'erotic reality' where the life instincts would come to rest in fulfillment without repression." [12] For Tieck, art failed to mediate satisfactorily between the beautiful and the real, and one of two desires must ultimately be suppressed: the desire for satisfaction on the human level; or the longing for immutable beauty.

Heine had an acute insight into the way repression operated in Tieck, and he describes in the *Romantic School* how

a strange misunderstanding has come between the reason and the imagination of this author. The former, or the reason of

Tieck, is an honest, sober, plain citizen, who worships practical economy and abhors the visionary. The other, that is, the Tieck imagination, is still, as of yore, the chevalresque lady with the flowing feather on her cap, the falcon on her fist. The pair lead a curious wedded life, and it is often sad to see how the poor dame of high nobility must help the sober citizen spouse in his household or in his cheese-shop. But often in the night, when the good man, with his cotton nightcap on, snores peacefully, the noble lady rises from the matrimonial bed of durance vile, and mounts her white horse and hunts away as merrily as of yore into the enchanted forest of romance. [HW 10:351; 5:288–89]

Tieck's need to repress his adventurous imagination is revealed by his turning toward realistic fiction. He felt compelled to modify the pleasure principle by social concerns; in the novel he could do this more easily than in the fairy tale, which is perhaps the least sublimated of literary forms.

But when measured by social needs, too often expressed by one or another form of utilitarianism, the whole aesthetic realm can be relegated to the trivial or illusory, or considered the domain of the social misfit. In this "all or nothing" context that irrevocably sunders art and life, the erotic impulse at the base of art is completely diverted into other activities. Tieck's Christian is allowed on the Runenberg that moment when sensation, aroused by the naked beauty of the Runenberg fairy, is totally freed from social repression. The result is that

within his soul, an abyss of forms and harmony, of longing and voluptuousness, was opened: hosts of winged tones, and sad and joyful melodies flew through his spirit, which was moved to its foundations: he saw a world of Pain and Hope arise within him; strong towering crags of Trust and defiant Confidence, and deep rivers of Sadness flowing by. [LT 44; 68]

Once returned to the flatlands, the sensations that had afforded him this visionary experience must find their outlets in more normal pursuits. But marriage and domesticity involve more repression than

Christian is aware of, and the stranger in his household—a guest who reminds him of some forgotten realm of existence—makes domestic happiness thereafter impossible.

Christian's aversion to domesticity had, of course, been revealed earlier and can be traced to those longings which prompted him to leave his father's home in the first place. But now his early feelings have been exacerbated by what he conceives to be his deception by the natural world. For the mutable joys of that world he has betrayed his "true" love, the Runenberg enchantress. He recalls for his father the day when he absentmindedly plucked a root from the earth and heard reverberate throughout its depths a tormented moan:

> I remember well that it was a plant which first made known to me the misery of the Earth; never, till then, did I understand the sighs and lamentations one may hear on every side, throughout the whole of Nature, if one but gives ear to them. In plants and herbs, in trees and flowers, it is the painful writhing of one universal wound that moves and works; they are the corpse of foregone glorious worlds of rock, they offer to our eye a horrid universe of putrefaction. I now see clearly it was this, which the root with its deep-drawn sigh was saying to me; in its sorrow it forgot itself, and told me all. It is because of this that all green shrubs are so enraged at me, and lie in wait for my life; they wish to obliterate that lovely figure in my heart; and every spring, with their distorted deathlike looks, they try to win my soul. [LT 53; 77]

The morbid sensibility of Christian, which allows him to see in the midst of spring "a horrid universe of putrefaction," recalls Tieck's letter to Friedrich Schlegel, in which he wrote that for no external reason he viewed life in pessimistic terms, focusing always on the mutability of all the seeming pleasures the world had to offer.

For Tieck art could be a refuge from such a life, and the tablet, which Christian first receives on the Runenberg, loses, and then finds again when he leaves his family, may symbolize the dazzling, immutable beauty of the aesthetic realm. Marcuse notes that in the age of Kant the original meaning of *aesthetic*, which referred to the senses, merged with a new meaning that pertained to beauty. He points out that for Kant the "aesthetic dimension is also the medium in which nature and freedom meet," a mediation which "is necessitated by the pervasive conflict between the lower and the higher faculties of man generated by the progress of civilization." [13] It does not matter whether one agrees that such a conflict is culturally determined or believes that it is inherent in human nature. More important is that the split itself is taken for granted by those artists who do not see how the imagination can reconcile fantasy with reality. Tieck perceived that the same sexual energies which most men devote to a "real," that is, nonartistic, existence also produce art. When he was frightened or guilty about his devotion to literature, he associated his talent with lower faculties controlled by demons; when he cast off his despair, poetry again seemed guiltless and allied with a noble human faculty that yearns for the ideal, as the letter to Schlegel implies. Such an attitude worked its way into *The Runenberg*, the writer's delusion being symbolized by the bag of worthless rocks that Christian in his insanity takes for precious jewels.

When Tieck told his brother in 1818 that art was a will-o'-the-wisp that lured men from their fellow beings, the period of his fairy tales was behind him and he had turned toward more realistic fiction. But, ironically, the precious gems in his literary canon were produced by that very conflict in which the delusive and real confront each other. *The Runenberg* is a fascinating, profound depiction of a quest for beauty whose asocial implications led Tieck to equate the aesthetic with the demonic.[14]

The Runenberg influenced E. T. A. Hoffmann's *The Mines of Falun*, although Hoffmann's primary source was a legend popular among German writers. G. H. von Schubert, in his *Ansichten von der Nachtseite der Naturwissenschaft* (1808), a quarry for German romantic ideas about the supernatural elements in nature, tells of a miner, killed in an accident, whose body was preserved for fifty years in vitriol water. When discovered, the corpse was claimed by a very old woman, the miner's betrothed, who had never ceased mourning his death.[15]

The legend is fraught with dramatic possibilities. The contrast between the young-looking body of the bridegroom and the aged bride would not be lost on those romantic artists keenly aware of earthly mutability. Johann Hebel's short story is largely taken up with recounting the historical events that occurred during the fifty years between the departure of the bridegroom for the mines and the strange reunion with his bride at the end of this period.[16] Achim von Arnim concentrated on the motives which lured the miner away from his bride. He conceived of his being seduced by the Queen of the Mines, who inspires him with the gold fever that leads to his doom.[17] Here the Tannhäuser motif has merged with the original legend. The emphasis is no longer on the event itself but a contrast between two worlds, one of which exerts a pernicious influence over a vulnerable hero.

Hoffmann's story resembles Arnim's treatment of the legend, for his interest was in precisely such a contrast. At the end of the story, which appeared in the framework of *The Serapion Brethren*, one of its auditors comments, "How often writers presented men who are in some dreadful fashion lost, since all their lives they are in conflict with themselves as though deluded by an unknown ominous power" (SB 197). Hoffmann's Elis Fröbom is a sailor recently returned from sea only to learn that his mother, his only living relative and tie to the world, is dead. Depressed, and unwilling to return to seafaring, he heeds the advice of a stranger who urges him to seek work in the mines at Falun. There he resides with the family of Person Dahlsjö, whose daughter Ulla becomes his betrothed. But at work in the depths of the earth, he glimpses the Queen of the Mines, who demands unswerving devotion from her servants. Thus Elis feels, on the eve of his marriage, as if the best part of himself belongs to the mines, while his lesser self remains content with the life promised by his bride; and he descends into the earth, supposedly to find a precious jewel to give Ulla as a wedding present. She does not see him again until his preserved body is recovered fifty years later.

The similarities to Tieck's *Runenberg* are obvious. The stranger who directs Elis Fröbom to the mines resembles the mysterious figure who tells Christian about the mountain. The Queen of the Mines has her counterpart in the fairy of the Runenberg, just as both Ulla and Elizabeth represent the heroes' attachment to this world. In both stories they waver between two women, only to capitulate in the end to demonic forces. And Hoffmann, as might be expected from these similarities, shares with Tieck many of his ambivalent attitudes toward art. But in Hoffmann's work, the main threat comes not only from the tormented soul of the hero but also from the Philistinism which drove so many romantics to seek another world.[18] Harvey Hewett-Thayer notes that the question "which perpetually tortured him" was, "how can a man of unusual gifts accommodate himself to the world of our everyday; how can he remain his real self when the forces of his environment constantly demand conformity at the expense of that higher self?" [19] In one sense it was a highly personal problem. Hoffmann's marriage was a dull one and to sustain it he worked as a civil servant. But that it was also a common predicament for the artist is evidenced by Keats's fears that marriage to Fanny Brawne would mean the end of his creative life.

Hoffmann's childhood also helps explain his acute sense of the distance between opposing modes of existence. When his mother's unhappy marriage ended, she returned with her son to her family home, where she went into a kind of permanent retreat, taking her meals alone and presumably living an almost entirely inward existence. Her son was left to his disciplined and unimaginative uncle, who stressed convention and conformity in his nephew's life. The contrast between introversion and extroversion is relevant to another crucial aspect of Hoffmann's life and career, his need to choose between music or literature.[20] Hoffmann thus occupies a very important place in German romanticism, where music was considered the proper medium for expressing *Sehnsucht*. Georg Brandes found this a contributing factor to what he calls the "extraordinary difficulty" of studying this period, because "the chief characteristic of the period is an absence of distinctly typical forms. The literature is not plastic; it is musical. French Romanticism produces clearly defined figures; the ideal of German Romanticism is not a figure, but a melody, not definite form, but infinite aspiration. Is it obliged to name the object of its longing?" [21] But literature is finally obliged to name the object of its longing, and for this reason it holds the artist earthbound in a way that melody does not. Music to Hoffmann was a key to the otherworld; presumably, then, the very act of writing stories was a tie to a more commonplace reality. Like Tieck, Hoffmann searched for antidotes to his otherworldly leanings and believed, as Ronald Taylor puts it, that essential to great art was the artist's ability "to control the forces of the imagination which welled up" within him.[22] This need for control provides *The Mines of Falun* with one of its dominant themes.

Hoffmann demonstrated his ties to reality by carrying out essentially uninspiring official tasks despite his artistic disposition.

Such a "classical" obedience to the regulated life is also reflected in his belief that the artist must dominate his material and not become prey to his own fancy. For this reason, perhaps, Hoffmann differs from Tieck in his use of the fairy-tale form. Unlike Tieck, who usually separates the real from the otherworld by some distance, Hoffmann locates the fantastic right in the midst of the real.[23] It was not his practice to send his heroes outside of the everyday world to find adventure, but to so intertwine the real with the fantastic that his hero frequently cannot separate the two. In *The Golden Pot*, for example, Anselmus meets a salamander, living and working as an archivist in his own town. Nevertheless, Hoffmann shares enough romantic assumptions to send his hero to Atlantis when he marries Serpentina, daughter of the salamander. He may have found her near home, but their love cannot flourish in such ordinary surroundings.

An understanding of how Hoffmann and Tieck differ in the settings of their tales makes particularly significant the locale of the mines at Falun. The mine is first a realistic phenomenon, although as conducive to fantastic as to naturalistic literature. The miner who descends into the earth each day to labor for his sustenance may appear unrelated to the sensitive artist whose imagination carries him far from such vulgar concerns as earning a living, but such is not the case. Heine's remarks in *The Hartz Journey* about the miners' life suggests that each is a potential Tannhäuser: I thought, he says, "how they had worked all day in lonely and secret places in the mines, and how they now longed for the blessed light of day, and for the glances of wives and children" (HW 3:84; 3:30). Tannhäuser, languishing in the Venusberg, which has an artificial splendor that resembles the jewels the miner digs out of the earth, longs for the life on earth, just as the miner looks forward each day to his return home. The mysterious depths of the earth and the brilliant jewels he digs out of it are far removed from earthly reality. Hence the mine, although a natural environment, has something fantastic about it, especially if you are a German romantic who believes the world is inhabited by elementary spirits and occult forces that frequently exercise an uncanny influence over man.

This is, of course, a highly romantic view of the miner's life, one unlikely to be encountered in Zola or Lawrence. But Hoffmann was working in a different tradition. In Novalis's *Henry von Ofter-*

dingen can be found an idealized version of the miner's life to compare with a more realistic account.

> How tranquilly . . . the poor, contented miner works in his deep solitudes, withdrawn from the restless tumult of the day and inspired only with desire for knowledge and love of concord. In his solitude he thinks of his companions and family with hearty affection and feels ever anew the interdependence and blood kinship of all mankind. His occupation teaches him tireless patience and does not permit him to distract his attention with useless thoughts. He is pitted against a singularly hard and unyielding power, which can be overcome only by stubborn diligence and constant watchfulness. But what a delightful growth blooms for him even within those gruesome depths, namely, a veritable trust in his heavenly Father, Whose hand and providence are daily visible to him in unmistakable signs.[24]

This depiction of solitude points to another symbol the romantic artist could find in mining. The depths of the earth can portray the inner life of man, his contemplative rather than his active nature. Not directly related to the miner, but relevant to this aspect of his life, is Novalis's critique of the practical versus the introspective existence:

> People born to carry on trade and business cannot early enough consider and come to grips with everything themselves. They have to take a hand in a great many things and hurry through a host of details. . . . They may not yield to the lures of a quiet contemplation. Their soul may not indulge in introspective reverie; it must be steadily directed outward and be an industrious, swiftly-deciding servant of their mind.[25]

For such a businessman, in short, the Philistine, the only charm of the mines is the wealth of precious metals and gems they yield; the beauty of the mineral world he could never appreciate for its own sake. Not so with the miner, who, for Novalis, is clearly a romantic, if not an outright artistic soul; with regard to the metals of the earth, their dazzling glamor has no power over his pure heart. Uninflamed by perilous frenzy, he takes more delight in their peculiar structures and their strange origin and habitat than in their possession which promises so much. They have no charm for him once they are turned into commercial articles.[26]

The interior world to which the romantic artist turns to escape the tumult and vulgarity of the common life is also dark, mysterious, frightening in its uncharted state—a world fraught with religious significance for Novalis, and like a mystic he was antagonistic to those worldly concerns that interrupted his reveries. The matter was not that simple for Hoffmann. Although he, like Novalis's miner, feared in the commercial world a destruction of aesthetic values, he also, like Heine's more naturalistic miner, yearned for the fresh air outside. Hoffmann was uneasily aware of the unhealthy state that resulted from a total commitment to the dark, the occult, the purely imaginative. In *The Mines of Falun* he was able to extract from the image of the mine a contrast between the fantasy life associated with the darkest recesses of the mind, and the mundane life which, although more healthy, was yet destructive of the artist's sensitive being. The mine, paradoxically, represents both modes of existence.

This double image of the mine creates the central ambiguity in Hoffmann's tale. And here again it is possible to make a significant comparison with Tieck, for whereas Tieck presents unresolved conflicts by opposing the life in the mountains to that of the plains, the life of the disciplined gardener to the wilder pursuits of the hunter, Hoffmann has skillfully manipulated the real and the illusory so that they emanate from the same source. For Elis Fröbom, the mines are *both* a means to make a living to support his bride, and a realm which corresponds to an inner being that shrinks from thoughts of domesticity. Both not only strain against each other but cancel each other out, and herein lies Elis's tragedy.

The duality is found in the initial advice about mining given to Elis when the old stranger tells him:

Follow my advice, Elis Fröbom! Go to Falun, become a miner. You are young, energetic. You will make a fine apprentice, then pickman, then miner. You will keep on moving up. You have some good number of ducats in your pocket which you can invest and which you can add to from earnings, and eventually you can acquire a small house and some land and have your own shares in a mine. Follow my advice, Elis Fröbom, become a miner. [SB 1:193; 176]

Elis's sensitive nature recoils from such commercialism:

What are you advising me? . . . Do you want me to leave the beautiful free earth, the cheerful sunny sky which surrounds me and quickens and refreshes me—I am to go down into the fearful depths of hell and like a mole grub around for ores and metal for a miserable pittance? [SB 1:193; 176]

The mines, the stranger assures him, yield other treasures than profit; and later in the story he will actually reproach the young man for materialistic concerns. Elis's occupation, he claims, will allow him "to recognize in the marvelous minerals the reflection of that which is hidden above the clouds" (SB 1:194; 176). This appeal to a transcendental vision, which seems to Elis to correspond to a world his dreams had already made familiar, finally convinces him that he must go to Falun.

Hoffmann reveals a correspondence between the dreamworld which emanates from man's inner self and that transcendent reality man has conventionally depicted as existing in the heavens. That is why the dark mines are able to reflect the mystery which exists beyond this world. The sea from which Elis has returned significantly lies between the two realms, for it mirrors what exists above and hides what lies below. In a strange dream, the three realms merge for Elis:

[Above] him he saw a dome of darkly gleaming minerals, which he had at first thought were clouds in the sky. Driven by an unknown power, he strode on; but at that moment everything around him began to stir and, like curling waves, there shot up all around him marvelous flowers and plants of glittering metal, the blossoms and leaves of which curled upward from the depths and became intertwined in a most pleasing manner. The ground was so transparent that Elis could clearly see the roots of the plants; but when he looked down deeper and ever deeper, he saw in the depths innumerable, charming female forms who held each other locked in embrace with white, gleaming arms, and from their hearts there sprouted forth those roots and flowers and plants; when the maidens smiled, sweet harmony echoed through the dome, and the wondrous metal flowers thrust ever higher and became ever more gay. [SB 1:195; *177–78*]

In this vision, sky, sea, and the depths of the earth are combined in an ecstatic evocation of the music which floods Elis's dream.

Hoffmann has described in fantastic, indeed phantasmagoric terms the dreamworld of Elis and, in invoking music at the end of the passage, has attempted to convey feelings better conveyed by melody alone. Music, as pure expression of emotion, alleviates the necessity for precise descriptions, for geographical distinctions. In contrast, the reality of the mines is depicted in coldly detached language:

As is well known, the great entrance to the mine of Falun is about twelve hundred feet long, six hundred feet wide, and one hundred and eighty feet deep. The blackish brown sidewalls at first extend down more or less vertically; about half way down, however, they are less steep because of the tremendous piles of rubble. Here and there in the banks and walls can be seen timbers of old shafts which were constructed of strong trunks laid closely together and joined at the ends in the way block houses are usually constructed. [SB 1:198; *180–81*]

But even this stark diction conveys the potential horror of the place and Hoffmann's writing goes on to become more excited, adjectival, and even allusive as he concludes the description by asserting that this was surely the place where Dante descended into the inferno.

Between the awful depths of the mines and the sky in which dreamers have usually pictured their heaven lies the real world. Here miners celebrate their prosperity and sailors rejoice in their safe arrival from foreign lands. It is a world of joyful ceremonies like marriage, of contented or frustrated old age, and also of tragic accidents. The death of his mother, his last living relative, has severed whatever ties Elis had to this material world, and when he is first introduced in the story he "had slipped away from the turmoil and was sitting alone on a bench by the door of the tavern" (SB 1:190; *172*). What singled him out as an ideal miner in the first place was his naturally melancholy and "childlike nature that is turned inward" (SB 1:193; *175*), the very qualities which buried him "in the wild loneliness in which he believed himself lost" (SB 1:191; *174*), and which caused him to yearn toward the love and domestic happiness offered by Ulla. For her Elis will descend into the mines to earn the living that will make their marriage possible. Unhappily, these same mines are a material expression of the lonely, asocial, deeply inner life he has always tended to live; so that to become a miner is paradoxically to commit himself more intensely to an existence inimical to his plans for earthly contentment.

Thus it is not merely a question of Elis's choice between his betrothed, Ulla, and the Queen of the Mines. Hoffmann has brilliantly presented the total irreconcilability of his hero's desires by providing the mines with a symbolic function that cancels out the literal one. Elis's doom is spelled out by the contradictory warnings he receives about his new craft. The old stranger who first directs him to Falun tells him to be "faithful to the Queen to whom you have given yourself" (SB 1:196; *178–79*). But Elis, by dreaming of a life with Ulla and of the money he can earn for her, evades his commitment to the queen, thus drawing the wrath of the stranger, who later appears to reproach him for his crass materialism:

> Oh yes, you want to win Pehrson Dahlsjö's daughter Ulla for your wife, and therefore you are working here without love or interest. Beware, you cheat, that the *Metallfürst*, whom you mock, doesn't seize you and hurl you into the abyss so that all your bones are smashed on the rocks. [SB 1:204; *187*]

But surrender to the queen is equally dangerous, as Ulla's father makes clear:

> There is an ancient belief among us that the mighty elements, among which the miner boldly reigns, will annihilate him unless he exerts his whole self in maintaining his mastery over them and gives thought to nothing else, for that would

diminish the power that he should expend exclusively on his work in the earth and the fire. [SB 1:201; *185*]

Self-control, in Pehrson Dahlsjö's terms, represents the betrayal of the queen's terms, for she demands the very submission Elis has been warned against by his future father-in-law.

Elis's struggle is similar to that depicted by Samuel Daniel in his poem about *Ulysses and the Sirens* and countered by Yeats when he spoke of the Gaelic muse as a malicious fairy. The sirens yield to Ulysses because they cannot dominate him, a classical conception which, when applied to art, makes necessary the artist's self-mastery. In contrast, Yeats suggests that inspiration comes to those who surrender to the destructive fairy who consumes her victims while she inspires them. This apotheosis of romanticism finds the demise of poetry in the domestication of the muse.

Elis Fröbom seems by nature to belong to the Queen of the Mines, for her realm corresponds to his essentially introverted nature. To struggle against her is hence to be false to himself. On his wedding day he turns from his bride, whose side he formerly could not bear to leave, because he recognizes in her a link to normalcy:

> He felt split in half; it seemed to him that his better, his true being, was climbing down into the center of the earth and was resting in the Queen's arms, while he was seeking his dreary bed in Falun. When Ulla spoke to him of her love and how they would live together happily, then he began to speak of the splendor of the shaft, of the immeasurably rich treasures which lay concealed there, and he became entangled in such strange, incomprehensible speeches that fear and anxiety seized the poor child and she did not know at all how Elis could have changed so suddenly into a quite different person. [SB 1:209; *193*]

Such a view of married life, of a dreary bed in Falun, is Elis's final capitulation to the otherworldly forces that oppose his domestic impulses.

Perhaps because so many of Hoffmann's stories are explicitly about artists, the critics have not viewed Elis as such. But Hoffmann's revulsion at a Philistine world and his uneasy aestheticism are both reflected in Elis's dilemma. For any artist anxious about the acceptance as well as the integrity of his work, the double motive with which Elis approaches mining is bound to seem applicable to the creative life. Can he make a living and still remain true to his "better" self? If not, how can he expect to live a normal life and still be an artist? Are normalcy and art incompatible? If so, how can the artist commit himself to an abnormal life without the struggle which itself was going to mar him. *The Mines of Falun* offers a critique of aestheticism without offering any alternatives. It would be interesting to know if Yeats, whose own career was marked by his concern that the poet must choose between art and life, ever came across the translation of Hoffmann's tale in the August 1876 issue of the *Dublin University Magazine*. Whether or not he looked at the back issue, another renowned nineteenth-century artist has left a very telling record of how Hoffmann's story could serve as a paradigm for an almost universal dilemma confronting the creative man. In his biography of Richard Wagner, Ernest Newman quotes from the composer's *Autobiography* a description of the way Wagner felt when about to be married to his first wife, Minna:

> At that moment . . . I saw clearly, as if in a vision, my whole being divided into two cross-currents that dragged me in completely different directions: the upper one, that faced the sun, swept me on like a man in a dream, while the lower one held my nature captive in a great and incomprehensible fear.[27]

It is not surprising that Wagner, at the point of marriage, recalled Elis Fröbom, who also faced wedlock with a sense of conflict and fear for his higher being. Although he never composed the opera, Wagner had by the time he married already written the scenario for *The Mines of Falun*.

VENUS and the POPE:
The Hebraic-Hellenic Dichotomy

Hoffmann in his writings combined two related aspects of nineteenth-century aesthetics: he is among those romantics whose escapism leads to self-conflict, and his distaste for Philistinism finds him in the company of artists whose preoccupations were somewhat different. The figure of the uncultured, middle-class citizen, who frequently appears in Hoffmann's stories and is so well described by Novalis in *Henry von Ofterdingen*,[1] has less to do with the romances of Fouqué or the poetry of Keats than with a cultural problem treated by Heinrich Heine and Matthew Arnold, who describe the contrast between Hebraism and Hellenism, that is, between prosaic morality and religion on the one side, and art and beauty, on the other.

In 1849 Matthew Arnold published a variation of the Undine motif. In *The Forsaken Merman* a woman from earth weds a merman, dwells in the sea, and bears him children.[2] In contrast to the mermaid who hopes to win a soul, Margaret fears she will forfeit hers, and returns to earth at Easter to pray with her kind. "Long prayers . . . in the world they say," muses her husband, for Margaret does not return to her family although she had promised otherwise.

The voice in the poem is that of the pathetic, forsaken merman, calling his children back to the sea from earth, where they seek their mother. She is theirs "no more," and the sounds of that Poe-esque phrase, and of words like "alone," "lonely," and "moan," seem to echo like the sea wind the desolation of the water folk. Meanwhile, on earth, Margaret is torn by conflicting impulses. During the day she joyfully celebrates the bright things of this earth as well as the "priest, and the bell, and the holy well," but at night

> She steals to the window, and looks at the sand,
> And over the sand at the sea;

And her eyes are set in a stare;
And anon there breaks a sigh,
And anon there drops a tear,
From a sorrow-clouded eye,
And a heart sorrow-laden,
A long, long sigh;
For the cold strange eyes of a little Mermaiden
And the gleam of her golden hair.[3]

Arnold's poem reflects that conflict which he also described in his essay on *Pagan and Mediaeval Religious Sentiment* and again in *Culture and Anarchy.* "Hebraism and Hellenism,—between these two points of influence moves our world,"[4] states Arnold, and it is possible that the contrast between the "gleam" of the mermaiden's "golden hair" and the "grey church" in which Margaret prays embodies the Hebraic-Hellenic dichotomy. The "cold eyes" of that same mermaid, however, point also to Arnold's characteristic reluctance to give undue weight to pure beauty (in much the same sense that Keats called the Grecian urn a "cold pastoral").

Many of Arnold's ideas about Hebraism and Hellenism were derived from Heine, for whom the Keatsian conflict between beauty and truth had a specific social context. In his last poem, *Für die Mouche*, a despairing summation of a life-long struggle, Heine imagines himself lying dead in an open tomb, around which are figures in bas–relief from both classical mythology and the Bible. In this

contrast glaring and grotesque,
Judea's Godward yearning was combined
With the Greek sense of joy!
[HW 20:264][5]

As the marble figures come to life and engage in contentious debate, the poet comes to a final realization:

O, well I know they never will agree;
Beauty and truth will always be at variance.

103

The army of mankind will always be
Split in two camps: The Hellenes and Barbarians.
[HW 20:267]

Whereas for the early romantics the struggle between beauty and truth was essentially an internal one, for later romantics the battle was with the public. An increasingly Philistine culture exacerbated the escapist tendencies of the romantic artist and provided him with a rationalization for turning his back on social responsibilities. Thus the dialogue of the romantic poet's mind with itself was affected by his confrontation with a hostile environment. This altered context is reflected in the treatments of the Belle Dame sans Merci story, but its relationship to the Hebraic-Hellenic dichotomy should be made clearer.

Hebraism and Hellenism can each be examined from at least two distinct points of view, both important because each bears a somewhat different relation to romanticism.[6] Hebraism has a decidedly otherworldly side and a this-worldly side, and in each instance Hellenism would represent the obverse. As is the case with the word *romanticism*, then, *Hebraism* and *Hellenism* must be used with caution. The nature of the conflict frequently differed for Heine and Arnold.

Hebraism is manifested first in its asceticism, in its tendency, as Arnold says, "to sacrifice all other sides of our being to the religious side."[7] For Heine this tendency is particularly marked in Germany, which, as far as he is concerned, absorbed all of the religious feeling banished from France by the Enlightenment: "When men repudiated spirit in France, it emigrated at once to Germany, and there repudiated matter" (HW 10:362; 5:293). Heine rejects this *contemptus mundi* philosophy, reflecting

> whether renunciation and abstinence are to be really preferred to all the joys of this life, and whether those who have, while here on earth below, contented themselves with thistles, will be on that account the more liberally treated with pine apples in the land above. No, he who ate thistles was an ass, and he who receives blows keeps them. [HW 12:305; 4:421]

He blames part of this spiritualism on the romantic school's tendency to relegate the natural world to mere symbolic reflection of the infinite. German romanticism, like medieval literature, had "risen from Christianity," and was "a passion-flower which had sprung from the blood of Christ" (HW 10:240; 5:217). Thus he believes the revival of interest in the Middle Ages in his own time can be traced to this unhealthy asceticism of the romantics, although in *The Elementary Spirits* he suggests another cause which he can endorse. The "mania for the Middle Ages was perhaps a secret prepossession for old German pantheism, or the remains of that old religion living on in the popular beliefs of a later age" (HW 11:109; 4:594). Pantheism is healthy in contrast to the renunciatory and politically reactionary views of Catholic romanticism, which attacked the rationality of Protestantism and the materialism of neoclassical culture. "The blooming rosy flesh in the pictures of Titian," says Heine, "is all Protestantism. The limbs of his Venus are more thorough *theses* than those which the German monk pasted on the church door of Wittenberg" (HW 10:256; 5:227).

Matthew Arnold was skeptical about this brand of Hellenism. His own could never be symbolized by the blooming rosy flesh of Titian's Venus, for he shared with orthodox Christianity the basic assumption that man's fleshly desires represented his lower nature. His critique of the philosophy propounded by Heine's brand of Hellenism exposes the essential weakness of its tenets: "Well, the sentiment of the 'religion of pleasure' has much that is natural in it; humanity will gladly accept it if it can live by it; to live by it one must never be sick or sorry." [8] As he thinks about "what human life is for the vast majority of mankind, how little of a feast for their senses it can possibly be," he understands the appeal held out by Christianity, which promises a better existence in an otherworld.[9] Ironically, Heine's own life confirmed Arnold's view. One of the more touching anecdotes about him concerns the last day before he became bedridden. In great pain and with difficulty, he made his way to the Louvre to bid a last farewell to the Venus of Milo, who he imagined looked at him with great pity and helplessness. She could not help him; did he not see she had no arms?[10]

Arnold's other criticism of the pagan existence is that, like Hebraism, it is addressed to only one side of man:

The ideal, cheerful, sensuous, pagan life is not sick or sorry. No; yet its natural end is in the sort of life which Pompeii and Herculaneum bring so vividly before us,—a life which by no means in itself suggests the thought of horror and misery, which even, in many ways, gratifies the senses and the understanding; but by the very intensity and unremittingness of its appeal to the senses and the understanding, by its stimulating a single side of us too absolutely, ends by fatiguing and revolting us; ends by leaving us with a sense of confinement, of oppression,—with a desire for an utter change, for clouds, storms, effusion, and relief.[11]

This passage could well gloss the Tannhäuser story in the works of Heine, Swinburne, and Wagner, each of whom deals with the ennui of life in the Venusburg. Heine's knight is so tired of Venus's kisses that he actually longs for the pains of an earthly existence.

In summary, then, one aspect of the Hebraic-Hellenic dichotomy emphasizes the conflict between spirit and matter. Hebraism, by turning away from the finite world, shares with romanticism its longing for an infinite perfection in some immaterial realm. Hellenism exalts the sensible world, even at times to the exclusion of those spiritual values materialism alone cannot provide. For Arnold man, whom he rather traditionally conceived of as being torn between flesh and spirit, could dispense with neither realm. Here he would have had no disagreement with Heine, for whom the battle between the pagans and Nazarenes was a reflection of an inner conflict. Nevertheless, Heine's quarrel with German romantic asceticism frequently caused him to find in materialism a self-sufficiency he knew it did not really possess.

The second aspect of Hebraism at issue here is—far from being otherworldly and *akin* to romanticism—closely associated with materialism and *antagonistic* to romanticism. But to begin an extended discussion of the connection between religion and the Philistine-producing commercialism in which nineteenth-century artists found a formidable enemy would involve the long, complex subject of the classic studies produced by Max Weber and R. H. Tawney. Briefly, however, each writer was concerned to show how religion, essentially otherworldly in its emphasis, was nevertheless a spur to capitalism. Tawney describes how, from the "reiterated insistence on secular obligations as imposed by the divine will, it follows that, not withdrawal from the world, but the conscientious discharge of the duties of business, is among the loftiest of religious and moral virtues." [12] The proper exercise of such duties is rewarded by earthly success, and thus, ironically, Hebraic spiritualism is transformed into materialism, into the beginnings of Philistinism. Arnold wrote, "The people who believe most that our greatness and welfare are proved by our being very rich, and who most give their lives and thoughts to becoming rich, are just the very people whom we call Philistines." [13] He thinks that Hellenism leads in contrast to a non-material pursuit of culture and inner perfection; that in his own age "it is a time to Hellenise, and to praise knowing; for we have Hebraised too much, and have over-valued doing." [14]

According to Tawney, in the religious conception of duty and industry were forged "some of the links in the Utilitarian coat of mail." [15] Utilitarianism shares with materialistic Hebraism its emphasis on outward appearance, on that which is tangible rather than spiritual, and its suspicion of an aesthetic experience which does not lead to some visible purpose. In contrast, there is Arnold's culture, "the disinterested endeavour after man's perfection." [16] But such an "idea of perfection as an *inward* condition of the mind and spirit is," Arnold realizes, "at variance with the mechanical and material civilisation in esteem with us." [17] There is a historical irony here. The Protestant conception of the direct communication between man and God fostered an emphasis on the inner being, on a perfection that could be perceived only through constant self-examination, a turning inward. This connection between Protestantism and romantic subjectivism will figure predominantly in my later discussion of Eichendorff. But the channeling of the religious life into business and the resultant materialism of the nineteenth century, with its emphasis on that which was useful, produced the anti-romantic Philistine. And the Philistine, in turn, helped produce a new kind of romanticism.

"Perhaps," said Heine, "it was irritation at this prevalent faith in money, or revolt at the egoism which they saw grinning out everywhere, which inspired certain poets of the Romantic school in Germany, who had deeply honourable feelings, to take refuge from the present in the past, and attempt the restoration of the Middle Age" (HW 11:50; 5:333). One might reply that to the genuinely romantic soul, there is always something in the world to cause revulsion, to encourage him to seek a Golden Age or create if necessary an imaginary realm of his own. But the commercialism which began to accelerate in the nineteenth century, especially toward the middle and end of it, had a particularly deleterious effect on art. E. D. H. Johnson has noted that the artists of the generation of Tennyson, Browning, and Arnold "were the first to face the problem of communicating with a modern reading public little sensitive to the life of the imagination." [18] This is not entirely so, for Peacock had already described how a new, inferior audience was moving into the space left by superior intellects, whose pursuit of science and moral philosophy left the artist without a cultured public. And still earlier Wordsworth in his preface to the *Lyrical Ballads* spoke about a multitude of hitherto unknown causes that were blunting the discriminating powers of the audience's mind. There is, however, no question but that the movement toward aestheticism as the century progressed can be traced to the artist's sense of alienation from his public.

Art for art's sake should be distinguished from earlier forms of romanticism. Keats and Tieck had worried about escaping into a dreamworld that shielded them from the suffering or annoyances of this world. They endeavored to move away from a subjective or lyric mode of writing toward drama or realistic fiction as a way of re-establishing ties with society. The "artsakist," to borrow a convenient word from Albert Guérard, similarly concentrates on objective form, but this formalism, far from being classical in orientation, is as much of an escape as the inwardness of the earlier romantics. Instead of feeling guilty about his evasion of social responsibility, the artsakist finds in an insensitive reading public justification for his retreat into form. "Elaborate technique, however," says Guérard,

> was but the veneer of Art for Art's Sake. The passion smouldering beneath the hard and polished surface was, we must repeat, the hatred of successful mediocrity, Philistinism. The deluded populace could be ignored: the enemy with whom there could be no truce was the middle class, with its undeniable cunning, its control of worldly goods, its capacity for aping the externals of culture. Thus it was that Art for Art's Sake assumed a non-moral, even an anti-moral attitude, for morality was the citadel of the Bourgeoisie. The victors

had seized it, as they had seized wealth, power, and all the strategic points in modern civilization. The triumph of materialism was actually heralded as the apotheosis of virtue. With a hypocrisy so ingrained that it was wholly unconscious, the Profiteering Motive and the sanctity of private greed were exalted as the highest principles.[19]

In short, if the reaction against Philistinism among earlier writers like Hoffmann took the form of a retreat into fantasy, the later reaction tended to be art– rather than poet–centered. Poetry was no longer the spontaneous, lyrical overflow of the subjective romantic poet, no longer the dialogue of his mind with itself, so much as artifice pushed to extreme as the artist inhabited a realm where form occupied those able to find pleasure in abstract beauty and eager to escape the dismal morality of their age.

When A. H. Krappe began his study of the Tannhäuser legend with a quotation from Swinburne,

> Thou hast conquered oh Pale Galilean,
> The world has grown gray from thy breath,

he suggested the inherent suitability of the legend for an expression of the Hebraic-Hellenic dichotomy, although his essay does not develop the point.[20] The *Hymn to Proserpine*, with its lament over the dethronement of the pagan gods by Christ, whose sad Virgin Mother has replaced Venus, is a eulogy to and elegy for Hellenism. The world has been emptied of beauty, has "grown gray" from the influence of Hebraism. The color is becoming a noteworthy adjective. In Arnold's *Forsaken Merman*, the gray church in which Margaret prays represents the force that keeps her from her family in the sea. Beauty loses ground in an age for which those things that are only beautiful are therefore *merely* beautiful. And religion, diverted into "useful" channels, as business allows man to serve God on earth, frowns upon pleasure, not because it is sinful so much as because it is purposeless. All of these forces feed Utilitarianism, which becomes art's most dangerous foe. Swinburne's *Poems and Ballads* was a notorious blow struck against a world permeated by gray Hebrist tendencies.

The Tennhäuser legend provided an ideal expression for the

Hebraic-Hellenic dichotomy, since the conflict between the old pagan gods and the Judeo-Christian God can be found in the opposition between Venus and the Pope. Tannhäuser's dissatisfaction with pagan sensuality bears witness to Arnold's warning that the stimulation of only one side of man's nature will lead to bitter frustration, while the knight's treatment by the Pope is a potential symbol of the artist's confrontation with an insensitive public.

In 1861 the magazine, *Once a Week*, published a translation of *Tannhäuser* from Arnim's and Brentano's *Des Knabes Wunderhorn*. The editors supplied some background to the poem:

> Venus, after the destruction of her temples, took refuge, with a licentious crew of nymphs, in an enchanted mountain, called the Mons Veneris, where she spends her time in riotous living. Woe to the rash, who, allured by the sound of the music and revelry, seek her attractive court. For them there is no escape. Pleasure may pall, conscience may awaken, but the captive knight cannot break his bonds, and escape from the arms of the vengeful goddess.[21]

Here are indications of the many directions the legend could take. The transformation of the goddess into a demon might serve as a basis for depicting the cultural transition from Hellenism to Hebraism. The romantic poet or "artsakist" might concentrate on Venus's attractive court, while the moralist could delineate the "woe" suffered by the captive knight. For those who, like earlier romantic artists, found the Hebraic-Hellenic dichotomy to be a reflection of an inner conflict, an identification with Tannhäuser, torn between flesh and spirit, would be easy to make. Because the legend was so fraught with possibility, it was very popular in the middle and late nineteenth century. La Belle Dame sans Merci, who had earlier appeared as Undine, Lamia, or the goddess of the Runenberg, now frequently appeared as the pagan goddess Venus.

EXILED GODS

Heine's chief quarrel with German romanticism concerned its otherworldly emphasis because he believed that its alliance with Roman Catholicism was destructive of those elements in life essential to man's well-being: pleasure, individual liberty, and reason. But in his preface to *The Romantic School,* Heine denies that he belongs to the materialists, who he claims "embody the spirit," in contrast to himself, who gives "the spirit back unto bodies. I spiritualise [them] again—I sanctify [them]" (HW 10:231; 5:528). Just how he does this beyond mere assertion is not always clear. In *The Elementary Spirits,* however, he follows the line of Paracelsus and, with perhaps less earnestness than his predecessor, tries to rescue the nature spirits from the taint of demonism with which Christians endowed them. The book is a loosely constructed anthology of stories about the relationships between supernatural and human beings. Heine's knowledge of such lore is extensive, ranging from folk tales to Spenser's *Faerie Queene.*

This range, however, is itself curious, for it takes a huge leap on the part of a reader to classify a simple folk tale with Spenser's complicated allegory in the manner that Heine does.

> If the elves were not already immortal by nature they would have become so through Shakespeare. They will live eternally in the Midsummer Night's Dream of poesy. And no more will Spenser's Fairy Queen be forgotten, so long as the English tongue is understood. [HW 11:127–28; 4:387–88, 598][1]

Kurt Weinberg has noted that in contrast to Jacob Grimm, who believed that folk literature had greater value than more sophisticated forms, Heine tended to blur the distinctions between "*Natur- et Kunstpoesie.*" [2] But such a blurring, if it does not result from a lack of discernment between distinct forms, invites further consideration.

The admixture of folk and art forms can probably be understood in terms of a marked ambivalence toward the German folk in *The Elementary Spirits.* At one point in the book Heine refers to a revival of the belief in witches and hence of witch hunting. This appalls him.

> Oh, ye black villains, and ye feeble-minded folk of all colours—go on, perfect your work, heat the brain of the people with old superstitions, drive it on to the road of fanaticism! Ye yourselves will be someday its sacrifice, ye will not escape that which befell the unskilled enchanter who could not control the fiends which he had raised, and was by them torn to pieces. Should the spirit of Revolution not succeed in arousing the German race by means of reason, it may be reserved for Folly to complete the great work.
> [HW 11:205–206; 4:616–17]

After this prophetic outburst, Heine catches himself and continues in a calmer tone: "But this is not the place for adjuration or exorcism, the more because it leads me from my theme. My business is to speak of simple tales, of that which is sung and told around the German stoves" (HW 11:206; 4:617).

Heine's attitude seems clearer after this passage. Rejecting most of the characteristics of German romanticism, he nevertheless shared its enthusiasm for nature and folk tales. This was partially so because the folk belief that nature was animated with spiritual beings led to an emphasis on this world rather than some immaterial otherworld. He preferred this pantheistic ethos to the asceticism of Christianity and noted with approval that "The German baker stamps on every loaf which he bakes the old Druid's foot, and our daily bread thus bears the sign of the German religion. What a significant contrast does this true bread offer to the dry sham bread with which spiritual culture would nourish us" (HW 11:109; 4:595). Yet Heine the romanticist, who himself used the folk vocabulary and rhythms in his verse, feared the underlying primitivism of the folk revival.

Beneath the artist, who found the materialism of the folk culture appealing and aesthetically satisfying, was Heine the social critic, who considered irrationalism a danger to man as a social and political being. The value of the folk revival for him lay more in what it countered than in what it affirmed.

Since the cultural significance of folklore existed for Heine in its symbolic protest against the arid Hebraism of his age, he discovered in fairylore meanings far beyond anything simple folk were likely to imagine. This may well be the reason that he made little distinction between the fairy tale and Spenser's epic. The value of fairyland, in short, is in the kind of symbolism it provides in his late poem, *Atta Troll.*

> And the lovely fay Abunde,
> Of the Nazarenes mistrustful,
> Through the sunlit hours seeks shelter
> In the Isle of Avalon.
>
> In that magic island hidden
> In the far and quiet ocean
> Of Romance, that none can win to
> Save the wingëd steeds of fable:
>
> By whose shore care never anchors,
> Where no steamer ever calls,
> Landing Philistines intrusive,
> Pipe in mouth, intent on prying:
>
> Where no echo ever pierces
> From our tiresome gloomy bells,
> With their dreary ding-dong jangle
> So detested by the fairies.
> [HW 18:277; 2:399–400]

Fairyland exists in the realm of art, and art, the product of man's imagination, is his bastion against Philistinism.

Much of Heine's writing, then, was an attack on Hebraism, both its religious aspect—he rejected the spiritualism of German romantics—and its commercial form—he also spurned Philistinism.

Nevertheless, he also understood, as his confrontation with the Venus of Milo in the Louvre reveals, that beauty was not self-sufficient in what it could offer mankind. Moreover, his revulsion from the anticultural elements in his own age frequently led him to a position which was no less otherworldly than those features of romanticism that he abjured. Perhaps this was inherent in his very choice of fairyland as a symbol for art. For the asceticism he abhorred he frequently substituted the aestheticism he could not at times help adopting.

That he was conscious of his equivocal position is clear from the frame he places around the Tannhäuser material in *The Elementary Spirits*. He invents a fictitious author, Heinrich Kitzler (Henry Tickler), who has just completed a treatise dealing with the magnificence of Christianity. Kitzler, however, faces a perplexing dilemma: whenever he concludes a work on some subject, he begins to anticipate objections to it, until he finally shifts his position. In his work on Christianity he says that

> I have shown how debauched and debased the Greeks and Romans became from the bad examples of those gods who, to judge by the vices attributed to them, were hardly worthy to be classed with men. . . . I have appropriately paraphrased the moral axioms of the New Testament, and shown how [they], according to the example of their divine prototype, in spite of the scorn and persecution which they thereby incurred, taught and practised the most perfect moral purity. [HW 12:301–02; 4:*419*]

His manuscript, however, was eventually consigned to fire, for, he says,

> I must confess that there at last stole over me a terrible pity for the remains of heathenism, for those beautiful temples and statues, for they no longer belonged to the religion which had been dead long, long before the birth of Christ, but to *Art*, which lives for ever. [HW 12:302; 4:*420*]

Heine expresses Kitzler's sentiments in his poem, *The Gods of Greece* (*The North Sea* cycle):

Gods of old time, I never have loved ye!
For the Greeks did never chime with my spirit,
And e'en the Romans I hate at heart;
But holy compassion and shudd'ring pity
Stream through my soul
As I now gaze upon ye yonder,
Gods long neglected,
Death-like, night-wandering shadows,
Weak as clouds which the wind hath scattered;
And when I remember how weak and windy
The gods now are who o'er you triumphed,
The new and the sorrowful gods now ruling,
The joy-destroyers in sheep-skins of meekness,
Then there comes o'er me the gloomiest rage;
Fain would I shatter the modern temples,
And battle for ye.[3]
[HW 4:205–06; 1:188–89]

The real question, says Heine, is "whether the dismal, meagre, over-spiritual, ascetic Judaism of the Nazarenes, or Hellenic joyousness, love of beauty, and fresh pleasure in life should rule the world." He notes that the triumph of Christ had consigned the Greek deities to the role of "sheer devils who hide by day in gloomy wreck and rubbish, but by night arise in charming loveliness to bewilder and allure some heedless wanderer or daring youth" (HW 12:307; 4:423). From the legends based on this popular belief, he continues, "our more recent German poets drew . . . the subjects of their most beautiful poems" (HW 12:307–08; 4:423). Included in his recounting of these stories is his own version of *Tannhäuser.*

The first two parts of the three-part poem reflect the dilemma of Heinrich Kitzler, who could not finally choose between his rejection of the immoral ancient deities and pity for the loss to the world of heathen values and beauty. At the beginning of the poem, Tannhäuser has rejected Venus because of the cloying pleasure of unrelieved sensuality.

O Venus, mistress fond and fair,
Of your wine so sweet in flavour,

Of your kisses warm, my soul is sick—
Some sourness I would savour.

Jested and laughed too long have we,
I yearn for weeping bitter;
I want no roses for my head—
A crown of thorns were fitter.[4]

Bored with the goddess, ready to accept even pain for the sake of change, Tannhäuser heaps insults upon his mistress:

Yea, when I think upon the gods
And heroes who have lusted
After your body lily-white,
My soul recoils disgusted.

This is too much for her, and she permits him to leave the Venusberg.

This *fin de siècle* languor and cynicism, which Swinburne would make the focus of his *Laus Veneris*, is confined, however, to the first part of the poem. In the second part Tannhäuser presents a very different picture of Venus to Pope Urban. At first his description is tender and gentle:

A lovely woman Venus is,
With many a grace to charm one;
Like sunshine and the scent of flowers,
Her voice can soothe and warm one.

As the butterfly, fluttering, sips from the cup
Of the fragrant flower posies,
So flutters my soul for ever round
Her lips as red as roses.

But as he describes the charms that made it so difficult to escape from the Venusberg, his memories renew his passion, and the intensity of his emotion is reflected in the imagery of wild nature that replaces the earlier descriptions of flowers and butterflies:

I love her with a boundless love,
Nothing will stay its urging;
'Tis like a swirling cataract,
You cannot stem its surging.

From rock to rock it leaps and foams:
The thunder-voices roar on;
If it broke its neck a thousand times,
The mighty flood would pour on.

This sweeping assertion belies the contrition that led Tannhäuser to Rome. He is trapped by his inability to accept either pagan joyousness devoid of higher meaning or Christian morality which demands asceticism as a price of salvation. Imprisoned in the Venusberg, Tannhäuser came to long for thorns of sorrow to alleviate his boredom. But faced with the spirituality of the Pope, which he hoped would lend meaning to his existence, his impulse is to defend the life of the senses, to rescue nature itself from any taint of sinfulness. Like Heinrich Kitzler, he reflects the internalized warfare between Hebraism and Hellenism, demonstrating the validity of Arnold's claim that each addresses itself too exclusively to one side of human life, and that both are needed. Moreover, the failure of Tannhäuser to resolve his conflict points to the emptiness of Heine's claim to have sanctified the body and foreshadows his ultimate confession of defeat in *Für die Mouche*, his despairing conviction that beauty and truth would never be united, that this world would forever be divided between Hellenes and Barbarians.

Parts 1 and 2 of the poem gloss the dilemma of Heinrich Kitzler, but part 3 continues to puzzle critics, who note in it a departure in tone from the rest of the poem and view Heine's description of Tannhäuser's journey back to the Venusberg as an excuse to satirize Germany and things German. Actually part 3 is not a departure from the rest of *Tannhäuser* so much as a continuation—however different in tone—of the main theme: the struggle between Hebraism and Hellenism.

The change that takes place in Venus herself is the essential part of this last section. Venus is no longer the goddess of parts 1 and 2, for she is neither the dissolute temptress who has bored the hero nor the beautiful embodiment of nature in either its milder or more exciting aspects. Instead, she is little more than an average, solicitous *hausfrau*.

> The knight awearied sank on the bed
> Ere a single word was spoken;
> To cook in the kitchen Venus went,
> That his fast might straight be broken.

> She gave him soup and she gave him bread;
> Herself his wounds washed featly;
> His matted hair she brushed and combed,
> And laughed the while full sweetly.

> Tannhäuser, noble knight, 'tis long
> Since you left me, and wandered forth, now;
> Oh, where have you been this weary while—
> In what land of the south or the north, now?

This transformation is reminiscent of Undine's after she marries Huldbrand. But whereas Fouqué's heroine has gained with her domestication that insight into the human condition which perhaps compensates for the dimming of her unearthly luster, Venus has acquired no such compensating qualities.

The domestication of Venus is best understood in the context of *The Gods in Exile*, which Heine began with the Tannhäuser material he had already included in *The Elementary Spirits*. In the earlier work he had endowed the Tannhäuser-Heinrich Kitzler connection with significance that went far beyond the conceptions of the folk, in whom he found little to praise save that by clinging to ancient beliefs they resisted the austere asceticism of Christianity. But there was another aspect of this resistance that drew Heine's attention. Folk literature reflected an imagination, vital and alive, which was unable to survive the stultifying modern, supposedly enlightened age.

A romantic nostalgia for some earlier time when primitive beliefs flourished marks Heine's introduction to the French version of *The Gods in Exile*:

> We are all passing away, men, gods, creeds, and legends. It is perhaps a pious work to preserve the latter from oblivion, so

that they are embalmed, not by the hideous process of Gannal, but by employing secret means which are only to be found in the *apotheca* of the poet. Yes, creeds are fleeting and traditions too; they are vanishing like burnt out tapers, not only in enlightened lands, but in the most midnight places of the world, where not long ago the most startling superstitions were in bloom. The missionaries who wander over these cold regions now complain of the incredulity of their inhabitants. In the report of a Danish clergyman of his journey in the North of Greenland, the writer tells us that he asked of an old man what was the present state of belief among them. To which the good man replied, "Once we believed in the moon, but now we believe in it no longer." [HW 12:295–96][5]

Here Heine has given this theme a double twist. His group of tales will relate the fate of the old pagan gods banished by the Christians; but since in this banishment Heine sees the demise of artistic beauty and imagination, he will actually be narrating imaginative stories whose symbolic import concerns the death of imagination.

The position of the Venusberg material in the earlier *Elementary Spirits* and the later *The Gods in Exile* becomes important here. *The Gods in Exile* was originally written in French and included the *Tannhäuser* ballad. In the German edition, Heine moved the ballad and its framework back to its original position in *The Elementary Spirits*. But his English translator and editor, Charles Leland, once more included *Tannhäuser* in *The Gods in Exile*. Since Venus is one of the exiled deities, she does seem to belong in the company of the other gods banished from their ancient temples. On close examination, however, we find her fate was not that of her fellow deities—at least not until part 3 of Heine's *Tannhäuser*. Although she was deemed an evil spirit by the Christians and relegated to a hell-like domain under the earth, the lot of the other gods was very different.

The theme of *The Gods in Exile* is not their metamorphosis into devils so much as it is their domestication. After the triumph of Christianity, says Heine,

Many of these poor emigrants, who were without shelter or ambrosia, were obliged to take to some everyday trade, to earn at least their daily bread. In such circumstances, many whose holy groves had been confiscated were obliged, among us in Germany, to work by the day as hewers of wood, and to drink beer instead of nectar. [HW 12:340; 6:79]

Apollo became a shepherd in Lower Austria, although he was discovered because of his singing and hanged. Mars became a mercenary soldier who served at the storming of Rome, where, Heine says, it must have been difficult for him to see the ruin of the temple in which he had been worshipped. Bacchus fared somewhat better, becoming a Franciscan monk who found means to conduct an annual orgy with his followers. Worst of all was the fate of Jupiter, who, confined to a lonely island at the North Pole, lived by the proceeds of sales from rabbit skins. Heine's comment on his end can be read as a general lament for the fallen gods:

> Such is the will of the iron law of fate, and unto it the grandest and highest of immortals must bow in suffering. He whom Homer sung and Phidias did counterfeit in gold and ivory, he who had but to wink to crush the world, he who had folded in his passionate arms Leda, Alcmene, Semele, Danae, Kallisto, Io, Leto, Europa—he must after all hide at the North Pole behind icebergs, and trade in rabbitskins like a beggarly Savoyard! [HW 12:374–75; 6:98]

In this text, part 3 of *Tannhäuser* begins to seem ironically clear. Although Heine had rejected Christian asceticism and particularly deplored its influence on German romanticism, he sympathized with the motivation that caused the modern age to look toward a medieval revival by way of a reaction against the commercialism of its time. This aspect of Hebraism, which subjugates to the profit motive all beauty, which reduces the aesthetic to the utilitarian, which results in a Philistine culture—this aspect of Hebraism and not its otherworldliness seems to be the target of *The Gods in Exile.* According to Heine's biting satire the pagan gods have been absorbed by a Philistine world. The metamorphosis of Venus into a demon is nowhere near as devastating a comment on a culture which has sought to destroy Hellenic joy and beauty as was her transformation into a *hausfrau*. The horror of the exiled gods is not in their banishment but in their assimilation.

Tannhäuser, then, can be seen as a link between *The Elementary Spirits*, which is a protest against worldly abnegation, one form of Hebraism, and *The Gods in Exile*, which attacks the other form, commercialism, the material by-product of a religion that debases culture. With mixed seriousness and frivolity, outrage and irony, Heine's writings had a satiric aim, and his cynical, mocking tone is never long absent. But beneath Heine the satirist is Heine the romantic poet, whose impulse to escape a crass and tormented world is no less strong than that of other romantic artists. Tannhäuser's sojourn in the Venusberg is thus as much an expression of this escapism as a similar journey to the otherworld had been for other romantic writers. The conflict between illusion and reality, art and life, takes on another dimension within the Hebraic-Hellenic dichotomy, but the fundamental issues concerning escapism frequently remain the same. Heine's connection with the earlier romantic writers can be seen in his ballet scenario, *The Goddess Diana*, which he says is a supplement to *The Gods in Exile*, and will save him from the necessity of making any further comment on that work. It is a ballet in which the Tannhäuser motif is used explicitly as an attack on Philistinism, but it also demonstrates that Heine's ultimate solution to his dilemma is a romantic, otherworldly solution.

The Goddess Diana is divided into four tableaux. The goddess herself is not the chaste Diana usually associated with ancient mythology but of a later tradition that brings her closer in conception to Venus. In the first tableau, a young German is about to sacrifice his life on her altar when she stops him, assuring him that his despair is unfounded. The old deities are not dead, but hidden in ruined temples and secret caves from which they emerge at night to hold festivals.

Tableau 2 finds the knight "brooding and melancholy" in a gothic castle, surrounded by "women affected, moral, and simpering" (HW 12:387; 6:105). A ball is about to start, and the knight and his wife begin with a "grave German waltz" (HW 12:388; 6:105). Soon a group of masked persons appear unexpectedly at the party and reveal themselves to be the pagan company of tableau 1. The wife becomes angry at the intrusion, and she and Diana engage in a significant exchange—a rare example of the confrontation between the real woman and the supernatural woman fighting for possession of the hero: "The chatelaine gives vent to her anger in the wildest leaps, and we see a *pas de deux* in which Greek and heathen divine joyousness dances a duel with German spiritual domestic virtue" (HW 12:389; 6:106). Diana, contemptuous of such mundane competition, leaves.

Tableau 3 introduces another figure from the folklore associated with the Tannhäuser legend: Trusty Eckhart, whose mission it is to guard the entrance to the Venusberg, warning victims lest they endanger their immortal souls.[6] Heine obviously sees in this figure not only the German domestic and spiritual virtues he dislikes but hypocrisy, for Trusty Eckhart kills the knight to keep him from joining Diana in the Venusberg, and "totters away clumsily, probably rejoicing that he has at least saved the soul of the knight" (HW 12:394; 6:108). This blow against Hellenic joyousness in favor of Hebraic morality will be rectified in tableau 4.

In the last tableau Venus and Tannhäuser make their appearance. The lovers quarrel and reconcile in turn, joined by a passion which is "by no means . . . based on mutual respect" (HW 12:396; 6:109). Soon Diana comes in, begging Venus to revive the dead knight, but Venus can only shrug her shoulders helplessly. Suddenly the music changes, and Apollo and the Muses appear. Their music momentarily rouses the dead hero, who, however, relapses into insensibility. But Bacchus's joyous tunes and the tambourine, which he almost bursts with his energy, permanently revive the knight, and he and Diana are reunited. They are crowned with wreaths from the heads of Venus and Tannhäuser, and Heine concludes the work with the words, "Magnificent transfiguration" (HW 12:398; 6:110).

The Goddess Diana is an apotheosis of Hellenic joy and the life-giving properties of art—not just any art but the wild, uninhibited, romantic art associated with Bacchus. However, the conflict between heathen joyousness and German domestic virtue has been resolved at the expense of the world. Only in the Venusberg is such a solution possible, and if Heine's ending is, as he claimed, a commentary on *The Gods in Exile*, then, ironically enough, he has concluded by following them in their banishment.

That Heine identified himself with Tannhäuser can be seen in the probably autobiographical element in *The Goddess Diana*. The alternately quarreling and reconciling lovers, whose union was based on physical passion rather than mutual respect, were almost certainly representative of himself and the tempestuous, uneducated girl he married. But that there is a more significant identification with his hero can be found repeatedly in the writings of his critics, who are always pointing out the conflict within him between Hebraism and Hellenism. Lord Houghton, whose own study of Venus in the Middle Ages was indebted to Heine's *Elementary Spirits*, wrote in his memoir of the German poet that in "his gay health and pleasant Parisian days the old gods haunted and enchanted him, like the legendary Tannhäuser in the Venus Mountain, while in his hours of depression, and above all in the miserable sufferings of his later life, the true religious feeling of his hereditary faith mastered, awed, and yet consoled him." [7] E. M. Butler, who has made a close study of Heine's shifting relationship to the gods of antiquity, notes that he had come to realize on his death bed "that the tumult in his soul, the conflict between beauty and truth, could only be stilled by death and would never cease from raging in this world." [8] This, perhaps, explains the final romanticism of *The Goddess Diana*. The ballet reflects a longing for some place beyond this world, one free from the fetters of Hebraic morality and commercialism, where the conflict between truth and beauty would be resolved.[9]

In *The Elementary Spirits* Heine mentions Joseph von Eichendorff as one of the several nineteenth-century German writers who had treated the legends about the exiled Venus's seduction of unwary youths. Eichendorff, in terms of the Hebraic-Hellenic dichotomy, seems to represent the polar opposite of Heine's materialism, and his book, *The Ethical and Religious Significance of German Romanticism*, is generally taken to be a belated defense of German spiritualism attacked in Heine's *Romantic School*. But just as Heine's Hellenism was never the self-sufficient philosophy he often pretended it to be, and Hebraism represented an internal need as well as a cultural force, so Eichendorff's Hebraism must be qualified. The problem is to reconcile his devout religious beliefs with his artistic commitment to earthly beauty.[10]

Eichendorff's novella, *The Marble Statue*, tells of the adventures of Florio in the city of Lucca, to which he travels after leaving the confines of his home (he is comparable in his wanderlust to Fouqué's Huldbrand and Tieck's Christian). As the story develops, Florio finds himself caught between two forces, each represented by a pair of figures: on the one hand, Fortunato, a singer whose position in

123

the tale might be described as a cross between Keat's Apollonius and Mann's Settembrini, and Bianca, an innocent young woman whose love for him will be returned when he successfully fights off the temptations that beset him; on the other hand, Donati, who proves to be Venus's emissary, and Venus herself. The plot of the story is based on an old belief that the statues of the pagan gods often come to life. Florio is for a time enthralled by an incarnation of Venus, and what he experienced is finally explained with reference to popular legend:

> It is said . . . that the spirit of the beautiful heathen goddess has found no rest. Every Spring the memory of earthly rapture makes her rise from the awful stillness of the grave, coming back to the green loveliness of her ruined home. There with devilish magic she practices the old seduction on young, careless spirits. And these then, departed from life yet not received into the peace of the dead, wander around, divided between wild desire and ghastly repentance, and consume their being in terrifying illusion. Quite frequently, it has been asserted, at that very place [where a ruined temple to Venus stands] people have seen evidence of temptation offered by spectres. Sometimes a wondrously beautiful lady, sometimes several alluring cavaliers, would appear, and lead the passerby into a phantom garden and palace presented to the eye. [EW 168–69; 2:344]

The locale of the story is of special interest. Italy frequently represented an otherworld or Venusberg to the German imagination, which often contrasts the northern and southern countries. (It is significant that scholars argue over whether the Tannhäuser legend is of Italian or German origin.) [11] For the Catholic Eichendorff, Italy takes on added significance, because its very history embodies the warfare in man between the spirit and the flesh. As the center of Roman Catholicism, it still contained the exotic remains of the older, heathen religions. Florio's travels to Lucca involve him in dangerous temptations about which he must be warned by Fortunato: "Have you ever . . . heard of the marvelous minstrel who by his notes lures youth into a magic mountain, out of which no one has ever come back? Be on your guard (EW 132; 2:308). Later, Fortunato's pious song will break the spell of Venus over Florio at that moment when

Eichendorff's hero is in greatest peril, for the song tells how the Virgin, her infant in her arms, comes into the world as the Goddess Venus hardens into stone. It is a song whose point of view reverses Swinburne's *Hymn to Proserpine*, which laments the demise of Venus and exalts her qualities over those of Mary.

The connection Eichendorff makes between Venus and spring, as well as his pervasive moral tone, lend substance to those who find a contradiction between his devout religious feelings and his artistic existence, which celebrates the beauty of this world. The theological assumptions of Eichendorff's faith, the emphasis of Roman Catholicism on the warfare between flesh and spirit and the fallen nature of the material world, lead to the asceticism against which Heine was reacting. Yet, Eichendorff's religious devotion is intimately bound up with his love of the natural surroundings in which he was raised (in this, perhaps, he is comparable to Words-worth).[12] One critic, Lawrence R. Radner, explains that Eichendorff believed that the material world led man closer to God and denies that his writings have any conflict between religion and art, claiming that where division appears, it is not a reflection of an internal split between Eichendorff the devout Catholic and Eichendorff the artist, but rather his portrayal of the essentially dual nature of man.[13] But since Eichendorff is a man, he is obviously subject to the basic human dilemma. And perhaps it is not unreasonable to take the next step and argue that as an artist he would have been more keenly aware than most men of the beauties of this world and hence of their tempta-tions. However much Radner tries to suggest that Eichendorff used rather than was subject to heathen forces, the portrayal of his hero's problems is more probably born of self-awareness than abstract theorizing. There are too many appearances of La Belle Dame sans Merci in Eichendorff's fiction and poetry for one not to believe that at least occasionally he felt keenly her seductive powers.[14]

There is nevertheless no question but that for Eichendorff religion was a means of resisting such seduction, a link for him between art, nature, and the invisible world manifested by the natural world. But the only valid religion for him was Roman Catholicism, which in its institutional form eliminated the subjectivity that comes from man's searching within for a sign of God's will. Thus, much of Eichendorff's literary theory is bound up with his Counter-Reforma-tion ideology, and his discussion of pre-romantic German literature concerns what he believes to be a search for unity and stability that can only be found in Christ, whose intermediary is the Catholic Church. When man lacks such mediation, he is thrown back upon himself, and the outcome of this is egotism. Eichendorff writes in his treatise on German romanticism that the Reformation had one chief characteristic: it had elevated the emancipation of subjectivity as a principle, in which it placed inquiry over churchly authority, the individual over dogma; and ever since all the literary movements of northern Germany had been more or less bold demonstrations of this direction (EW 4:428). His views link what is rarely examined in close juxtaposition, Protestantism and romanticism. In reacting against the subjectivity inherent in Protestantism, Eichendorff is also repudiating a major aspect of romantic literature. Moreover, his study of German romanticism does much to shed light on one of the chief themes of *The Marble Statue.*

Romanticism and Protestantism share an emphasis on the inner man.[15] The result of the introspection that occurs when one turns inward to find reality or an ethical guide is frequently isolation, since no third party can sanction the validity of what one finds. This isolation leads both to melancholy and to a still further disintegration of social ties. One's fellow beings are almost irrelevant to one's present and future life. Eichendorff directed his own writing, both in the aesthetic and ethical realms, precisely against these ideas. His hero in *The Marble Statue* begins his adventures by severing his ties to home. Florio, like the heroes of Fouqué and Tieck, is a romantic figure who longs for what is remote from the world he knows:

> For the present . . . I have chosen to travel, and feel as if released from a prison; all old wishes and delights are now set free at once. I was raised quietly in the country. How many years I have gazed with longing on the far off blue mountains, when Spring, like an enchanting minstrel, walked through our gardens, and sang enticingly of the wondrously beautiful distance and of great, immeasurable desire. [EW 132; 2:307–08]

Parallel situations in the tale are the spring awakening of Florio's romantic *Sehnsucht* and Venus's coming to life to cause gullible youths to forget their proper relationship to the world.

The result of Florio's longing is his imprisonment in a dreamworld in which he unhealthily sinks further and further into himself. The alienation and sadness he will come to feel are foreshadowed in a dream he has on his first night away from home.

> Gradually it seemed to him as if he were voyaging alone with swan-white sails on a lake silvered by the moon. Softly the waves struck against the ship; out of the water rose up sirens, who all looked like the beautiful girl with the flower-garland of the preceding evening [Bianca]. They sang so marvelously, mournfully and without end, that he thought he would die of sadness. The ship bowed forward imperceptibly, and slowly kept sinking ever deeper and deeper. [EW 140–41; 2:316]

That he could confuse the innocent Bianca with sirens points to the extent to which illusion has usurped the place of reality. His romantic self-centeredness makes him incapable of seeing her in any but his own delusive terms:

> For the one whom he really had in mind had long since ceased to be the charming little girl with the flower-garland. The music among the tents, the dream in his chamber, and his own heart repeating in vision the sounds and the dream and the charming appearance of the girl—all these had imperceptibly and marvelously changed her image into a much more beautiful, grand, and splendid one, such as he had never yet seen. [EW 142; 2:317–18]

This transformation of Bianca into some ideal but nonexistent woman is further evidence that Florio is more in love with his own dreams than with her, that his inner life has more meaning for him than the external world. When the previous two passages are viewed in conjunction, one finds an implicit connection between romantic idealism and demonism. It is as if Shelley's Intellectual Beauty had been transformed into La Belle Dame sans Merci.

Eichendorff does not depend on his narrative alone to point out the dangers of romantic subjectivity. Fortunato's speeches emphasize Eichendorff's lesson by describing Venus's cavalier Donati, for example, as a "chaser of phantoms, a languishing fool, a braggart about his melancholy" (EW 140; 2:316). He has described a satirically conceived epitome of the romantic hero as well as the condition of Florio, whom he hopes to keep from degenerating into such a figure. And so he ridicules Florio's romantic attachment to the moon, an attachment Fortunato believes is totally misguided; the morning, he asserts,

> is a thoroughly healthy, wildly beautiful companion, as he comes down rejoicing from the highest mountains into the sleeping world and shakes the tears from the flowers and trees, and surges and blusters and sings. He doesn't pander to emotions, but he grips all our limbs coolly, and laughs in our faces, when we, tense and still under the spell of the moonlight, step into his presence. [EW 143; 2:319]

He advises Florio, "Drop it, melancholy, moonlight and all that rubbish; and even if sometimes things go a little awry, just get out eagerly into God's free morning, and there shake off your anxieties with a fervent prayer" (EW 144; 2:320). Such words alone do not influence Florio, but later, when Fortunato's pious song breaks Venus's spell, Florio, standing in the midst of her palace, is able to see beneath the illusion she creates its evil deception. He imagines that all the knights on the tapestries that surround him take on his own likeness and mock at him maliciously. His inner condition has in effect been projected outward so that he might view the absurdity of his own state in an objective fashion and examine the unpleasantness at the base of his dream life.

Eichendorff's attacks on romantic subjectivity can be related to the importance for him of nature itself. There are two aspects to the natural world that are significant in his works. First, he, like other German romantics, views this world as symbolic of the infinite, which the ending of *The Marble Statue* suggests:

> The morning, coming shooting over the plain, shone right into their faces with long, golden rays. The trees rose up bright in the glow; countless larks were singing as they whirred through the clear air. And so the happy lovers journeyed

merrily through the gleaming meadows out into the flowery regions of Milan. [EW 170; 2:346]

The descent of the sun's rays and the ascent of the trees and larks may symbolize a reconciliation of the natural and divine worlds, casting a final approving aura about the lovers. But nature does more than lead those who are appreciative of God's creation to God himself. It is this other aspect of the natural world in Eichendorff's story that is decidedly anti-romantic. The natural world leads man out of the labyrinth of his own mind, turning his gaze away from himself to the outer world. The lark that ascends to the sky is contrasted in *The Marble Statue* to the swan, which is associated with Venus and with Florio's strange dreams of sirens.[16] The swan's gaze is downward into the water that reflects its own image, and in that sense it symbolizes the narcissistic romantic hero who cannot look away from himself.[17] As soon as Florio is free of Venus, external reality becomes even more beautiful than was the illusory world of the pagan goddess, and his appreciation of Bianca is renewed: "Florio's glance rested well pleased on that lovely shape. A strange infatuation had hitherto covered his eyes as if with a magic mist. Now he was downright astonished to see how beautiful she was" (EW 170; 2:345). This healthy relationship to the natural world also becomes a sign of his eventual happiness in another, not because of an ascetic negation of the earth but because a clear-sighted approach to the world allows man to serve God in this life.

    Nature's role in *The Marble Statue* nevertheless remains ambiguous. When Florio first hears the religious song that breaks Venus's spell, he murmurs a prayer: "Lord God, let me not become lost in the world!" (EW 163; 2:338). To be lost in the world is to be separated from God, to wander about like Venus's victims, departed from this life yet not dead. One is, however, so lost to God precisely because one has become lost *in* the world, that is, so delighted with its transitory joys that one ignores its proper place in God's scheme for man. In this state, it is easy to adopt the *carpe diem* philosophy of Venus, who advises Florio to "take the flowers of life gladly as the moment gives them, and [not to] ask about the roots underground, for below everything is joyless and still" (EW 155; 2:330). The basic hopelessness of this doctrine will be the focus of Swinburne's treatment of Venus's realm, but Eichendorff, who has a specific alternative to the *carpe diem* philosophy, is less concerned to expose the futility of paganism than to demonstrate how man may walk the path to God. Thus, while his view of nature does not include man's giving up this world to gain the next, he shows that too great a joy in the here and now can prove detrimental to salvation.

For nature is also a temptress inhabited by demonic powers ready to enthrall the unwary. Behind this other view of the natural world probably lies Eichendorff's belief in original sin, and this is, in turn, related to his suspicion of the subjective principle in Protestantism. The elevation of the individual gave sanction to modern and supposedly enlightened doctrines which held that man's instincts were to be lauded, that man was at his best when he was "natural." In his book on German romanticism, Eichendorff writes that in the previous seventy years man's primitive power, prophetic faculty, divination, instinct, in short, the demonic in him, commonly considered genius, are—counter to all tradition—supposed to produce an entirely original creation, like nature (EW 4:429). He not only disputes that man can create in the sense that God can but also makes an implicit connection between nature and those instincts in him which lead to such egotistic and arrogant assumptions.

Eichendorff believed that what man finds within himself when he turns away from a secure faith in God—that is, one firmly anchored in Roman Catholicism—is a link to the demonic forces which are unfortunately also present in his beloved nature. He would thus deny, for example, Coleridge's theory of the imagination, which, owing much to Kant and thus to the philosophical tradition Eichendorff is negating, states that man participates in the creation of the universe. Such an idea Eichendorff would consider allied with the egotism born of subjectivity. In *The Marble Statue*, Fortunato speaks of the "genuine poet," who "can venture a great deal, for art that is without pride and sin charms and restrains the wild earth-spirits, who reach out for us from the depths" (EW 169; 2:344). Thus the total experience that Florio has undergone in his trip to Italy has meaning not only for mankind in general but also for the artist in particular.

The specific meaning of *The Marble Statue* for the artistic life has not been the focus of critical attention. Yet, Florio's youthful attempts at song and the redeeming power of Fortunato's art unmistakably stamp upon the work an aesthetic theme. Eichendorff has been at pains to demonstrate a double concern with literature. The first is his distrust of romantic subjectivity; the second is that his story itself contains the paradigm for the correct relationship of artist to audience.

Although a moralist, Eichendorff, one of the most renowned of German romantic lyric poets, did not object to art whose only function is to produce pleasure. A lighter scene in *The Marble Statue* is one in which it "had been arranged that every one in the circle should pledge his sweetheart with a short improvised song. The soft singing, which only playfully like a spring wind touches the surface of life, without sinking into its depths, merrily enlivened the circle of happy faces around the table" (EW 134–35; 2:310). Shortly thereafter Eichendorff describes some festivities in Lucca by noting that "dance music, even if it does not stir and change our inmost feelings, comes over us with pleasant spell, just like the Spring, gentle and powerful" (EW 152; 2:327). Although this second passage contains a subtle warning, in both instances Eichendorff has described an essentially healthy, communal situation in which the cares of life are lifted temporarily by the cheer spread by song. But each time he also reminds the reader that such art does not go very deeply into man's nature to effect profound changes.

The contrast to be made is *not* between entertainment and a more elevated art, which both entertains and effects a moral change, but between both of these on one side, and, on the other, pure romantic lyricism, which is not directed at any audience at all. Thus a distinction can be drawn between the song Florio sings to Bianca as part of the improvised sport devised by the young people and the later song he sings alone under the moonlight when Bianca undergoes a transformation in his mind into some unknown ideal. Such a song, after which he "could not help laughing at himself . . . since he did not know to whom he was offering the serenade" (EW 142: 2:317), is pure self-expression, turned neither to the enjoyment of others nor to a higher ethical purpose. As such it is a song sung to one's self and shares the narcissistic qualities of the swans who constantly face their own images. Such art exists for its own sake in the most literal sense, and these products of romantic artists are frowned upon by Eichendorff as he frowns upon subjectivism itself, although his own frequently subjective approach to the ballad form shows that he too was capable of singing to himself and knew well the enticements of pure art.

Romantic poetry, sung to one's self in the absence of an audience and without any purpose save self-expression, is, in its spontaneity, frequently devoid of form. In his treatise on German romanticism, Eichendorff approves of Lessing's attention to form, because it had loosened the bond between German poetry and French influences which held that beauty is its own justification (EW 4:436). He discovered in form that concern for order which he would advocate as an antidote to aestheticism. As it was, romantic lyricism was devoid of moral purpose and thus far from what he considered art's highest function.

Eichendorff's conception of the artist's role was one that traditionally combined teaching with entertaining. Significant art, unlike love songs and dance music, *will* effect a change in the reader by revealing the ethical significance of the events he experiences. Thus Eichendorff stands in relation to his reader as does Fortunato to Florio. The latter's adventures, which involve a learning process, contain a lesson for all young men, emphasized by Venus when Florio tells her he thinks he has seen her before their first meeting: " 'Forget all that,' said the lady at this point absent-mindedly, 'everyone thinks he has seen me some time before, for, beyond question, my image looms dimly and blossoms in all the dreams of youth' " (EW 162–63; 2:338). Florio goes through the events in the story with the air of bewilderment that the novella intentionally evokes in the reader as well. When Fortunato warns Florio about the mysterious minstrel who lures youths into a magic mountain, Eichendorff writes, "Florio did not know how he was to interpret this speech of the stranger" (EW 132; 2:308). Even when he is exposed to temptation, he remains confused, so that when Venus tells him that all young men think they have seen her at one time or another, it is again said that "the lady's last words, which he did not know how to interpret rightly, troubled him strangely" (EW 163; 2:338). When his experience with Venus is finally explained by the old legends, both Florio and the reader are enlightened, and to both an important lesson has been imparted. Fortunato's song, which breaks the charm that beclouds Florio's vision, is thus a virtual microcosm of the entire *Marble Statue*.

This traditional attitude toward his role as artist and teacher is Eichendorff's means of reconciling his religion and his art. Just as the delights of the natural world point to the glory of God, so does the pleasure of art lead in the same direction by helping man to live a moral life. That Eichendorff as man and artist experienced temptations is, again, clear from the subject matter of his work and his own delight in lyricism and fantasy. But even if he did find his muse occasionally threatening to become a Belle Dame sans Merci, he was able with the help of his faith to resist. By exposing his temptation in literature he also wrote for the edification of others. And by admitting his share in the human predicament and by turning his art into useful channels by giving it a moral direction, Eichendorff maintained his link with both the human world and God. He rejected romantically morbid introspection and turned toward the outer world with optimistic security. *The Marble Statue* alone among the well-known German romantic tales concludes with a happy ending in *this* world. Eichendorff's novella therefore serves to focus by way of contrast on the dilemma of the romantic artist who has lost his belief in any institutionalized faith that would tie him to the social realm, and has, as a consequence, lost any firm conception of his artistic function with regard to this realm.[18]

7

MORE PAGAN RUINS

Eichendorff's tale ends on a note of domestic bliss for his hero, who has come to acknowledge the superiority of his earthly sweetheart to the pagan goddess of love. The Venusring story, of which Eichendorff's is a variant, can also lend itself to a cynical view of marriage. In the legend of the bridegroom who pledges himself to Venus, the institution of marriage is intrinsic to a theme that could easily be adapted to the general attack on Philistinism. Middle class morality, which artists interpreted as another term for middle class insensitivity, channeled love into marriage as its only proper outlet. Prosper Mérimée, who admits in his *Letters to an Unknown* that nothing makes him so melancholy as a wedding, reproaches his beloved for her fear that their meeting will result in something "improper." This could only be so in the eyes of society, he tells her, a society that makes us unhappy from the day of our birth, when we put on uncomfortable clothing according to its dictates, to the day of our death.[1] Mérimée, creator of that most notorious of nineteenth-century *femmes fatales*, Carmen, who would prefer death to surrendering her right to choose and discard lovers at will, also invokes for himself the old dichotomy between love and freedom, on the one hand, and marriage, on the other. He believed that betrothals were fatal, since it is a law of nature to recoil from whatever is imposed as an obligation. If she were really engaged to another, he tells his Unknown, then surely she would love *him*, to whom she had promised nothing.[2] Marriage, highly romanticized in so much literature, was also a bond from which the romantic soul could shrink. At least as far back as the courtly love tradition of the Middle Ages, marriage had been held inimical to passion, which must freely follow its own bent. In addition, as Tieck's *Runenberg* reveals, married life is another source for an increased awareness of earthly mutability—the young bride and groom must age—and wedded life, as in the case of Hoffmann and to a lesser degree Keats, can be the foe of an artist whose need to earn a living, especially if he undertakes domestic responsibility, will force him into a dull mundane existence. Again, marriage is the moral staple of a society the artist had learned to view with hostility. Therefore, since the pagan goddess of the Venusring story was pitted specifically against wedded life, and not only—as in the Tannhäuser legend—against the Christianity that sanctioned it, the story and its analogues can be found in the works of writers like Mérimée and Hardy, for whom the question of marriage was at best problematic.

Lord Houghton, a friend of Hardy's, told the Venusring story in his essay *The Goddess Venus in the Middle Ages*, and used its theme again in the long narrative poem, *The Northern Knight in Italy*. The poem is comparable to Eichendorff's tale of the marble statue, but differs in that the traveler recognizes immediately the source of his temptation:

> A ruin'd temple of the Pagan world,—
> Pillars and pedestals with rocks confused,—
> Art back into the lap of nature hurl'd,
> And still most beautiful, when most abused
>
> . . . .
>
> Amid this strife of vigour and decay
> An Idol stood, complete, without a stain
>
> . . . .
>
> He knew the glorious image by its name—
> Venus! the Goddess of unholy fame.[3]

The story is told to the narrator by a mature knight, who looks back on his experience from the vantage point of a happy, idyllic married life:

> He told it me, one autumn evening mild,
> Sitting, greyhair'd, beneath an old oak tree,
> His dear true wife beside him, and a child,
> Youngest of many, dancing round his knee.[4]

Whatever he has lost in youthful illusions is amply compensated for by present contentment. The domestic scene is to be contrasted to the "palace of sensual delights," where, according to Houghton's essay, Venus enticed "brave and noble souls" in order to "keep them there till they became debased and brutalised and altogether lost." [5]

The matter was not that simple, however, for William Morris, and when he included the Venusring story in *The Earthly Paradise*, he portrayed a bridegroom whose yearning romanticism makes doubtful his readiness for marriage:

> [Some] men's lives were like a dream,
> Where nought in order can be set,
> And nought worth thence the soul may get,
> Or weigh one thing for what it is.
> [WM 6:138]

Venus here has not seduced the unwary but claimed what is rightfully hers; and the wedding ring is only a symbol of the bridegroom's true desire. "I love thee well," says Morris's Venus,

> And thou hast loved me ere to-night,
> And longed for this o'ergreat delight,
> And had no words therefor to pray.
> [WM 6:151–52]

It is not to his bride but to the goddess who has long been his ideal that he is unfaithful. His is the conflict of Hoffmann's Elis, who believes his marriage to Ulla will result in betrayal of his true nature, which he thinks belongs to the Queen of the Mines at Falun.

Morris's conception of the story, rather than Houghton's or Eichendorffs, is comparable to Hardy's *The Well-Beloved*, both the novel and the poem of the same title. Like Keats's *La Belle Dame sans Merci*, Hardy's poem depicts a man whose seduction by unworldly forces makes him unfit for a real existence. But the novel is less compelling, for the Venus myth seems employed merely to explain the marriage shyness of its hero, the sculptor Jocelyn Pierston. Hardy, for whom the Tannhäuser motif underscored the tragedy of

The Woodlanders, treated similar motifs in his later novel with a levity that makes doubtful his intention to engage the reader's deep sympathies on behalf of his artist-hero.

Jocelyn Pierston pursues his well-beloved, his ideal woman, in a succession of mortal ladies in whom the sprite takes only temporary residence. In particular, he falls in love with both the daughter and granddaughter of a sweetheart whom he had failed to marry. Thus, even in the temporal realm his well-beloved never ages. An explanation for Jocelyn's inability to love any one woman for long is to be found in the setting of the novel, the Isle of Slingers, where "tradition urged that a temple to Venus once stood at the top of the Roman road leading up into the isle; and possibly one to the love-goddess of the Slingers antedated this." [6] Jocelyn believes that the goddess has claimed him as her own and that his fickleness is a chastisement for his tendency to mistake any real love for his ideal love: "Aphrodite, Ashtaroth, Freyja, or whoever the love-queen of his isle might have been, was punishing him sharply, as she knew but too well how to punish her votaries when they reverted from the ephemeral to the stable mood." [7]

Tone is very important here. The narrator's unconcern for the precise identity of Jocelyn's Belle Dame sans Merci is matched by the closing words, where stability is conceived of as a mood, apparently not to be taken too seriously and, ultimately, changeable. Jocelyn may or may not deserve to be punished for his temporary infidelity to his ideal, but precisely this shifting of moods makes it unnecessary for his goddess to be too harsh. If he represents the artist's dilemma, Jocelyn does so without becoming a tragic figure. For while the sculptor is frequently wistful about his lonely life, he is never driven by a conflict that will finally kill him or drive him mad.

The Well-Beloved may have its source in *Epipsychidion,* a poem in which Shelley expresses disappointment in his marriage:

> In many mortal forms I rashly sought
> The shadow of that idol of my thought. [8]

This late work picks up the themes of *Alastor,* where the poet who is the subject of the work spurns earthly love to pursue his shadowy ideal to an early death. The preface to *Alastor* makes clear, if not the poem itself, that Shelley was ambivalent about his hero, whose "self-centered seclusion was avenged by the furies of an irresistible passion pursuing him to speedy ruin," but whose genius was, nevertheless, "led forth by an imagination inflamed and purified through familiarity with all that is excellent and majestic, to the contemplation of the universe." [9]

This disparity between the worthiness of the goal and the danger of its pursuit provides the tension in Hardy's ballad of *The Well-Beloved*, which describes a young bridegroom hastening by night to wed "the God-created norm / Of perfect womankind!" [10] On his way to the town where she lives, he passes close by an ancient hill where a pagan temple had once stood. But if he "quick and quicker walked," it is because of his eagerness to greet his bride and not out of fear of the influences that emanate from the hill. When a "shape" approaches him out of the darkness, he mistakes it for his beloved.

His real error, the mysterious figure explains, was to think in the first place that the shape was his fiancée, to confuse the ideal and the norm:

> Thou hast transferred
> To her dull form awhile
> My beauty, fame, and deed, and word,
> My gestures and my smile.

Troubled, he miserably allows her to instruct him:

> O fatuous man, this truth infer,
> Brides are not what they seem;
> Thou lovest what thou dreamest her;
> I am thy very dream!

When, in response, the bridegroom asks to wed her instead, she tells him she never has and never will marry a mortal, and disappears "near where, men say, once stood the Fane / To Venus, on the Down." He continues on to his wedding, but when he meets his bride,

> Her look was pinched and thin,
> As if her soul had shrunk and died,
> And left a waste within.

This meeting is comparable to the one between Thomas Rhymer and the Elf Queen. When Thomas takes her for the Virgin Mary, Queen of Heaven, she almost humbly corrects him to say that such a name does not belong to her. Hardy's Venus is more arrogant in her correction, for, after all, she is the ideal to which from her point of view the inferior real has been compared. And the hero's final perception of his bride bears out her contention. Yet this difference between Hardy's ballad and the medieval one serves to emphasize the dilemma of the modern age. Thomas's perceptions, even when mistaken, can be precisely measured against the opposing values represented by the Elf Queen and the Virgin, against values clearly differentiated in the earlier age. There were the spiritual realm and the underworld represented by the fairies; and each corresponded to antagonistic elements in man, his reason and his passion, which was allied with the world of fantasy. Marriage at that time had a positive function with regard to this internal warfare, a function specifically hostile to the fairies or to Venus. Within this framework one can understand the medieval Venusring story. So long as the bridegroom places his ring upon the pagan statue's finger, he is not yet ready to be a proper husband. Eichendorff, a devout Catholic, understood this, and Florio must be disillusioned in a literal sense in order to understand the value of Bianca and domesticity as a means of living the moral life in this world.

Hoffmann's Elis had inverted this traditional world view when he decided that his higher nature was allied with the Queen of the Mines, and that Ulla, his bride, represented his lower desires. His belief logically follows the romantic exaltation of the imagination and elevates the artistic life above all earthly concerns. But despite this inversion of older values, and the dilemma it posed for the artist who sometimes yearned for normalcy on the world's terms, Hoffmann's hero is never confused about which is his real and which his ideal love.

Hardy's poem, in contrast, deliberately confuses illusion and reality not only for the hero of the poem but for the reader also, who must come to terms with its ending: a peculiar variation of the Duessa motif, in which what was formerly viewed as beautiful is no longer so. Again, for Spenser the matter is relatively simple: the metamorphosis reveals the truth. In Hardy's poem, the bridegroom's view of his fiancée is true only insofar as, for example, Tieck's morbid concentration on the seeds of decay in all earthly beauty reveals the "truth" about nature. But is not such truth distorted? James Southworth has quoted from Hardy's notebooks to claim that the author felt "it was the incompleteness that is loved, the less than perfection, when love is genuine and sincere. An ideal lover could possibly prefer perfection, but not the real lover. A practical man may well see . . . 'the Diana or the Venus in his Beloved, but what he loves is the difference.' " [11] But *The Well-Beloved* by no means expresses such a theme. And if it did, could the reader conclude that this complex treatment of the ideal and the real was merely a device to portray an insincere lover?

Venus cannot be dismissed that easily. True, her beauty's steadfastness costs her lover infinite frustration. Embodying man's dreams, she will wed no mortal and thus offers no more substance for his life than those very dreams. And yet there is something to be said for such dreams, as Jean Giraudoux implies in *Amphitryon 38*, when Jupiter says of Alkmena's preference for her mortal husband that she lacks all imagination and is perhaps not too bright. This is not an overtly condemnatory observation, because Jupiter loves Alkmena for those earthly virtues of loyalty and devotion that make her indifferent to the love of gods. But that her qualities result from a limited vision both Jupiter and a mortal can recognize. Here again is the Shelleyan dilemma, the conflict between the worthiness of the goal and the price of the quest. And at stake is a search for values in a world where defining what is or is not real is problematic as it was not for earlier times.

It is therefore ironic that the romantic attack on marriage can trace its ancestry to the medieval theoreticians of courtly love. And yet even here the contrast is telling. Whether or not courtly love was anything more than a literary convention, its attitude toward marriage is in any event clearly spelled out. What was probably a game for the past became a potentially tragic conflict for the romantic who had turned inward and away from convention to find direction. He could choose a normal domestic life, which he unhappily viewed as an alliance with Philistinism and bourgeois morality, or decide in favor of art and imagination in a life devoid of more basic joys.

Such domestic joys are hardly to be glimpsed in Prosper Mérimée's treatment of the Venusring story. Nor is the conflict between marriage and a more ideal existence to be found as theme in *The Venus of Ille*. What seems instead to be revealed is Mérimée's cynicism, his tendency to look at marriage and passion as irreconcilable. Passion is the dominant theme of his works: the passion for honor that causes Mateo Falcone to execute his only son when the latter breaks the code by which his family lives; or the passion for revenge behind Colomba's determination to involve her brother in a vendetta; or the passion for freedom of Carmen, who would prefer death to surrendering her liberty; or the jealous passion of Don José, who murders his paramour. Mérimée's characters are driven by obsessive feelings rather than by an introverted quest for the ideal and, in contrast to such extreme emotions, marriage appears in his work as the paltry thing he believed it to be. Moreover, an aversion to wedded life can be found throughout his work.

In *Lokis*, the narrator postpones his marriage to pursue scholarly interests. He tells the story of a count whose mother was abducted by a bear right after her marriage, the event causing her subsequent madness. The count himself disappears immediately following a wedding night that leaves his own bride dead and mutilated. In *The Venus of Ille*, the narrator is depressed by merely having to attend a wedding, which also ends with the violent death of one of the wedded couple. Interestingly enough, in *The Blue Chamber* when a night of love that threatens to be disastrous ends happily, the couple involved are lovers rather than husband and wife. In another story spun about jealous passion, *The Etruscan Vase*, the death of the hero prevents his marriage to a woman with whom he had been having a happy love affair. It is believable that the lover's violent death, followed by the death of his mistress after a long bout with grief, averted what Mérimée would view as more calamitous, the disintegration of their love into mediocrity and boredom. Where marriage appears to be the happy outcome of a Mérimée story, as in *Il Viccolo di Madama Lucrezia*, it is perhaps so because it is considered the lesser evil. Here the bridegroom had been destined by his family for the celibate life of a priest.

Mérimée's *Venus of Ille* more than expresses the dislike of marriage he admitted so openly in his letters; it also epitomizes his era's sense of the disparity between utility and art. And if, despite this, his supernatural horror story lacks truly philosophical complexity because of its lack of ambiguity, it perhaps for that very reason displays more starkly the Philistinism from which Mérimée recoiled. The narrator of the tale is an archaeologist from Paris who has come to Ille in order to meet M. de Peyrehorade, recommended to him as a learned antiquarian. This provincial gentleman has found a statue of Venus buried on his property and has devoted much time and speculation to interpret an inscription engraved on its arm. Meanwhile, the natives of Ille are suspicious of this idol that has already been a source of injury, breaking the leg of one of the excavators. But M. de Peyrehorade is delighted with his find, and even invokes blessings from the statue for the marriage of his son, M. Alphonse, to a pretty Catalan heiress.

The narrator's observations about the household he is visiting provide the contrast between the husband's interests in classical antiquity and the provincialism of Mme. de Peyrehorade. At the same time, Mérimée is able to score some points about the less romantic aspects of marriage: "His wife was rather too stout, like most Catalan women over forty, and she seemed to me an out-and-out provincial, completely taken up with the cares of her household" (VI 4: *412*). This Hebraic sense of housewifely duties is also reflected in her devout religiosity: "Do you know," her husband informs the narrator, "my wife wanted me to have my statue melted down to make a bell for our church?" (VI 7; *414*). This predilection on the part of Mme. de Peyrehorade echoes what the narrator had already heard from a villager, that the head of the household had found an idol made of copper, enough for hundreds of coins and as heavy as a church bell. And, finally, after the catastrophe that appears traceable to the statue, which the bride claims has murdered her husband, this masterpiece of Greek sculpture does end up as a bell in the local church belfry. The story concludes with this ironic comment on Hellenic art being turned to Christian worship: "Since that bell began to ring in Ille, the vines have twice been frost-bitten" (VI 32; *436*).

The failure of the community to appreciate the artistic magnificence of the statue, and the tendency to see its value only in religious or commercial terms, betray a Philistinism that is focused upon in the character of young M. Alphonse. The narrator describes the future bridegroom as a peasant dressed like a dandy, and the contrast between the Parisian refinement of the former and the provincial vulgarity of the latter is revealed in the conversation about a ring. M. Alphonse has added diamonds to an otherwise plain and tasteful piece of jewelry intended for his bride-to-be. The narrator believes these stones "have detracted slightly from its original character," but the bridegroom is not to be swayed by this example of urbane fastidiousness and responds, "I think that she will be glad to have it in any case. Twelve hundred francs on one's finger is very pleasing" (VI 17; *423*).

The bride is an heiress, and the narrator who finds her enchanting has no doubt that it is her wealth that attracts M. Alphonse. This realization adds to his gloom during the wedding reception, where he notes that the coarse jokes bandied about leave "only three grave faces at the table—those of the bridal couple and mine. I had a splitting headache; besides, I don't know why, a wedding always makes me feel melancholy. This one disgusted me slightly too" (VI 24; *429*). The disgust is exacerbated when he imagines the wedding night of the young couple: "What an odious thing," he muses, "is a marriage of convenience! A mayor puts on a tricolor sash, and a priest a stole, and the most innocent of girls may be handed over to the Minotaur" (VI 26; *431*).

The vulgar Philistinism of this provincial family is hardly offset by the Hellenic values of the antiquarian father of the groom. First, it is not made clear if M. de Peyrehorade is a good scholar, and the narrator is skeptical of his interpretation of the inscription on the statue's arm. More important, the statue itself suggests the diabolism that makes plausible the fate of M. Alphonse:

> It was not at all the calm and austere beauty of the Greek sculptors, whose rule was to give a majestic immobility to every feature. Here, on the contrary, I noticed with astonishment that the artist had deliberately set out to express ill-nature raised to the level of wickedness. Every feature was slightly contracted: the eyes were rather slanted, the mouth turned up at the corners, and the nostrils somewhat distended. Disdain, irony, cruelty, could be distinguished in that face which was, notwithstanding, of incredible beauty. Indeed, the longer one looked at that wonderful statue, the more distress one felt at the thought that such a marvellous beauty could be united with an utter absence of goodness. [VI 11; *418*]

The sculpture, in short, reflects the demonic Venus conceived by Christians to be seductive and evil. Ironically, Mme. de Peyrehorade has been justified by Mérimée's very depiction of the statue.

How, then, is the reader to interpret Mérimée's Hellenism? His willingness to allow his story to sustain the ideas of the antiquarian's wife, although he despised her religious views? The dilemma can be resolved only by ignoring altogether the conflict between Hebraism and Hellenism in the *Venus of Ille* and looking at the story in terms of its failure to deal with themes it nevertheless introduces. Frank P. Bowman explains Mérimée's conception of Venus and the ending of the story by claiming that the tale portrays its author's general view of love: "It must be concluded that the myth of the Venus of Ille was for Mérimée the myth of love in its pure state. Love leads to destruction; Venus, a terrible and vengeful goddess, accepts only one tribute, that of human life." [12] Mérimée provides the basis for such an interpretation when his narrator says of the bride whom he finds generally appealing that "her expression was kindly, but nevertheless was not devoid of a slight touch of maliciousness which reminded me, in spite of myself, of my host's Venus" (VI 17–18; *424*). The trouble with the interpretation, however, is that love is hardly an element in this story, except for a brief mention of the difference between marriage for love and marriage for wealth. Indeed, M. Alphonse seems to feel hardly any passion much less love for his bride.

The answer perhaps lies in the general cynicism of Mérimée, a cynicism that renders shallow his conception of Hellenism in *The Venus of Ille*. His Venus is a demon because she can hardly be anything else. The culture of the ancients was never felt by him to be a genuine alternative to modern reality, as Peacock, for example, made it. And although Mérimée urges his Unknown to learn Greek so that she may read Homer in the original, and instructs her that the ancients were more amusing than their own contemporaries because the former did not occupy themselves with trivialities[13] he cannot in fact provide anything substantive to take the place of the Philistinism he so despised. Thus, there is little conflict in *The Venus of Ille*, and the bridegroom's father is only making a coarse joke when he claims that his son has chosen a Catalan Venus over the Roman one because the former is made of warm flesh and blood (VI 24; *429*). With the Parisian sophistication of his narrator, Mérimée views from an uninvolved distance the seeming pettiness of ordinary life and, because of this distance, never allows himself the pain of those who, like the Shelleyan hero, pursue their dreams at a cost they cannot avoid recognizing, or turn to flesh and blood with a pervasive sense of lost ideals.[14]

The conflict between flesh and blood and art is contained in the distinction between Roman and Greek paganism in Henry James's *The Last of the Valerii*.[15] The counterpart to young M. de Peyrehorade here is Count Valerio, who wins for his bride the young American heiress who is drawn to both his sexual attractiveness and his heritage in an old world culture she can never really share with him. His Roman paganism, his sensuality, is such that her godfather, the narrator of the tale, worries lest she may someday seek for mind and spirit in a man who is in fact a dull sensualist. Ironically, however, the goddaughter's insistence on using her money to dig for buried treasure in the grounds of her husband's family villa results in unearthing the ancient statue of Juno that turns Count Valerio into a Hellene and makes him almost profound, even at times witty. Awakened in him is an anger for the demise of the banished gods: "It was in caves and woods and streams, in earth and air and water, they dwelt. And there—and here, too, in spite of all your Christian lustrations—a son of old Italy may find them still!" he tells the godfather when the latter urges him to seek the aid of a priest or doctor to exorcise the powers that are transforming the count into a stranger to his wife.[16] In his worship of the statue he rejects her not only, one suspects, because her flesh and blood reality palls before the symbol of his heritage but because her very wealth is the result of a Christian tradition he now spurns. She cannot worship his gods—only pay to excavate them. And so the young American, understanding now the only way to keep her husband, arranges to have the statue buried again: all that remains to Count Valerio is its marble hand.

The story is told by an American who has little sympathy for the count's obsession with the dead gods, and the happy ending is essentially the result of that point of view. Although an artist, the narrator would never have chosen such an exotic husband for his goddaughter, preferring that she marry one of her own countrymen. Her choice of the Italian count instead leaves him no other option than to impress on her that her husband must be the last of the Valerii, and he watches with satisfaction the exorcism of what he considers the demonic influence of the past and the return to domesticity of the bridegroom. Count Valerio, however, has the last word in the story. When asked whether the marble hand of the statue is the relic of ancient Roman statuary, he replies, with a frown, "A Greek." [17]

The ending of James's tale suggests some doubt about the value of the count's "rehabilitation" and some regret about the necessity of suppressing his awakening Hellenism so that he may be a good husband to the pretty American heiress. For ambiguity to exist in the Venusring story, the writer treating it must have a genuine concern for the realm of culture and art symbolized by the statue, and genuine regret for the demise of Hellenism, however much he may deem it necessary to subordinate the aesthetic realm to the requirements of ordinary life. But when the realm of the goddess is reduced to the triviality of everyday concerns, or is appropriated by Philistines, as Heine sees it, the result is not so much ambiguity as farce. This is the reduction that lends Anthony Burgess's *The Eve of Saint Venus*[18] its comic dimensions.

Burgess claims that he took the Venusring legend from Burton's *Anatomy of Melancholy*, but there is something disingenuous about this claim for a book that abounds in literary allusions. It is difficult not to believe that there lies behind Burgess's novel, although unacknowledged, a large section of the nineteenth-century tradition of the Venus myth. There is a strong if satiric similarity between M. de Peyrehorade in Mérimée's *Venus of Ille* and the bride's father, Sir Benjamin Drayton, in *The Eve of Saint Venus*. Both inordinately treasure the statue of Venus that has come into their hands, and each is a somewhat ineffectual member of his family. Moreover, Burgess is clearly familiar with the folklore surrounding the pagan gods and the manner in which they were transformed into demons after the triumph of Christianity, although this lore is expressed in the highly amusing, original language that characterizes the novel. The vicar who intends to exorcise the power of the statue over the bridegroom who places his ring on her finger assures the family and friends of the affianced couple that

> I used to study this sort of thing, you know. The origin of devils. The ancient gods never died. They joined the opposi-

tion when the new administration took over. Devils were once gods. Devil—the very term means "little god." This poor boy's bewitched. Possessed by a little god. Or goddess. But they can't have sex, can they? But, of course, it's the form they take. A devil disguised as a goddess. Dear, dear, dear.[19]

But the reference to Burton's *Anatomy of Melancholy*, where the Venusring legend is recounted immediately after the one concerning Lamia, links Burgess's novel in a more serious fashion to Keats's poetry and strengthens any belief one might have that his title is not only the translation of a Latin Hymn to Venus, as he claims,[20] but also a deliberate variant of *The Eve of St. Agnes*. The novel furthermore bears an interesting relation to Keats's poem.

Few readers of *The Eve of St. Agnes*—Jack Stillinger is notable among them—have understood the important point that Madeline should be compared to the dreamers of Keats's other poems, for it is she, not Porphyro, who cannot reconcile herself to the real world and prefers her dreams to their embodiment in human beings.[21] Burgess seems to have used a similar insight into Keats's poem to conceive of the possibility that it is not the groom alone in the Venusring story who may be a romantic attempting to flee the ordinary. It is the bride in *The Eve of Saint Venus* and not her fiancé who is marriage shy and fears that she will sacrifice her talents and career in order to marry and lead a rather mundane life. Burgess's joke is that her talent is but a mediocre one, and her final capitulation to marriage is hardly to be viewed as any loss to the world of art about which she has so many pretensions.

Do not "maken ernest of game," says Chaucer in one of his tales, and any extended analysis of Burgess's "romp for the happy reader"[22] might be doing just that. The author has used the Venus legend to satirize the English upper-middle class, woman's liberation movements, and even love, concluding, however, on a kindly if serious note. Sir Benjamin Drayton views the present and future with appropriate alarm, worried because he had heard that it was possible to bring "the past perpetually up to date" (as Burgess has the Venus legend) and that the ancient "gods in the garden . . . were dead," [23] so that there was no longer any escape. But the next day would bring his daughter's wedding, and thus a new beginning instead of the catastrophic end of things. He thus rejects his fears as a touch of heartburn and retires to bed with his placid, intelligent wife. On this note, which also foreshadows the life his daughter is to lead, the book ends.

The Venusring story is the most optimistic of the medieval legends concerning the pagan goddess. The groom's dilemma is usually a temporary one and, except in those rare instances (like Mérimée's) where the supernatural proves deadly, the bride triumphantly receives her husband back and settles down with him to a contented if unexciting existence. For the writer whose hatred of Philistinism leaves no room for such a placid acceptance of ordinary domestic life, the legend was necessarily of less interest than the more popular story of the tormented knight, Tannhäuser, who could neither accept nor abjure a world in which there seemed to be no place for the dead or exiled gods.

FAIRIES and SAINTS

The death of the gods took on an added poignancy for Gérard de Nerval, revolted by a materialistic world and temperamentally unsuited to the reality of contemporary life, as he visited middle eastern and oriental sites. Churches had replaced ancient temples, and ruins existed only to announce the passing of deities that once were worshiped there. Naiads no longer inhabited their grotto, and Pan had died as only a god can die, through ingratitude and forgetfulness (GN 2:83). Nevertheless, in his sonnet *Delfica*, he expresses his confidence that

> They will return, those gods . . .
> Time will bring back the order of old days;
> Earth has trembled with a sigh of prophecy.
> [GN 221; 1:5]

But it is not really an old order that Nerval longs for; instead it is an ideal order in which the old gods will not dethrone the new, but rather merge with them.

Nerval [1] published his prose versions of Heine's *Traumbilder* [Dream images] in the *Revue des Deux Mondes* by introducing the poems with a description of the terror that he found lurking behind them.[2] The first poem, he says, is a somber beginning, with the enveloping charm of dangerous flowers whose perfume is extracted from death. It is the Venus Libitina who, from her violet lips, gives the poet the last kiss. For Heine, Venus Libitina could represent women in general; Nerval records the German poet's feeling that woman is man's chimera, or his demon, if you will—an adorable monster, but a monster. Heine had quipped that Mélusine's husband was fortunate to love a woman who was only half-serpent. He, Nerval, has a very different view:

> A woman is love, fame and expectation;
> To the children she brings up, to the consoled man,
> She lifts the heart and calms all suffering,
> Like a spirit of heaven exiled on the earth.
>
> [GN 247; 1:42]

And while it is true that the siren with her seductive dangers is a frequent image in Nerval's writing,[3] his work more characteristically transforms the mortal into a goddess, not a seductress, and a goddess quite distinct from the Venus Libitina.

In the records of his travels in Greece, Nerval writes of the *Trois Vénus*, the three aspects of the pantheistic deity who presided over the sky, the earth, and the underworld (GN 2:77). This tripartite division of the goddess is traditional among mythologists:

> [Venus] Urania, or the celestial [Venus], was the goddess of pure and ideal love. [Venus] Genetrix or Nymphia favoured and protected marriage; unmarried girls and widows prayed to her in order to obtain husbands. [Venus] Pandemos (common) or [Venus] Porne (courtesan) was the goddess of lust and venal love, the patroness of prostitutes.[4]

A significant analogy can be made between the three forms of Venus and the three most important women in Nerval's writing: Adrienne, Sylvie, and Jenny Colon, whom he calls Aurelia. Adrienne is the beautiful girl he compares to Dante's Beatrice. She has been consecrated by her family to the life of a nun, and thus to a love as pure and ideal as that represented by Venus Urania. It is Adrienne who attracts Nerval away from Sylvie, the sweetheart of his youth, whom he associates with the normalcy of home and family, of a life represented by Venus Genetrix. Jenny Colon is an actress, a member therefore of a profession against which Nerval had been placed on his guard by one of his uncles, who, he writes in *Sylvie*, "had early warned me that actresses were not women and that nature had denied them hearts . . . he had told me so many stories of illusions and deceptions" (GN 50; *1:242*). In this description it is not difficult to find Venus in her lowest form.

Actually he need not have worried about his uncle's judgment, for it was not the actress whom he loved with a hopeless longing for the unattainable, but the ideal he had created for himself. In *Aurelia*, which records both the experience of his madness and the most extreme idealization of his love, he displays true insight into his own fantasies, realizing that the metamorphosis of Jenny into Aurelia is the product of his own imagination: " 'What madness,' I told myself, 'to go on platonically loving a woman who no longer loves you. This is the evil result of your reading. You have taken the conceits of poets quite seriously and fashioned for yourself a Laura or a Beatrice out of an ordinary person of the present century' " (GN 116; *1:360*). He writes in *Sylvie* that this passion had its seeds in the memory of Adrienne. And here too Nerval is keenly aware of the incongruity of his position: "To love a nun in the form of an actress! . . . but what if they were one and the same!—It was enough to drive you mad! That fascination is fatal in which the unknown leads you on like a will-o'-the-wisp hovering over the reeds in still water" (GN 55; *1:247*). But if Aurelia is Adrienne, so then by an almost geometric logic is she Sylvie, for Nerval had mused, "Adrienne or Sylvie—two halves of a single love. One was the sublime ideal, the other the sweet reality" (GN 83; *1:272*). A total synthesis is achieved in *Aurelia* as Nerval describes a dream:

> Three women were working in the room. . . . Their facial contours changed like the flames of a lamp, and all the time something of one was passing to the other. Their smiles, the color of their eyes and hair, their figures and familiar gestures, all these were exchanged as if they had lived the same life, and each was made up of all three, like those figures painters take from a number of models in order to achieve a perfect beauty. [GN 130; *1:372–73*]

With all feminine beauty and virtue finally bestowed upon Aurelia, there was in effect only one Venus. This, Nerval claims, was also the case for the Greeks, because they, although recognizing the triple aspect of the goddess, addressed themselves principally to the austere, ideal, and mystical Venus, whom the Neoplatonists of Alexandria were able to hold up without shame to the Virgin of the Christians. Mary, more human, easier to understand, had finally defeated the philosophical Urania (GN 2:77–78). Since Nerval's desire is to synthesize opposites, he does not set up here a conflict between pagan and Christian divinity, nor does he lament, as Swinburne does, the overthrow of Venus by the Virgin Mary and the implications of her defeat for an age in which the change of order spells the death of beauty and passion. Rather, Venus in her highest form is not only comparable to Mary but is the same as Mary, both manifestations of Isis, who, in turn, is both goddess and woman in her most exalted forms. He writes in *Aurelia* (GN 168; *1:404*): "I turned my thoughts to the eternal Isis, sacred mother and spouse; all my aspirations, all my prayers were mingled in that magic name, and I seemed to live again in her; sometimes she appeared to me in the guise of Venus of the ancients, sometimes as the Christian Virgin." Each of his loves had been but a mortal form of eternal Isis: "During my sleep I had a marvellous vision. It seemed to me that the goddess appeared to me, saying: 'I am the same as Mary, the same as your mother, the same being also whom you have always loved under every form. At each of your ordeals I have dropped one of the masks with which I hide my features and soon you shall see me as I really am'" (GN 162; *1:399*).

His syncretism frequently disturbed Nerval, as when he writes in *Aurelia*, "I have preferred creature to Creator; I have deified my love and adored with pagan ritual her whose last sigh was consecrated to Christ" (GN 150; *1:389*). Even worse, in his most desperate agonies he wonders how Isis, his amalgam of Venus and Mary, can help him: "What can she, conquered as she is and perhaps oppressed, do for her poor children?" (GN 168; *1:404*). Like Heine, who dragged himself to the Louvre only to confront a Venus of Milo helpless to ease his pain, Nerval also experiences despair over the probable inability of Isis to alleviate the misery of her mortal worshipers. But such doubts are usually rejected, and, unlike Heine, who saw an unending battle between the forces of Hebraism and Hellenism, Nerval professes in *Aurelia* that "My own role seemed to be to re-establish universal harmony by means of Cabalistic arts and to seek a solution in summoning the occult powers of the various religions" (GN 165; 1:402).

This difference between Heine and Nerval, one despairing of synthesis, the other searching for it with a fervor that leads to insanity, may account for their differing treatments of La Belle Dame sans Merci. Nerval's translation of two Heine poems that depict the seduction of mortals by water fairies provides by way of contrast a means of looking at his own treatment of similar themes.

In the poem Nerval translates as *Les Ondines*, a young knight lies upon a beach, lost in reverie.[5] Six water fairies, believing him asleep and ravished by his charms, approach. Their gestures toward him become more intimate until the sixth kisses his face and lips. All the while the knight feigns sleep; he is not a fool; he keeps himself from opening his eyes and quietly allows himself to be kissed by the beautiful undines in the moonlight. There is nothing sinister about the episode, but the passivity and revery of the knight seem ultimately dangerous. Like so many others enthralled by these immortal enchantresses, he is content to neglect whatever duties await him in order to luxuriate in voluptuous delight. The peril lurking beneath this situation is fully exposed in *Harald Harfagar*. King Harald lives with his fairy mistress from the sea, and the years come and go like waves of the ocean. Seduced by the charms and enchantments of the undine, he can neither live nor die. Occasionally, however, he is aroused from his amorous languor by cries of war, or is reminded of his former exploits when he hears sailors chanting war songs. But on each of these occasions the king, sighing, returns to the arms of his fairy mistress. One wonders if Nerval was at all conscious of the irony of including this poem in the July 1848 issue of the *Revue des Deux Mondes*, where he begins his piece on Heine by asking if, at a moment when Europe is on fire, it does not take some courage to present not the political and republican Heine "but a simple bouquet of flowers of fantasy, of penetrating perfume, of bright colors."[6] Perhaps because Nerval considered himself a faithful devotee at "the altar of poetry" in those troublesome times, and not a mere escapist, his own undine, who appears in his pseudo-folktale, *The Queen of the Fish*, completely lacks the fatal seductiveness of Heine's sea maidens.

Nerval was deeply involved in the folklore of his country, specifically the Valois region—an involvement to which, Aristide

Marie has claimed, his "Germanism" can be traced. There, as Marie depicts it, the undines of Montefontaine whispered to him the songs that he would later hear from the nixies of the Rhine,[7] But his Queen of the Fish is noticeably different from the seamaids that had found their way to Heine's verse.[8]

The Queen of the Fish can be summarized as follows: On the banks of a small river in the Valois, a young boy and girl meet from time to time. He is obliged to work for his uncle at collecting dead wood, while she is sent by her parents to collect eels and crayfish. But the poor girl, overcome by pity at the contortions of the fish she captures, often throws them back into the water. The boy, however, is subjected to the reproaches of his uncle for not gathering enough wood or for spending too much time talking to the girl.

One day a week the two do not meet—and here Nerval alludes to the mythical origins of his tale—the same day, doubtless, that the fairy Mélusine turned into a fish. After one of these mysterious absences, the two meet and describe their respective dreams. She had appeared to him as a beautiful red fish to whom the other fish paid court. In the girl's dream he was on the shore and resembled a beautiful green oak whose top branches were of gold, an oak other trees bowed to in salutation. They wonder at this miracle, that they could have met each other in this mutual dream.

At that moment they are interrupted by his uncle, who reprimands him for not tearing off fresh branches from trees to include among the dead fagots. The young boy claims that he can hear the trees complain, and the girl comes to his defense by admitting the same concern for her fish. Menacingly, the uncle reveals that the girl is the Queen of the Fish and threatens to kill her on one of those days when she assumes her fishlike shape. But when he later attempts to do so, she is defended by his nephew. This young King of the Forest is protected against his uncle by the passive masses of trees, while the Queen of the Fish implores the aid of neighboring rivers. The nature myth behind the story fully emerges: the uncle is the destructive sun, and the trees are saved from his ravages by the flooding rivers. The girl and boy are no longer a fishergirl and woodsman, but an undine and sylph whose union is later legitimized.[9]

Nerval's sea fairy can be distinguished from Heine's nixies by the total lack of evil or ambiguity in her nature. Even in the comparison to Mélusine, Nerval has softened his portrait,[10] alluding to Mélusine's weekly metamorphosis into a fish, whereas in fact the legend specifies a serpent. It is true that illustrations of the story frequently depict Mélusine as a mermaid, but Nerval was familiar enough with the details of the legend. His handling of the material is consistent, because he had used the same method when he focused the triple aspect of Venus on her highest nature, the pure and ideal Urania, who could be compared to the Virgin Mary.

The redemptive qualities of Nerval's Queen of the Fish are reflected in Octavie, one of the *Daughters of Fire*. He describes how, during his travels to Italy, he met when bathing in the blue waters of Marseilles a young English girl whose slim body broke through the surface of the water. This water maiden, Octavie, came to him one day delighted by a strange catch she had made. She held in her hands a fish that she then gave to him (GN *1:285*). Such an image for medieval Christianity would have been ominous, because the fish was a symbol of the soul, and in church carvings a mermaid grasping a fish was a warning to man.[11] But Nerval's Octavie is different from the evil sea fairies who destroy their victims. She is a human manifestation of his Queen of the Fish, and she uncomplainingly cares for, first, her sick father and, then, her invalid husband. It does not matter that Nerval probably did not know the medieval bestiaries and their conception of the mermaid. He did not have to. He knew Heine's nixies and the story of Mélusine, which he had gone out of his way to soften. In short, the manner in which Gérard de Nerval idealized and idolized woman is reflected in his very treatment of the Belle Dame sans Merci story.

Such an idealization of woman resulted in her becoming unattainable, allowing Nerval to place her beyond the ordinary functions of home and family. For if, as he said in his poem *A Woman Is Love*, wife and mother are "like a spirit of heaven exiled on the earth," his returning woman to her rightful place was also a way of protecting himself from the crass materialism of bourgeois life. Such a Philistine existence was represented in the *Queen of the Fish* by the young woodcutter's uncle and the fishergirl's parents, who see in nature only goods to be exploited for money. Nerval's solution to this story is similar to that of Hoffmann's *The Golden Pot*: mortal and nature spirits are united and sent beyond the human realm to find their happiness. Wagner, too, will bypass the real world when, in *Tannhäuser*, he poses the supernatural Venus against the heavenly

Elisabeth. Although Nerval differs from Wagner in that he attempts to synthesize the temptress and the saint by making them, finally, one, he nevertheless is comparable to the German composer in his failure to provide a place for those women who represent the natural world. Wagner finally came to understand the value of Elsa, who for him epitomized "die Weib"; in *Sylvie* Nerval confesses to the stubborn aversion of his romantic age to the values of the real woman:

> Material man longed for the bouquet of roses which would regenerate him from the hands of the divine Isis; the goddess in her eternal youth and purity appeared to us by night and made us ashamed of our wasted days. We had not reached the age of ambition, and the greedy scramble for honors and positions caused us to stay away from all possible spheres of activity. The only refuge left to us was the poet's ivory tower, which we climbed, ever higher, to isolate ourselves from the mob. Led by our masters to those high places we breathed at last the pure air of solitude, we drank oblivion in the legendary golden cup, and we got drunk on poetry and love. Love, however, of vague forms, of blue and rosy hues, of metaphysical phantoms! Seen at close quarters, the real woman revolted our ingenuous souls. She had to be a queen or goddess; above all, she had to be unapproachable. [GN 50–51; 1:242]

Geoffrey Wagner has claimed that more than anyone else Nerval was responsible for the phrase "ivory tower." [12] Certainly, it seems to be a fact that Nerval was a writer not in the least abashed about dwelling in it. In this connection it is interesting to note that he was obviously impressed by a folksong of the Valois that appears twice in his writing. Presented in full in *Angelique*, the first tale in *The Daughters of Fire*, the song tells of a princess locked up in a tower for choosing a love her parents do not approve of, and of how, after seven years of suffering, she still prefers her confinement to acquiescence (GN *1:195–97*). In *Sylvie*, the song is only alluded to as Adrienne "sang one of those old ballads, full of melancholy and love, which always tell of the sufferings of a princess confined in a tower by her father as a punishment for having fallen in love" (GN 54; *1:245*). Forced to decide between the presumably mundane life which her parents have in mind for her, the princess prefers her tower and, implicitly, her reveries about a more romantic existence. That it should be Adrienne, the ideal woman who detracts Nerval's attention from the more real Sylvie, who sings this particular song is noteworthy. She, destined for the life of a nun, represents Nerval himself, who prefers his ivory tower to the realities of domestic life.

Sylvie herself plays a double role. On one hand, she represents a life that at times beckons to Nerval, so that after she has married someone else and borne two children, he visits the family and wonders, "Perhaps this is happiness; and yet . . . ," leaving the thought unfinished (GN 84; 1:273). Once in their youth, he and Sylvie played at marriage, dressing in the wedding garments of her aunt and uncle and listening to the aunt recite the "simple epithalamion, which accompanied the young couple as they went home after the dance." Nerval tells how "we repeated the artless rhythms of these verses, with the pauses and assonances of their time, flowery and passionate like the Song of Songs. We were the bride and bridegroom for a whole summer morning" (GN 65–66; 1:256). This ability to romanticize the past, on the other hand, is the most significant advantage that Sylvie allows Nerval. He is drawn from the materialism of Paris to the primitivism of the Valois region where he spent his childhood. Sylvie was the love of those earlier, more innocent years:

> Sylvie's enchanting gaze, her wild running, her happy cries, once gave such charm to the places I have just been through. She was still a wild child, her feet were bare, her skin sun-burnt in spite of the straw hat whose long ribbon streamed out carelessly with the tresses of her black hair. We used to go and drink milk at the Swiss farm, and they told me: "What a pretty sweetheart you have there, little Parisian!" Oh! No peasant boy would have danced with her then! She only danced with me, once a year, at the Festival of the Bow. [GN 73; 1:262]

It is therefore not completely true, as critics generally have it, that Sylvie, in contrast to Adrienne and Aurelia, represents reality, sometimes a seductive reality when measured against Nerval's search for the ideal. Were these remembrances of his childhood not as romantic as his transforming of Jenny Colon into Aurelia? Sadly,

Nerval watches Sylvie change. As she grows older, she ceases to be a peasant and dresses like a fine lady from the city. She cannot understand why he is dismayed when she uses her fine voice to sing arias from modern operas instead of the old songs from the Valois. And instead of making lace in the old fashion, she now helps support her family by sewing gloves with modern implements that suggest a machine world. Yet her transformation is but the signal for an entire cultural change, and Nerval looks back with nostalgia at an era that no longer exists. Sylvie will help him evoke memories of an Eden whose ponds are now only "expanses of stagnant water disdained by the swans" (GN 84; *1:272*).

In Nerval's writings the lament for this vanished pastoral age is expressed through the familiar symbol of the dead gods. He is himself, he explains in *Isis*, the child of a century inimical to their return. He moves between two contradictory educations, that of the revolution, which denied everything, and that of a reaction, which pretended to gather together Christian beliefs. But worst of all is modern reason itself, under which perished Christ, who had already overthrown the other gods (GN *1:299–300*).

It is the skepticism of the age that impedes his pursuit of the ideal. Was he not, alas, the son of a century robbed of illusions, a son who needed to touch in order to believe, and to dream of the past on its physical remains? (GN *2:67*). The physical world, reality itself, drew Nerval with its own seductive force as he struggled to escape from its bourgeois influences. In one sense, the attraction is healthy, as he suggests when he praises Heine for the use in his poetry of concrete images of nature. Nerval tells the reader that in his most abstract revery, interiorized passions, and desperate melancholy, Heine recalls the eternal signs of the human drama.[13] But such a tie to the physical world has made it difficult for him, Nerval, to lose himself completely in that dream world he found more real than the waking one:

> When I found myself alone, I pulled myself together with an effort and set off again in the direction of the star, from which I had never removed my eyes. As I walked along I sang a mysterious hymn which I seemed to remember having heard in a previous existence, and which filled me with ineffable joy. At the same time I took off my terrestrial garments and scattered them about me. The roadway seemed to lead

continually upwards and the star to grow bigger. Then I stood still, my arms outstretched, waiting for the moment when my soul should break free from my body, attracted magnetically by the rays of the star. A shudder went through me. Regret for the earth and for those I loved there gripped my heart, and so ardently within myself did I beseech the Spirit drawing me up towards it that it seemed as if I went down again among men. [GN 120–21; 1:363–64]

The alternating attraction of dreams and reality that he describes in *Aurelia* worked itself out in Nerval's life through his mental breakdowns. He calls this insanity the "long illness which took place entirely within the mysteries of my soul" (GN 115; 1:359), but says that when his dreams began to overflow into real life, "everything took on at times a double aspect—and did so, too, without my powers of reasoning ever losing their logic or my memory blurring the least details of what happened to me. Only my actions were apparently insensate, subject to what is called hallucination, according to human reason" (GN 120; 1:363). Once more we note that Gérard de Nerval showed amazing insight into the nature of his own fantasies, especially in separating the real from the imaginary. Human reason will not always tolerate ambiguity, however, and when he recovers to describe his experiences in *Aurelia*, he tells how in his madness his imagination provided him with infinite delight. "In recovering what men call reason, do I have to regret the loss of those joys?" (GN 115; 1:359).

The life of Nerval perhaps indicates a tragic realization of the plight of Tieck's Christian, who is maddened by his search for an ideal that would lift him above his dependence on a mutable and often prosaic world. Christian's last desperate return to wife and family can be compared to those flashes of insight that Nerval records as occurring in the very midst of his insanity. He tells how in one dream he meets an uncle who responds to Nerval's plaint that he is tired of life by reminding him that he still belongs to the world above (GN 125; 1:368). Was his agony, Nerval wonders in *Aurelia*, a punishment for attempting to penetrate the mysteries of the universe in order to find those correspondences which exist between the real and invisible worlds? Was such harmony to be denied man so long as he dwelt on earth, and must man reconcile himself to unending conflict?

This was, of course, Heine's question. And in part 2 of *Aurelia* Nerval's conflicts focus to a considerable extent on the split between Christianity and paganism. Like Heine, who at the end of his life turned more and more to traditional religion for solace, Nerval begins to visit cathedrals, where he implores the Virgin Mary for help. But his background had not prepared him to accept any solace she might offer. In addition to the revolutionary doctrines in the air during Nerval's youth, the chief influence on his early education had been an uncle whose researches into pagan antiquity inspired his nephew "with more veneration than did the poor Christian images in the church and the two battered saints in its portico" (GN 156; *1:394*). In Isis, who sometimes appeared to him as Venus and at others as Mary, he worshiped his personal synthesis.

To seek in *Aurelia*—a work that Nerval admits is a record of his mental illness, a work whose mood and thought foreshadow his suicide—a solution to his conflict between the real and the ideal, between Hebraism and Hellenism would be a mistake.[14] It was a conflict that resulted in Nerval's impulse toward syncretism, and his aim was the reconciliation of opposites on the highest level he could conceive. Thus, he idealized woman, and thought of both Christianity and paganism as emanations of a universal religion that had splintered in an imperfect world. But where reconciliation seemed impossible, where the supernatural and the divine seemed to represent opposing values, he, Nerval, could only continue to seek for harmony. And so he dreamed in the grottoes where the sirens swam, and, vanquished. twiced crossed the Acheron, where

> On Orpheus' lyre in turn I have sent
> The cries of faery and the sighs of a saint.
> [GN 213; *1:3*] [15]

Wagner's rendition of the Tannhäuser legend is made unique by his treatment of fairy and saint. The contrast is not between the real and the supernatural worlds, as it is for Tieck, Hoffmann, or Keats; nor is the conflict between Hellenism and Hebraism in the sense that such a conflict is revealed in Heine or Eichendorff. Rather, *Tannhäuser* contrasts two *unearthly* realms, one represented by

Venus and the other by the redemptive figure of Elisabeth. The real world is virtually bypassed.

A comparison with Eichendorff may help to make the point clear. Venus in *The Marble Statue* is otherworldly in that she lures Florio away from reality toward a deceptive fantasy that reflects his antisocial inner life; but she remains part of the real world in that she also symbolizes those earthly delights that were likely to divert her victims from the path to eternal salvation. Obversely, Bianca is this-worldly in that she represents Florio's healthy attachment to this world, the home, the hearth; but she also represents the otherworld to the extent that marriage to her is consonant with religious duty. In either event, this world and the other are conceived of as antagonistic only so long as Venus is on one side and Bianca on the other. For Eichendorff's point is that Bianca stands for a wholesome instinct for life even when she signifies its religious path. In contrast, Wagner presents two otherworlds, the Venusberg and Heaven, as Elisabeth's redemptive love for Tannhäuser culminates in their deaths. Neither Venus nor Elisabeth has any connection to the natural world which Tannhäuser longs for as he lies bored in the arms of the goddess. The life instinct which this love of nature points to, the one fulfilled in Eichendorff's tale, is to the end thwarted in Wagner's *Tannhäuser.*

Wagner's creation of Elisabeth, the woman who helps save Tannhäuser's soul despite the Pope's obduracy, has caused many to see in the opera a strongly religious theme, one, indeed, which they have not always found to their taste. May Morris says, for example, about Tieck's influence on her father's version of Tannhäuser, that she will "always be grateful for the preservation of the Venusberg legend as it was before Wagner's hand—which had not yet attained its later mastery—stamped it for always in people's minds as 'the' story of material and ideal love. The intrusion into this splendid legend of the holy Elisabeth and all she stands for in the operatic world of sentiment is not to be borne without protest" (WM 6:xxvi).

Wagner, however, denied the presence of any Christian theme in the opera, claiming that those critics were absurd who, "drawing all their wit from modern wantonness, insist on reading into my 'Tannhäuser' a specifically Christian and impotently pietistic drift!" (RW 1:323; 4:279). His essay, *A Communication to My Friends,* supplies, albeit in retrospect, a more interesting interpretation of his work, one which depicts his own artistic search. By understanding the dilemma he was faced with when he composed *Tannhäuser*, we can understand why two otherworlds vie with each other in his opera.

Three motifs are introduced in act 1 of *Tannhäuser*, and of them the religious is the least significant. When Venus, about to release her lover, warns that the outside world has nothing to offer him, he responds that his hope is in the Virgin Mary. This claim harkens back to those versions of the Tannhäuser ballad in which the knight is able to break the spell of Venus only by invoking the Virgin's name. But this is the extent to Tannhäuser's religiosity in act 1. What has really impelled him to leave the Venusberg is the motive that Wagner found in Heine's ballad—boredom. The Venusberg, it is true, stands in contrast "to the cold and joyless earth" from "whence every smiling god hath flown" (T 50–51). Nevertheless, Wagner writes in his stage notes, "when the Bacchic frenzy is at its height, a sudden lassitude is seen to spread amongst the dancers" (T 26). They seem to reflect the mood of Tannhäuser, who finds that this is no element for his human nature:

> A god alone can dwell in joy—to mortal frail its blisses cloy; I would be sway'd by pain and pleasure, in Nature's sweet alternate measure! I must away from thee, or die—oh, Queen belov'd! Goddess, let me fly! [T 34–35]

Just as strong as his ennui is his longing for the natural world:

> The radiant sun I see no longer, strange hath become the heavens' starry splendor—the sweet verdure of spring, the gentle token of earth's renewing life; the nightingales no more I hear, who sing of hope and promise! All these delights, are they forever lost? [T 30–31]

When Venus rejects his argument, he has no recourse but to repeat it:

> But far from these, thy rosy bowers, I long to meet the breath of flowers, long for the enfolding heavenly blue, long for the verdure fresh with dew—carols of birds, so sweet and tender, earth's fair expanse in noontide splendor. [T 38–39]

But Tannhäuser's return to earth from the Venusberg is not a return to nature, as Wagner himself later made clear in his essay when he compared Elsa, earthly wife of Lohengrin, to Elisabeth, earthly beloved of Tannhäuser. Where Elsa drew Lohengrin to "earth's warm breast," Elisabeth was the one who "star-like, showed to 'Tannhäuser' the way that led from the hot passion of the Venusberg to Heaven" (WP 1:340; 4:295).

That Wagner must bypass the "real" world altogether in *Tannhäuser* can be explained by the disaffection and alienation he felt during the composition of his opera. In 1843, two years before the work was completed, he had been appointed Royal Kappellmeister for life in Dresden. For the frequently poverty-stricken artist, this represented the possibilities of untold luxuries, and he did not at first recognize their danger to his artistic integrity. He describes his awakening to peril in the communication to his friends:

> Through the happy change in the aspect of my outward lot; through the hopes I cherished, of its even still more favourable development in the future; and finally through my personal and, in a sense, intoxicating contact with a new and well-inclined surrounding, a passion for enjoyment had sprung up within me, that led my inner nature, formed amid the struggles and impressions of a painful past, astray from its own peculiar path. A general instinct that urges every man to take life as he finds it, now pointed me, in my particular relations as Artist, to a path which, on the other hand, must soon and bitterly disgust me. This instinct could only have been appeased in Life on condition of my seeking, as artist, to wrest myself renown and pleasure by a complete subordination of my true nature to the demands of the public taste in Art. [WP 1:322; 4:278]

The analogy between Tannhäuser and Wagner at this point is unmistakable. Dresden theatrical life, like the Venusberg, satisfied a desire for luxury. But it was inimical to real art in that such a life demanded conformity to a loathed Philistinism. This false and deceptive culture also meant that in actuality the real world was parading about in the guise of a seductive otherworld, that there was virtually no distinction between them. To what then could he escape?

Wagner's dilemma can be explored by considering his adoption into the Venusberg story of another popular tale only tangentially related to it: Hoffmann's *The Singer's Contest.* A reading of Hoffmann's version of the *Sängerkrieg* legend reveals more clearly than Wagner's opera alone the extent to which the composer could find a reflection of the artist's plight in his sources. In *Tannhäuser,* the knight returns from Venus's mountain and takes part in a minstrel's contest. The winner will receive the hand of Elisabeth, a young woman he loves. Tannhäuser's entry *into* the contest is a song fraught with sensuality, proving him unworthy of her pure love and of the forgiveness he will later seek in Rome. The distinction between a healthy and a sick art was found by Wagner in Hoffmann's portrayal of the struggle between two renowned German poets, Heinrich von Ofterdingen and Wolfram von Eschenbach.[16]

Hoffmann's Heinrich von Ofterdingen represents the almost typical romantic artist. Hoffmann writes: "See the pale handsome lad: how his eyes flame, and the muscles of his face are drawn with pain—as if some invisible being were sitting behind him and torturing him." [17] His songs are born of his inner suffering and appeal in turn to the inner life of his audience: "Heinrich of Ofterdingen's songs went straight to the depths of the soul. Wasted and worn himself by pain and longing, he knew how to stir the deepest sorrow in the hearts of men; how often there rang through his music harsh accents coming from the torn and wounded breast." [18] His longing seems born of "some foul enchantment" and the "deceptive visions of a paradise on earth—of vain, mundane pleasure." [19] It is not surprising that this minstrel should sing songs in praise of the Venusberg and merge with the legendary Tannhäuser to become the hero of Wagner's opera.

In contrast to the tortured Ofterdingen are the other masters of song, whose individuality was submerged by their social interrelations:

Each of them had a "manner" of his own, as it was called, a "style" as we should more probably term it; but just as each note of a harmony differs from all the rest, and yet they all unite in forming the beautiful chord, so the various "modes" or "styles" of these masters harmonized completely together, and seemed but diverse rays of the same star of love.[20]

Their songs were from holy writ or sung in praise of fair ladies. Wolfram's songs, "breathing of grace and peaceful clearness, were like the pure blue skies of his beautiful native land, his 'manner' had in it the sounds of the cattle-bells, and of herdsmen playing their reeden pipes; but yet the wild waterfalls lifted their voices, and the thunder rolled among the mountains." [21] How different is such art from the songs of Ofterdingen, which "bewailed the immeasurable pain of earthly existence, and were often like the wailing cry of one who is mortally hurt, and longs in vain for death to deliver him." [22]

Hoffmann's contrast between the introspective artist whose unhealthy isolation from society is manifested by his sensuality and the healthier singer whose work is in touch with nature and his community is comparable to that presented in Eichendorff's *Marble Statue*. Wagner, more sorely in conflict than Eichendorff, had to battle his own cravings for luxury as well as his own romantic desire for isolation from an uncomprehending public, while searching for an artistic medium which would both satisfy his own integrity and still allow him to maintain contact with the world of men. By nature like Ofterdingen, he longed to be an Eschenbach. At the time of his employment in Dresden he could identify with his own Tannhäuser, who turned away in disgust from the Venusberg. Yet Wagner could conceive of only one alternative to the vulgar art appreciated by the Dresden public—pure art, symbolized by Tannhäuser's pure love for Elisabeth. "If at last," he writes in *Communication*,

I turned impatiently away, and owed the strength of my repugnance to the independence already developed in my nature, both as artist and as man: so did that double revolt, of man and artist, inevitably take on the form of a yearning for appeasement in a higher, nobler element; an element which, in its contrast to the only pleasures that the material Present spreads in modern Life and modern Art, could but appear to me in the guise of a pure, chaste, virginal, unseizable and unapproachable ideal of Love. What, in fine, could this love-yearning, the noblest thing my heart could feel—what other could it be than a longing for release from the Present, for absorption into an element of endless Love, a love denied to earth and reachable through the gates of Death alone? . . . a love that could *never* come to fruitage on the loathsome soil of *modern* sentience? [WP 1:322–23; 4:279]

This, he concludes, is what he really meant in *Tannhäuser*, his Christian theme existing only as an allegory for a personal dilemma. But Wagner's suffering, like Ofterdingen's, culminated in a death wish that was inimical to the healthiest impulses of the composer.

Wagner notes that after the composition of *Tannhäuser*, when he turned to the composition of *Lohengrin*, he "was now so completely awoken to the utter *loneliness* of my position as an artist, that the very feeling of this loneliness supplied me with the spur and the ability to address myself to my surroundings" (WP 1:339–40; 4:294). In short, the strongly romantic otherworldliness that Wagner had felt in his revulsion against Dresden society, and which was expressed in Tannhäuser's relationship with Elisabeth, was now being countered by a strong attraction *to* the world, and in *Lohengrin* would find its mythical expression in the motif of the supernatural being who longs for union with a mortal.

> In *Tannhäuser* I had yearned to flee a world of frivolous and repellent sensuousness,—the only form our modern Present has to offer. . . . By the strength of my longing, I had mounted to the realms where purity and chastity abide: I felt myself outside the modern world, and mid a sacred, limpid aether which, in the transport of my solitude, filled me with that delicious awe we drink-in upon the summits of the Alps, when, circled with a sea of azure air, we look down upon the lower hills and valleys. . . . The desire, however, that had driven *me* to those heights, was a desire sprung from art and man's five senses: it was not the warmth of *Life*, I fain would flee, but the vaporous morass of trivial sensuousness whose exhalations form *one definite* shape of Life, the life of modern times. [WP 1:339–40; 4:294–95]

The almost predictable metamorphosis of Tannhäuser into Lohengrin is suggested here. Seen in conjunction, the two legends are comparable in significance to the dual aspect of La Belle Dame sans Merci, the demon and the penanced elf, representing the artist's guilty desire to escape the world and his equal yearning to create an art in touch with mankind. Wagner's Lohengrin, like Mann's Little Mermaid, wishes to be on familiar terms with the world of men, and Wagner recognized in this desire the essentially classical instinct that holds man, the artist in particular, bound to earth. The motif, he points out, is the invention of man, who recognizes in it something central to his very humanity.

Who had taught Man that a God could burn with love toward earthly Woman? For certain, only Man himself; who, however high the object of his yearning may soar above the limits of his earthly wont, can only stamp it with the imprint of his human nature. From the highest sphere to which the might of his desire may bear him up, he finally can only long again for what is purely human, can only crave the taste of his own nature, as the one thing worth desiring. [WP 1:335; 4:290]

Wagner recognizes that it is in this world, not the other, that man must realize himself. And now he claims to recognize the true significance of the "real" woman, who had appeared before in his operas but without his understanding her true function. Elsa, he says, made him a revolutionary at one blow. "She was the Spirit of the Folk, for whose redeeming hand I too, as artist-man, was longing" (WP 1:347–48; 4:302).

The folk was Wagner's tie to the real world, the world for which Tannhäuser longed from the Venusberg. Now the composer need not move from one otherworld to another, but back to earth itself, with which the romanticized folk were associated. Of course, this folk was as much of a mythical abstraction as the figures in his operas. Longing like Tannhäuser to escape a modern Philistine world, and longing like Lohengrin to join society, Wagner had to appeal beyond the superficial appearances of modern society to a spirit that united him with Germany in such a way that he need not remain isolated and lonely in the ethereal existence of pure art.

It would require a separate study to examine Wagner's relationship to Germanic myth and folklore. Nevertheless we can find in the relationship of Tannhäuser to his antithesis, Lohengrin, a key to the composer's conception of the *Gesamtkunstwerk*, which would unite in a single production the different art forms.[23] Ernest Newman has pointed out that even the youthful Wagner tended toward an art which was communal. For this reason he preferred Meyerbeer's music, which stressed harmony, to Rossini's, which emphasized melody.

Melody, he explains, is the "immediate expression of a sensibility in isolation" (like Ofterdingen), while "harmony is more communal in its nature" (like Eschenbach).[24] The isolated romantic lyricists represented the aestheticism against which Wagner reacted despite his hatred of Philistinism. The *Gesamtkunstwerk* suited Wagner's purpose for two reasons. First, it was directed toward a large audience, and, as Alfred R. Neumann has noted, "in its extroversion, the *Gesamtkunstwerk* is opposed to the *l'art pour l'art* attitude."[25] Second, it united words with music. Baudelaire, in his study of Wagner's *Tannhäuser*, quotes from the composer's *Letter on Music*, in which Wagner shows how the duality between nature and spirit, which in one form or another had bothered all romantic artists, could be synthesized through such a union:

> I recognized in fact that it was precisely at the point at which one of these arts reached impassable frontiers that the sphere of action of the other started, with the most rigorous exactitude; and that in consequence, by the intimate union of these two arts it was possible to express what neither of them could express in isolation; and conversely that any attempt to render by means of the resources of one of them what could only be rendered by the two together was doomed to lead at first to obscurity and confusion, and then to the degeneration and corruption of each art individually.[26]

The romantic longing that drew Tannhäuser away from the world, first toward the Venusberg and then toward the deathly redemption of Elisabeth, finds its theoretical outlet in music, which was held by romantics to be the purest form of art because it is the least representative of this world. Conversely, Lohengrin's attraction to the earth is expressed by the artist through word, action, or myth. In *Lohengrin*, Wagner had come to that revolutionary understanding whose absence had stamped upon *Tannhäuser* the theme of aestheticism. The theme, inherent in the legend, was intensified when Wagner posed against each other two otherworlds, each irreconcilable to the life-giving earth to which he later turned by embracing the German *Volksgeist*. Yet, significantly, *Lohengrin* is as much a tragedy as *Tannhäuser*, Elsa's distrust exiling from her forever her Swan Knight husband, whose quest is hence frustrated. Tannhäuser and

Lohengrin are in the end finally one, neither able to live in a world whose hostility they cannot surmount. Wagner could not get beyond the knowledge Keats possessed, that mortals starve and die in the realm of the ideal, and that divinity could not breathe below in the world of men. Through form, the *Gesamtkunstwerk*, Wagner might at least in theory reconcile these opposites, but his success, both materially and ideologically, would still depend upon an audience that might or might not be sensitive to what he was trying to achieve.

ART and MORALITY

Yeats wrote in *The Second Coming* about a world in which things fall apart, describing a process of fragmentation that for many characterizes modern times. It is not that earlier artists lived in simpler times, but that complexity and change themselves became paradoxically the only constants in a world which becomes increasingly like the one that has learned to recognize and define future shock. Jerome H. Buckley points out that John Stuart Mill thought his generation had a quite "unprecedented awareness" of time and change.[1] One concern, however, remained the same: writers still worried about their responsibility to society. Nevertheless, poets like Swinburne, Morris, Davidson, and Yeats do not form as coherent a group as do Keats, Hoffmann, and Tieck, for example, perhaps because the middle and late nineteenth century saw the development of two distinct and even contradictory outgrowths of romanticism, while at the same time earlier romantic tendencies persisted. On the one hand, there was aestheticism with its offspring, decadence. If these exaggerated certain features of romanticism, realism, on the other hand, was in part a reaction against them.

Realism might appear to be an incongruous element in stories about fairy mistresses. But just as Hoffmann had based his supernatural fantasy on the realistic features of mining, so more than a century later would Thomas Mann endow a tuberculosis sanatorium with the features of a Venusberg. In one way or another the pull of reality that had drawn the lover of La Belle Dame sans Merci back to his own domain had been reflected in the forms of the stories in which she appeared. John Davidson's version of the Tannhäuser ballad reveals a curious intermingling of the material world with the supernatural.

In contrast to realism, essentially antiromantic, is aestheticism, which Albert Guérard has described as a newer and "purer" form of romanticism:

It is more frankly an escape and not a quest. The Shelleyans were reaching for a new heaven and a new earth; they were only a few steps ahead of the practical reformers. Their grandsons remembered obscurely the harsh lessons of 1848. Not the hope, and not even the dream could satisfy them; for hope and dream, if brought to consciousness, were found to be merely distorted reality. The aim of the Symbolist movement was not to attain but to flee.[2]

Guérard's claim, although interesting, should probably be qualified insofar as he neatly divides the earlier romantics from their successors. The element of escape is equally important in considering Shelley's poetry, and it would not be easy to decide whether Keats's *Endymion* was about a quest or a flight. William Morris was influenced by Keats's poem,[3] and *The Earthly Paradise* is about, if indeed it is about any one thing, the very relationship of quest to flight. What was the earthly paradise for Morris—the medieval past or the socialist future? Was it Endymion's fellowship with pure essence that attracted him, or Keats's lesson that human beings only starve and die in an ideal atmosphere too rarefied to breathe in?

For if a pronounced aestheticism is one of the characteristics of the middle and late nineteenth century, an equally strong reaction against it is also representative of the period. *The Wanderings of Oisin*, usually taken as an example of Yeats's youthful Pre-Raphaelite aestheticism, points in fact to the gay acceptance of tragic reality that marks his late poetry. This negation of the escapist impulse defines a notable circularity in the nineteenth century, because it links late century writers like Yeats and Hofmannsthal to their predecessors, Keats and Hoffmann. The earlier romantics who feared that a withdrawal from reality might lead to increasingly unhealthy results for art find their fears confirmed by those who can look back at their writings and discover prophecy. The difficulty experienced by Hugo von Hofmannsthal when he tried to adapt Hoffmann's *Mines of Falun* reveals an important struggle, for his reluctance to finish the play can be read as a counter-gesture to Elis Fröbom's final commitment to the Queen of the Mines.

Clearly, most stories concerning La Belle Dame sans Merci end with the defeat of the hero, who cannot reconcile his conflicts, and with the triumph of Philistinism or other hostile forces. Elis's return to the queen points not so much to the preservation of his higher being as it does to Hoffmann's belief in the need to isolate this being in order to preserve it. Hofmannsthal willingly published only act 1 of his play, and the other acts came out in mixed order over the course of some ten years. It was not until after his death that the drama was published in its entirety.[4] The English edition of his works includes only act 1, apparently in accordance with his wishes.[5] Hofmannsthal considered the play to be the last phase of an early period marked by a pronounced aestheticism, against which he struggled for the rest of his career.[6] To surrender his hero to the otherworld and to La Belle Dame sans Merci, who demands his absolute allegiance, would have been a profound admission of defeat.

If aestheticism was a problem for artists, decadence provided and still provides a knotty one for critics.[7] In Swinburne's early poetry decadence is an almost literal phenomenon in which sterile paganism leads to a decaying world. But it is usually difficult to keep the word *decadence* literal or descriptive,[8] to use it without the pejorative overtones of a Robert Buchanan, who in *The Fleshly School of Poetry* wrote that "sensualism, which from time immemorial has been the cancer of all society, is shooting its ulcerous roots deeper and deeper, and blotching more and more the fair surface of things." [9] Keats had asked for a life of sensation rather than of thought, but this alone by no means characterizes his beliefs, and, in any event, he had not meant to confine sensation to sexual pleasure or the cultivation of the exotic. How the change took place is difficult to explain, as Donald Davidson notes: the "Tragic Generation," by dissociating itself from social concerns, "had nothing left but an appeal to Beauty—which, alas, in a way that nobody was quite clear about, had somehow got allied with sin." [10]

Historically both Keats and Pater have been associated with decadence in England. The equation of beauty and truth in the *Ode on a Grecian Urn*, if taken literally, would result in a relativism that itself makes the very use of the word *decadent* meaningless.[11] As C. E. M. Joad puts it,

A thing is judged to be decadent by reference to some standard of what is good and valuable which the judger

172

recognizes, even if his recognition is unconscious. Now if the existence of objective value be denied, there are no standards of independent valuation which can be legitimately invoked.[12]

Pater's role in the concept of decadence points in another direction from the Keatsian equation of beauty and truth. According to Holbrook Jackson, decadence began in England "by accident" with *The Renaissance* (from the phrasing it seems that Jackson is anxious not to blame Pater).[13] It is not the art for art's sake philosophy propounded in *The Renaissance* that is decadent, unless one considers aestheticism and decadence virtually synonymous, but the emphasis on the hard gemlike flame, the ecstasy of sensation produced by art. The focus has shifted from the work, the source of the sensation, to the sensation itself. This affective theory substitutes ends for means, and eventually quantitative distinctions usurp qualitative ones. Any means of achieving sensation becomes legitimate, and it is impossible to separate the beautiful from the merely sensual.[14]

The argument over a definition of decadence would remain the province of critics alone were it not for a legal concern about one particular form that decadent art takes, pornography. There are two questions that are difficult to answer. First, is it possible to say anything about pornography and still avoid being judgmental or moralistic? Second, is pornography art, or are their realms mutually exclusive? Or, to put it another way: as soon as one starts to talk about pornography as art, has not one ceased to talk about it as pornography?

For David Loth, the word *pornography* has no meaning outside legal contexts. In his use of the term he means "those writings about sex or eliminative functions which past or present officials or influential groups have suppressed or tried to on the ground that they were morally corrupting or degrading."[15] But the contention by Justice Felix Frankfurter that obscenity is utterly without redeeming social value[16] is not a purely legal one, since he has unwittingly employed the criterion that lies at the heart of all writers' concern for their role in society. For many, escapism is itself obscene. In contrast to these legal considerations, Steven Marcus, one of the first critics to venture into this touchy area in *The Other Victorians*, defends pornography on the grounds on which it is usually condemned:

If it is permissible for works of literature to move us to tears, to rouse our passions against injustice, to make us cringe with horror, and to purge us through pity and terror, then it is equally permissible—it lies within the orbit of literature's functions—for works of literature to excite us sexually.[17]

Marcus's final rejection of pornography is based on aesthetic criteria. Pornography is boring and ultimately fails on its own terms if it makes any pretense to literary quality. For him the categories of literature and pornography are mutually exclusive, not because pornography is a purely legalistic concept but because it lacks the form necessary for deeming a work art.

The Venusberg story is perfectly adaptable to pornography, because it needs only to spell out in detail the pleasures that await the hero in the arms of his supernatural mistress, and to emphasize the sexual nature of the fantasies that are symbolized by the knight's journey to the otherworld. It is therefore striking that Tannhäuser suffers from the boredom that Marcus feels will overcome any sensitive reader who exposes himself to pornography. The reader becomes Tannhäuser, and what Marcus calls pornotopia is his Venusberg. In pornography there is an absence of human conflict and even characterization, since, according to Marcus, the pornographic work is more concerned with sexual organs than people. Similarly, the Venusberg is an escape from earthly conflict and human interrelationships that cause suffering and pain. Anger, betrayal, fear, despair, anguish, none of these are to be found in the otherworld. In that sense, then, it is hardly a realm inhabited by human beings but rather the abode of ideal abstractions parading in human garb. As Blake realized, without contraries there is no progression, and indeed this lack of conflict ultimately makes the Venusberg unsatisfying. Everything is given; there is nothing to strive for, no goals to be achieved. There are no prizes to be won, because everything is a prize. The dream takes its value from its counterpart, a reality often harsh. Without the one, the other becomes meaningless—and, again, boring.

When Heine and then Wagner introduced into the Tannhäuser legend the theme of ennui,[18] they were also introducing into literary versions of the tale a possibility for morality without didacticism. Marcus's aesthetic standards, in other words, can easily be turned to the uses of ethics. For no Christian condemnation of the

Venusberg on grounds of sin could compete in effectiveness with its condemnation on the grounds of boredom. Unfortunately, an audience used to an admixture of the moral and didactic is likely to miss the point. When Swinburne's *Poems and Ballads* were published, even his friends, Edmund Gosse says, considered that *Laus Veneris* was the most dangerous poem in the volume.[19]

The whole volume had outraged a public already shocked by Swinburne's frank glorification of sexual pleasure. Such frankness alone would have elicited their indignation, but combined with Swinburne's equation of pain and pleasure, this openness caused Robert Buchanan, for example, to use adjectives like "blasphemous" and "atrocious," although in *The Fleshly School of Poetry* he also claimed that Swinburne's "hysterical tone slew the animalism," thus reducing "the first feeling of disgust" to one of "comic amazement." Swinburne was, he concluded, "only a little mad boy letting off squibs; not a great strong man, who might be really dangerous to society." [20] Critics over the years, however, have generally avoided Swinburne's poems as if they were indeed dangerous, and only recently has Cecil Y. Lang been able to proclaim gladly that the "old order is yielding place, and it is about time." [21] Is he consciously echoing the theme of one of Swinburne's best known poems? In reading the modern scholarship that he introduces, one might indeed believe that the prophecy which ends the *Hymn to Proserpine* was being fulfilled, and that the pale Galilean was being replaced by a triumphantly returning Venus.

However welcome the change for a general understanding of Swinburne's poems, that such a process does true justice to *Laus Veneris* (or even the other *Poems and Ballads*) is not certain. True, the volume was Swinburne's counteroffensive to the Philistinism of his time, which he had attacked in a defense of Meredith's *Modern Love* by appealing to the autonomy of art and by hinting at an impotence disguised as an assertive morality:

There are pulpits enough for all preachers in prose; the business of versewriting is hardly to express convictions; and if some poetry, not without merit of its kind, has at times dealt in dogmatic morality, it is all the worse and all the weaker for that. As to subject, it is too much to expect that all schools of poetry are to be for ever subordinate to the one just now so much in request with us, whose scope of sight is bounded by the nursery walls; that all Muses are to bow down before her who babbles, with lips yet warm from their pristine pap, after the dangling delights of a child's coral; and jingle with flaccid fingers one knows not whether a jester's or a baby's bells.[22]

Yet in 1876, ten years after the publication of *Poems and Ballads*, Swinburne seems unwilling to be associated with these poems in particular. He had been linked with the Pre-Raphaelites Rossetti and Morris, and protests that he cannot see any principle of classification that could bring together the authors of *The Earthly Paradise* and *Songs before Sunrise*.[23] He is correct in claiming that the revolutionary spirit of this latter volume has little in common with Morris's writing (or his own defense of Meredith), but *Poems and Ballads* bears comparison with *The Earthly Paradise*, if for no other reason than that in each is a version of the Tannhäuser legend that suggests the poets' general dissatisfaction with the Venusberg.

It can even be said that Tannhäuser's anxiety to be free of the otherworld has an analogy to Swinburne's wish to be dissociated from his erotic *Poems and Ballads*. But if he preferred to be remembered as the poet of *Songs before Sunrise*, modern scholarship has not heeded his wish. In a volume of essays intended to celebrate the centennial of its publication, none have to do with the poems being celebrated, while many are focused on *Poems and Ballads*, *Laus Veneris* having received much of the attention.

This criticism of *Laus Veneris* tends to view Swinburne's Tannhäuser as a dramatic character who errs in his Christian view of Venus as a demonic force. In this context, Tannhäuser is victimized by the dualism of flesh and spirit promulgated by Christianity, and the viewpoint through which Swinburne observes his knight is indebted to Blake, who would marry heaven to hell and restore what Venus represents to its rightful place as a healthy, creative, life-giving influence rather than a deadly one.[24] *Ave atque Vale* reveals that Swinburne was familiar with the process by which Venus was transformed from the pagan goddess of love to the demon associated with sinful lust.

Insofar as *Laus Veneris* is placed in a religious-moral context, this view of the poem can be supported by Swinburne's attitude toward Victorian Hebraism. But as soon as it is argued that

Tannhäuser represents the nineteenth-century artist resisting his own aestheticism, then it can be seen that in a world in which religion is losing ground, it is easier to patch up the quarrel between flesh and spirit than it is to solve the dilemma of the writer torn between conflicting and perhaps irreconcilable views of art. It can even be claimed that there exists an inverse ratio between a strict moral system and the artist's uncertainty about his role in society. To obliterate one dichotomy (between flesh and spirit) is perhaps to open up another (between art and morality). *Songs before Sunrise,* which followed soon after *Poems and Ballads,* stands in ethical relation to the earlier volume in much the same way that Rome does to the Venusberg. And if the later poems are not the most typical or even the best of Swinburne (to judge by their critical neglect), then Swinburne's predicament as a Tannhäuser whose efforts at redemption have been repulsed is only emphasized that much more. He tried hard in *Poems and Ballads* to expose the sterility Venus alone represents, and yet in the eyes of modern critics he remains bound in her embrace.

Venus's role in *Poems and Ballads* is best understood in relation to the role of Proserpine, who should be interpreted in the context of Swinburne's general approach to time and creativity in these early poems. In *At Eleusis* Ceres herself describes how she, in the grief that followed the kidnaping of her daughter, allowed the earth to become a wasteland. She then turns her attention to the youth Triptolemus, who is identified with the remission of Ceres's harsh decree, in short, with spring. This dissociation of her daughter from that part of the myth dealing with her annual return to earth has a particular significance for the entire volume of poems, with its recurrent denial of the hope usually associated with the seasonal cycle. Hence, Swinburne writes most of the poems as if unaware that to Proserpine is due not only winter and death but spring and rebirth.

The Garden of Proserpine depicts the goddess as waiting "for all men born," but forgetting

> the earth her mother,
> The life of fruits and corn.
> [SP 1:301]

177

It is as though Swinburne saw in the end of the year the end of time itself. In *A Ballad of Burdens* the seasons appear as a progression that ceases with a deathly vision of winter and the cessation of human aspiration:

> Rain in spring,
> White rain and wind among the tender trees;
> A summer of green sorrows gathering,
> Rank autumn in a mist of miseries,
> With sad face set towards the year, that sees
> The charred ash drop out of the dropping pyre,
> And winter wan with many maladies;
> This is the end of every man's desire.
> [SP 1:257]

The Triumph of Time makes clear that emotion which dies will not be revived: "It will grow not again, this fruit of my heart, / Smitten with sunbeams, ruined with rain" (SP 1:169).

Such an approach to the seasons is contrary to that found in poets for whom the cyclical process is itself a source of hope in a mutable world. Shelley's optimistic belief that if winter comes, spring cannot be far behind, finds a more ambiguous echo in Swinburne's image of "the hounds of spring . . . on winter's traces" (*Atalanta in Calydon*; SP 7:271). But *Poems and Ballads* provides no hope, and when occasionally Swinburne presents the seasons as a cycle instead of a linear progression from spring to winter and death, he does so only as a reminder that the things to which man is attached are denied the renewal afforded the earth. In *The Year of Love*, the very title of which is significant, Swinburne traces the decay of feeling, concluding,

> And now the time is winterly,
> The first love fades too: none will see,
> When April warms the world anew,
> The place wherein love grew.
> [SP 2:50]

Felise presents spring as almost a mockery, since the lovers' passion is dead; and in *Anactoria* Sappho pretends to take consolation in her belief that man will say in future years that "earth's womb has born in vain / New things," since never again will appear songs like hers (SP 1:198). Similarly, Swinburne's elegy for Walter Savage Landor complains that

> In many a tender wheaten plot
> Flowers that were dead
> Live, and old suns revive; but not
> That holier head.
> [SP 1:265]

The vision of these poems is the end and not the beginning of things, an apocalyptic vision from which, however, rebirth is rigidly excluded. This finality is paradoxically conceived as blessed relief from the pains of a sensibility tortured with the knowledge that all things perish, for if beauty dies, so does its beholder, whose anguish ceases with his life. *Ilicet* says that

> There is an end of joy and sorrow;
> Peace all day long, all night, all morrow,
> But never a time to laugh or weep.
> The end is come of pleasant places,
> The end of tender words and faces,
> The end of all, the poppied sleep.
> [SP 1:207]

The Garden of Proserpine rejoices at this release:

> From too much love of living,
> From hope and fear set free,
> We thank with brief thanksgiving
> Whatever gods may be
> That no life lives for ever;
> That dead men rise up never;

> That even the weariest river
> Winds somewhere safe to sea.
> [SP 1:301]

From a Christian point of view, the hopelessness which finally seeks respite in death demonstrates the emptiness of paganism with its exaltation of mutable pleasures. The Christians offered eternal happiness for what to them was the relatively cheap price of ascetic withdrawal from the world, and the pagan speaker of the *Hymn to Proserpine*, who denies the Christian promise and exalts Venus over Mary, can in the end only confirm their basic premises. For his supplication of Proserpine is the final mark of pagan defeat, suggesting not only the political but the philosophical triumph of the new faith as well.

The opening lines of the *Hymn* contain the feelings and ideas expressed throughout *Poems and Ballads*:

> I have lived long enough, having seen one thing, that
>   love hath an end;
> Goddess and maiden and queen, be near me now and
>   befriend.
> [SP 1:200]

The plaint is that of a man for whom all pleasures have faded, who is "sick of singing" and "fain / To rest a little from praise and grievous pleasure and pain"; he knows that love does not endure (SP 1:200). Hence the "Proclamation in Rome of the Christian Faith," which has inspired his hymn, is both a historic and a symbolic event. The dethronement of the pagan deities by the followers of the pale Galilean proves to him that nothing endures, and he predicts that these new gods too will be succeeded by others. On this level, his claim that "love hath an end" alludes as well to the replacement of Venus by Mary, an event that epitomizes for him the whole transition from Hellenism to Christianity.

But his efforts to disparage Mary by an exaltation of sensual beauty are doomed to frustration, for he also knows that all "love hath an end," and thus the historic event is symbolic of a truth he cannot evade. Therefore the famous lines,

Thou hast conquered, O pale Galilean; the world has
grown gray from thy breath;
We have drunken of things Lethean, and fed on the
fulness of death,

are followed by two which denigrate the value of what has been lost:

Laurel is green for a season, and love is sweet for
a day;
But love grows bitter with treason, and laurel
outlives not May.
[SP 1:202]

The tension which can be found in the relationship of Venus to
Proserpine is intimated in this paradoxical juxtaposition of ideas and
images in the *Hymn*. The very ambiguity of the phrase "love hath an
end," suggesting as it does both the deposition of Venus and the
ultimate emptiness of what she stands for, points to the spiritual
despair of one who laments the end of that whose value he can hardly
sustain.

Later Swinburne called the *Hymn to Proserpine* the
"deathsong of spiritual decadence" in contrast to the *Hymn to Man*
(included in *Songs before Sunrise*), which is the "birthsong of spiritual
renascence." [25] The *Hymn to Proserpine*, its speaker rejecting the new
faith as he defiantly asserts that "I kneel not neither adore you, but
standing, look to the end" (SP 1:202), proclaims a vision literally
decadent, because the pagan, in denying rebirth, knows only decay.
Beyond the eternal sea where the "foam of the present . . . sweeps to
the surf of the past" is a place where "death waits" and "waste water
washes" (SP 1:202). Associated with this waste are "unspeakable
things" and waves that roll "white-eyed and poisonous-finned, shark-
toothed and serpentine-curled," and the spray is "bitter as blood"
(SP 1:203). From this sea beyond which all decayed matter is swept
was born Venus, who, though she is "fair as the foam," cannot be
dissociated from the wasting of the earth, which only for awhile "grew
sweet with her name" (SP 1:204). The very historical process,
described by Swinburne in *Ave atque Vale*, through which the

Botticellian Venus deteriorated into the demon feared by Christians, reflects the decay of Western civilization.

Because of the pagan's bitter and hopeless outlook, the *Hymn to Proserpine* reveals him turning away from Venus to Proserpine, goddess of the underworld. Once again, she is carefully dissociated from the seasonal cycle:

> Thou art more than the day or the morrow, the seasons
>   that laugh or that weep;
> For these give joy and sorrow; but thou, Proserpina,
>   sleep.
>   [SP 1:200]

She is, finally, the fairest of all the pagan deities, because she delivers men from their pains and in the end she of all "shall surely abide" (SP 1:205). Here is the pagan's final though dubious triumph: death is stronger than all gods, for even the new faith cannot promise material immortality. The speaker's own superiority over the new order is asserted through his recognition of the way things are. But surely his is a sad, perhaps tragic certainty; since his vision cannot transcend a world in which nothing endures, he knows only that he "shall die as my fathers died, and sleep as they sleep; even so" (SP 1:206). To Proserpine eventually come all lovers of Venus, and the hymn itself, although it extols the fairness of the goddess of love and beauty, finally rejects her. Such, then, is the meaning of the mutual presence of Venus and Proserpine in *Poems and Ballads*: the value of the former is negated by the eventual longing for the latter.

Although the limited vision of the pagan who worships Proserpine leaves him no other hope than death, his ethical choices are uncomplicated so long as he devotes himself to the religion of pleasure. A vision which attaches itself only to the end of things reinforces the belief in *Ilicet* that "the goodness of a man shall perish, / It shall be one thing with his sin" (SP 1:210). Within a pagan context, the hedonistic logic of the *Hymn to Proserpine* is difficult to dispute:

> Nay, for a little we live, and life hath mutable
>   wings.

A little while and we die; shall life not thrive
    as it may?
For no man under the sky lives twice, outliving
    his day.
        [SP 1:201]

Christianity, in its claim that man does indeed "live twice"—although only once and eternally in the true sense if he will renounce the pleasures of earth—resolved the philosophical futility of the pagan doctrine but complicated the ethical realm for man, who, torn between the spirit and the flesh, did not find it easy to reject even this mutable world. The pagan is trapped in the contradiction of his own dead-end philosophy when he adopts a hedonistic stance that negates the very thing he worships, but he has not willfully, like Tannhäuser, denied the faith that was once a part of him. The hedonism of a Christian, then, should lead to an entirely different way of perceiving the worship of Venus.

    Tannhäuser, in *Laus Veneris*, points out precisely that distinction between himself and the one who might have been the narrator of the *Hymn to Proserpine*:

For I was of Christ's choosing, I God's knight,
No blinkard heathen stumbling for scant light.
        [SP 1:154]

He is the potentially tragic figure Swinburne describes in his explanation of the poem:

To me it seemed that the tragedy began with the knight's return to Venus—began at the point where hitherto it had seemed to leave off. The immortal agony of a man lost after all repentance—cast down from fearful hope into fearless despair—believing in Christ and bound to Venus—desirous of penitential pain, and damned to joyless pleasure—this, in my eyes, was the kernel and nucleus of a myth comparable only to that of the foolish virgins, and bearing the same burden. The tragic touch of the story is this: that the knight

183

who has renounced Christ believes in him; the lover who has embraced Venus disbelieves in her. Vainly and in despair would he make the best of that which is the worst—vainly remonstrate with God, and argue on the side he would fain desert. Once accept or admit the least admixture of pagan worship, or of modern thought, and the whole story collapses into froth and smoke.[26]

But Swinburne's analysis seems more applicable to the Tannhäuser legend than to his own poem, because despite the distinction his hero makes between himself, a knight of "Christ's choosing," and a "blinkard heathen stumbling for scant light," the voice in *Laus Veneris* is essentially the same voice as that heard in the *Hymn to Proserpine*.

The most obvious reason for the similarity is that *Laus Veneris* lacks any truly spiritual focus. Christ's knight, Tannhäuser, is a thoroughgoing materialist, whose life before enthrallment by the goddess of love reveals his essential worldliness. Languishing in the Venusberg, he recalls not his previous religious devotions but rather "the clean great time of goodly fight."

> I smell the breathing battle sharp with blows,
> With shrieks of shafts and snapping short of bows;
> The fair pure sword smites out in subtle ways,
> Sounds and long lights are shed between the rows
>
> Of beautiful mailed men; the edged light slips,
> Most like a snake that takes short breath and dips
> Sharp from the beautifully bending head,
> With all its gracious body lithe as lips
>
> That curl in touching you; right in this wise
> My sword doth, seeming fire in mine own eyes,
> Leaving all colours in them brown and red
> And flecked with death; then the keen breaths
> like sighs,
>
> The caught-up choked dry laughters following them,
> When all the fighting face is grown aflame
> For pleasure, and the pulse that stuns the ears,
> And the heart's gladness of the goodly game.

Let me think yet a little; I do know
These things were sweet, but sweet such years ago
   Their savour is all turned now into tears;
Yea, ten years since. . . .
                                        [SP 1:154]

All of the senses are included in the smell of the battle, the sight of
the "beautiful mailed men," the sounds of shafts that seem to
"shriek" as they leave their bows, the "touch" of lips which curl like
the "gracious body" of the warrior, and even the hint of taste as
Tannhäuser laments that the "savour" of these "sweet" things is now
the cause of tears. No suggestion of past asceticism separates this late
servant of Christ from the sinner bound to Venus, and so it is difficult
to credit Swinburne's argument that when the knight compares Christ
unfavorably to Venus, he is arguing on the "side he would fain
desert":

Alas, Lord, surely thou art great and fair.
But lo her wonderfully woven hair!
   And thou didst heal us with thy piteous kiss;
But see now, Lord; her mouth is lovelier.

She is right fair; what hath she done to thee?
Nay, fair Lord Christ, lift up thine eyes and see;
   Had now thy mother such a lip—like this?
Thou knowest how sweet a thing it is to me.
                                        [SP 1:147]

   Here is no Tannhäuser reluctantly forced to play devil's
advocate, but an echo from the *Hymn to Proserpine*, where the
virtues of Mary are denigrated by the praise of Venus:

Not as thine, not as thine was our mother, a blossom
      of flowering seas,
Clothed round with the world's desire as with raiment,
      and fair as the foam,

185

And fleeter than kindled fire, and a goddess, and
mother of Rome.
[SP 1:204]

Nothing in *Laus Veneris* offers Christianity as a viable alternative to
paganism; there is nothing save the ennui and hopelessness of
Tannhäuser to weigh the decision in favor of Christ.

But in treating the Tannhäuser legend, Swinburne had to
deal with its Christian context, with the Pope, whose staff miraculously flowers after he refuses Tannhäuser God's forgiveness. The
manner in which Swinburne handles this aspect of the legend is
consistent with *Poems and Ballads* as a whole. Just as the poet negates
the cycle in which winter will progress toward spring, so in *Laus
Veneris* does Tannhäuser stubbornly deny that any miraculous
flowering of the Pope's staff can occur. And since the poem is a
dramatic one and Tannhäuser's the only point of view, to all intent
and purposes the Pope's staff never does blossom in this version of the
Tannhäuser legend.

> Yea, what if dried-up stems wax red and green,
> Shall that thing be which is not nor has been?
>   Yea, what if sapless bark wax green and white,
> Shall any good fruit grow upon my sin?
>
> Nay, though sweet fruit were plucked of a dry tree,
> And though men drew sweet waters of the sea,
>   There should not grow sweet leaves on this dead stem,
> This waste wan body and shaken soul of me.
>
> Yea, though God search it warily enough,
> There is not one sound thing in all thereof;
>   Though he search all my veins through, searching them
> He shall find nothing whole therein but love.
>   [SP 1:159–60]

Tannhäuser denies the rebirth which the staff symbolizes. By substituting for it his own wasted body and shaken soul, and insisting that
no renewal is possible for him, he comes close to denying God
Himself, negating not only the possibility of his own salvation but the

whole promise of Christianity as well. Even the fires of hell to which he alludes have for him no theological significance, existing merely as a metaphor for his own burning lust and frustrated existence. He already dwells in hell. Thus, like the pagan of the *Hymn to Proserpine*, his vision is strictly limited to the end of things, and the poem concludes with a defiant commitment to Venus:

> I seal myself upon thee with my might,
> Abiding alway out of all men's sight
> Until God loosen over sea and land
> The thunder of the trumpets of the night.
> [SP 1:161]

But the trumpets announce nothing save themselves in this poem, because night, like winter, in *Poems and Ballads*, is an end beyond which nothing is imagined.

    Laus Veneris, therefore, proves to be another hymn to the goddess of death. Tannhäuser, bored and "satiated with things insatiable" (SP 1:151), envisions the figure of love—a parody of Christ crowned with gilt thorns—laboring in a dream while he weaves man's amorous destiny, "Till when the spool is finished, lo I see / His web, reeled off, curls and goes out like steam" (SP 1:148). This analogy to the fates is, however, ironic, for if ever character seemed to determine fate, it is that of Swinburne's Tannhäuser: he has "sealed" himself upon Venus to the end of time; he has denied the possibility of miraculous redemption. Bound to Venus as to his own nature, he sees no release from his agony save death. And even this is conceived of in sensual terms:

> Ah God, that sleep with flower-sweet finger-tips
> Would crush the fruit of death upon my lips;
> Ah God, that death would tread the grapes of sleep
> And wring their juice upon me as it drips.
> [SP 1:151]

Proserpine's realm, then, provides the only hope for Swinburne's Tannhäuser, who has also learned in his boredom that "love hath an end" and, recognizing the hopelessness of his own philosophy, longs for death.

Swinburne intensified the element of ennui already introduced by Heine's satiric treatment of the Tannhäuser legend, and makes explicit this interpretation of the knight's predicament in a letter to Lord Houghton. Referring to Titian's Venus, he notes, "I think with her Tannhäuser need not have been bored—even till the end of the world: but who knows?" [27] Indeed this reading of the legend provides an insight into the role played by religion. For one reason or another, La Belle Dame sans Merci almost invariably loses her lover. In Keats, Tieck, and Hoffmann the imaginative impulse is always countered and sometimes checked by a reality principle inimical to what the fairy represents. Religion is another expression of this principle, and in effect fills a vacuum left by the temptress herself. Just as Christianity grew out of the despair of pagans who found their philosophy inadequate and the anguish of Jews who saw in the course of history the frustration of their hopes, religion in the Tannhäuser legend is less the reason Tannhäuser turns away from his mistress than a reflection of Venus's failure to satisfy anything but his physical needs. What she offers is subject to the natural processes of decay, and what happens to her at the hands of Christianity, her denigration from goddess to demon, is inevitable so long as pagans assert that her value is self-sufficient. But Swinburne need not have tried to place his work in a Christian context it did not fit and which he actually slighted, since he did not believe in it. Even without the threat of eternal damnation, even without the affirmation of Christian hope through the flowering of the Pope's rod, his Tannhäuser was not likely to win servants for Venus among his readers, that is, from among perceptive readers who could get beyond the sensuous appeal of Swinburne's verse to the implications behind it.

The difficulty with *Poems and Ballads* is that if the volume as a whole points to the rejection of Venus, she nevertheless remains the muse of Swinburne's poems. Like Heine's Tannhäuser, who in the process of describing his passion for Venus to the Pope finds his ardor renewed, Swinburne's verse celebrates the delights of sensuality at the very same time that it reveals the sterility that results from a love which, having no end but itself, finally cloys. In *Dolores* he tells of "things monstrous and fruitless" (SP 1:286), but the reader is more likely to be titillated by the "monstrous" than warned away by the cautionary "fruitless." Similarly, the dark image of night in the closing lines of *Laus Veneris* is less likely to impress than the opening stanzas, which find Tannhäuser studying the sleeping Venus:

Asleep or waking is it? for her neck,
Kissed over close, wears yet a purple speck
    Wherein the pained blood falters and goes out;
Soft, and stung softly—fairer for a fleck.

But though my lips shut sucking on the place,
There is no vein at work upon her face;
    Her eyelids are so peaceable, no doubt
Deep sleep has warmed her blood through all its ways.
[SP 1:146]

The analogy to Tannhäuser's minute scrutiny is the obvious pleasure Swinburne has derived from his attention to detail. What was implicit in Keats's *La Belle Dame sans Merci*,

She took me to her elfin grot,
    And there she wept, and sigh'd full sore,
And there I shut her wild wild eyes
    With kisses four,
[KP 442]

has been made explicit in Swinburne, and even more graphically in Beardsley's *Story of Venus and Tannhäuser*. The poet is Tannhäuser, bound to a muse who has too frequently permitted sensuality to replace imagination.

La Belle Dame sans Merci was for many writers the symbolic queen of their imagination, the erotic components of which cannot be denied in light of the figure who rules over it. In *Poems and Ballads*, however, imagination seems threatened by reduction to the merely erotic, almost justifying the medieval belief that imagination is a product of the senses and like them to be condemned as unhealthy and evil. Robert A. Greenberg has convincingly argued that a Blakean unity of flesh and spirit is the theoretical ideal behind the *Triumph of*

Time,[28] but it is difficult to read "All senses mixed in the spirit's cup /
Till flesh and spirit are molten in sunder" (SP 1:180) without thinking
that spirit has been lost in the mixture. The verse suggests that the
poet's own bondage to the senses has destroyed his vision. But perhaps
this is fortunate. Because Swinburne's Belle Dame sans Merci
represents a particular kind of art, an art of the senses cut off from
direct social concerns, rather than art per se which she represented for
Keats, it would be possible for Swinburne to reject her without
rejecting poetry itself. It can be argued that the aesthetic of *Poems
and Ballads* was closer to what was frowned upon by the critics of the
time than the aesthetic of favorable critics today who consider *Songs
before Sunrise* a departure from Swinburne's most effective mode of
expression. A recent essay on his poetics takes for its premise that
aestheticism can be stripped of its pejorative connotations and be
viewed as an alternative in no way inferior to, for example, the poetics
of Arnold.[29] Undoubtedly a useful and perhaps valid tenet for the
modern reader of *Poems and Ballads*, who may thoroughly enjoy the
sensual experience offered by it or even achieve the transcendence
from flesh to ideal beauty, this belief was apparently not self-con-
fidently held by the poet who went on to compose *Songs before
Sunrise.*

Thus, we see that the muse of *Poems and Ballads* is not the
goddess envisioned by the ancients as rising fresh from the sea, but the
Venus whom the Christians banished to the depths of the earth. The
historical process, lamented in the *Hymn to Proserpine,* is reflected in
the contrast between the Venus of that poem and the more demonic
goddess of *Laus Veneris.* But even in the former poem the decadent
vision of the narrator, who describes the waste matter of the sea,
points to the transformation of Venus. What her metamorphosis
implies for the poet is suggested by Swinburne in his elegy for
Baudelaire, *Ave atque Vale:*

> And one weeps . . . in the ways Lethean,
> And stains with tears her changing bosom chill:
> That obscure Venus of the hollow hill,
> That thing transformed which was the Cytherean,
> With lips that lost their Grecian laugh divine
> Long since, and face no more called Erycine;

A ghost, a bitter and luxurious god.
Thee also with fair flesh and singing spell
Did she, a sad and second prey, compel
Into the footless places once more trod,
And shadows hot from Hell.
[SP 3:50]

In the midst of his elegiac tribute to Baudelaire, there is a suggestion
of self-criticism, and self-protection as well. Baudelaire "also" had
dwelled among the "shadows hot from Hell," but it would be
inappropriate in this tribute for Swinburne to chastise the aesthete
who had bound himself to a "luxurious god." Although he thus spares
himself, Swinburne nevertheless denies—like his own Tannhäuser—
the possibility of miraculous redemption:

And now no sacred staff shall break in blossom,
No choral salutation lure to light
A spirit sick with perfume and sweet night
And love's tired eyes and hands and barren bosom.
There is no help for these things; none to mend
And none to mar; nor all our songs, O friend,
Will make death clear or make life durable.
[SP 3:50]

The last words are comparable to Morris's uneasy Apology to *The
Earthly Paradise*, where he calls himself an idle singer of an idle day,
one who cannot ease the sufferings of man. Swinburne also recognized
that so long as his poetry was bound to the senses, which alone led
only to satiety and ennui, his muse was not the fair Cytherean, but a
ghost who led the poet into meaningless, "footless places." The sacred
staff of poetry would blossom only when his art took another form.

Songs before Sunrise is dedicated to Swinburne's hero,
Mazzini, by whom he had been urged in a letter to abandon his
"songs of egotistical love and idolatry of physical beauty," in order to
become the "apostle of a crusade," writing poems which would be
"the watchword of the fighting nations and the dirge of the
oppressors." [30] As in *Poems and Ballads*, the vision of the new volume

is apocalyptic; the end, however, is always the prelude to a new beginning. Even the title anticipates renewal as part of the natural order of things, and so will the songs, as Swinburne says in the *Epilogue*, "strain eastward till the darkness dies" (SP 2:289). The volume celebrates *The Eve of Revolution*, revolution that finds its metaphor in the sunrise, as the people too are "risen up" (SP 2:281). In contrast to the gloomy and futile hedonism of *Poems and Ballads*, Swinburne advances a new ethic in *Prelude*:

> A little time that we may fill
> Or with such good works or such ill
> As loose the bonds or make them strong
> Wherein all manhood suffers wrong.
> [SP 2:75]

Some critics did not find such a difference between the morality of the two volumes, considering that Swinburne had merely shifted his libertinism from the realm of sex to that of politics.[31] Nevertheless, the differing treatment of cyclical time in *Poems and Ballads* and *Songs before Sunrise* indicates that Swinburne believed his philosophy had shifted significantly. Yet the very end of the later volume contains an echo from the former: if his hopes in man be wrong, if change does not mean progress but only decay, then let the end come—not just the end of love and beauty but the end of man, of history, of time itself. "Let man's world die like worlds of old, / And here in heaven's sight only be / The sole sun on the worldless sea" (SP 2:299).

Poems and Ballads, then, contains neither the dangerous sensuality rejected by Swinburne's own age nor the supposedly healthy defense of Venus celebrated today, but is rather a work in which the ambiguity of attraction and repulsion, sensuality and morality, reveals the depth of Swinburne's self-awareness. To reduce this ambiguity to singularity on either side would be to deprive the poet of a seriousness that demands critical attention and to relegate him once more to that area of general neglect from which he seems lately to have been rescued. Nevertheless, the new emphasis on the Blakean exaltation of sexual instincts in Swinburne has had the beneficial effect of turning critical attention to the form rather than to the supposedly sinful content of his work. In any event, it is difficult in an age of X-rated movies to look very far askance at *Poems and Ballads*, which by today's standards is a masterpiece of indirection and innuendo. No such claim, however, can be made for Aubrey Beardsley's *Story of Venus and Tannhäuser*, often called by the title of its bowdlerized version, *Under the Hill*. Beardsley's friend and biographer, Haldane MacFall said of the work that "it was so obscene, it revealed the young fellow revelling in an orgy of eroticism so unbridled, that it was impossible to publish it except in the privately printed ventures of Smithers' underground press," and that it expressed "the sexual ecstacies of a mind that dwells in a constant state of erotic excitement." [32] Its confessional quality, however, redeems it for MacFall, who invokes an expressive theory of art to assert that Beardsley's story of Tannhäuser qualifies as true literature.

Today Beardsley's unfinished piece of fiction still confronts the reader with the question of pornography and its relation to art. Of course it is possible to avoid the matter altogether, as Annette Lavers does when she alludes only to the "extreme outspokenness" of Beardsley's work and goes on to discuss the artistic form and merits of the piece without any concern for the level at which sexual description becomes pornographic.[33] That she cannot entirely evade the issue is revealed in a footnote when she speaks of John Glassco's conclusion to Beardsley's story: "The contrast between the genuine psychological motivations apparent in the first part [Beardsley's] and the mechanical devices in the continuation admirably shows the difference between an erotic novel and a pornographic one." [34] There is some confusion here between form and content, however, which raises more questions than are answered by the assertion alone.

If it were true that Beardsley's section of the work involved psychological motivation lacking in Glassco's conclusion, then in terms of content one would have to argue that Beardsley's *Story of Venus and Tannhäuser* discloses that element of human conflict which would usefully distinguish the erotic from the pornographic novel. But it is Glassco's section, however ill– or well–written, and not Beardsley's that introduces a feature in the Tannhäuser legend which proved crucial to its psychological impact on the nineteenth-century writers who made wide use of it. Glassco's Tannhäuser, languishing in the Venusberg, bored with its pleasures, searching for something to give meaning to his existence, announces to Venus that he thinks it would be well for them to have a child. No children, she responds, are born in the Venusberg; it is against the rules.[35] The sterility of the otherworld, perhaps rendered too literally by Glassco, was impressed on writer after writer otherwise attracted by its allure. It can hardly be a coincidence that Yeats not only omitted from his version of *Oisin* the children who, according to the legend, were born to the hero and Niamh but also added to the story a scene in which Oisin's harp is destroyed by the fairies who effectively silence the creative mortal whose art cannot flourish in their world. In short, if content alone is invoked as a standard for distinguishing between literature and pornography, then possibly Glassco has the edge over Beardsley, who in his fragment had not yet arrived at a motive for Tannhäuser's dissatisfaction with the Venusberg.

On the other hand, Lavers's reference to "mechanical contrivances" in Glassco's writing has to be considered within the context of the criticism leveled against Beardsley's best known piece of writing. The question, much debated among aestheticians, is whether or not form as form is a sufficient criterion for judging a work of art. To Steven Marcus it is at least a standard for distinguishing between art and pornography. He feels that the language of pornography renders it inartistic, because it consists "almost entirely of clichés, dead and dying phrases, and stereotypical formulas." [36] In this sense, Beardsley's *Story of Venus and Tannhäuser* must be considered art, for it is written in such an extraordinary style that, as Osbert Burdett claimed, "only the punctuation is ordinary." [37] The problem is that one of the common descriptions if not definitions of *decadence* concerns its elaborate attention to style, its refinement of language for its own sake. Can we conclude that because of its elaborate style, Beardsley's work is not pornographic but only decadent? Both evaluations seem equally negative and equally useless for interpretation; *pornography*, it might be added, has as a descriptive term the virtue of specificity lacking in *decadence*.

Actually the language of *The Story of Venus and Tannhäuser* is not so much extraordinary as it is dandified, like Beardsley's hero:

The Chevalier Tannhäuser, having lighted off his horse, stood doubtfully for a moment beneath the ombre gateway of the

Venusberg, troubled with an exquisite fear lest a day's travel should have too cruelly undone the laboured niceness of his dress. [VT 19]

"Laboured niceness" is an apt description of the prose in this work; adjectives like *delicious, graceful, adorable, delightful, dainty, exquisite, sumptuous, elegant* serve to rob even the sexual descriptions of their potential eroticism. Swinburne describes Venus's neck, bruised, "wherein the pained blood falters and goes out" (SP 1:146), while Beardsley describes "Tannhäuser's scrumptious torso" (VT 66). Where the former is passionate, Beardsley is, in spite of his obsession with sex in the Venusberg, more likely to be cute. So, for example, there is the suggestive ingenuity of his description of the buttons on Venus's dress, buttons "so beautiful that the buttonholes might have no pleasure till they closed upon them" (VT 28–29).

Beardsley here is an artist working outside his natural element, attempting to make words do the work of his pen. The completed sections of his work are hence a series of pictures or scenes varying only in the degree of salaciousness one finds in them. Descriptions exist for their own sake, the following a typical example:

The breakfasters were scattered over the gardens in têtes-a-têtes and tiny parties. Venus and Tannhäuser sat together upon the lawn that lay in front of the Casino, and made havoc of a ravishing déjeuner. The Chevalier was feeling very happy. Everything around him seemed so white and light and matinal; the floating frocks of the ladies, the scarce robed boys and satyrs stepping hither and thither elegantly, with meats and wines and fruits; the damask tablecloths, the delicate talk and laughter that rose everywhere; the flowers' colour and the flowers' scent; the shady trees, the wind's cool voice, and the sky above that was as fresh and pastoral as a perfect fifth. And Venus looked so beautiful. Not at all like the lady in Lemprière.
    "You're such a dear!" murmured Tannhäuser, holding her hand. [VT 75]

"You're such a dear"—rarely has the goddess of love and beauty been damned with such faint praise. Indeed, one hardly knows whether the bathos of the Chevalier's remark is intended as satire (Holbrook Jackson claimed that the work satirized "all the weaknesses of the decadence, by pressing them to their logical conclusion in the negation of all spontaneous desire"),[38] or whether it is in its banality the only comment that the previous passage, void of all save description, could produce. Although the passage describes the scene as "pastoral," Beardsley's Venusberg is not a place where nature, however idealized, is held up as a criticism of life but is, rather, a celebration of artifice so empty and repetitious that the novel finally threatens to lapse into formlessness.

If artifice as artifice is enough to rescue a work from the label of pornography, then *Venus and Tannhäuser* must be described as decadent but not pornographic. But, we have already noted that these labels are not helpful, and some extra-aesthetic standards must be invoked to criticize the work. Marcus in fact does this when he speaks of the conflicts one finds in good literature, because such conflicts are drawn from life, to which he has ultimately turned for a standard of judgment. Similarly, it can only be charged that Beardsley's language is empty or decadent by appealing to human experience. Words themselves are not usually decadent except in instances when their contexts have unmistakable and generally agreed upon connotations. There is nothing wrong with speaking of a "delicious dinner," although references to a "delicious person" may say more about the speaker than his object. The suitability of an adjective usually depends on what is being described and the tone the adjective suggests, but such criteria are, again, drawn from life. In *Venus and Tannhäuser*, so far as Beardsley completed it, artifice has replaced life. As Burdett claims, it is "all technique and no humanity";[39] and if technique is to be synonymous with art, then there really is no distinction between Andrea del Sarto and Raphael.

Both technique and humanity are obviously required if art is to be more than a producer of sensations—or mere fun (for Beardsley's *Venus and Tannhäuser* is amusing and can be fun). If sensation alone is the end of art, then no aesthetic standards can be applied, and dirty jokes, skin flicks, pushpins, and drugs will do as well. The part of the work completed by Beardsley fails as significant art because it lacks humanity. And humanity is lacking because there is no conflict or necessity for choice on the part of its hero. Its language fails to redeem it as art because the language too seems very remote from the supposedly intense experiences to which it is applied. Edmund Wilson has claimed that Beardsley's Venus is harmless when compared to Swinburne's,[40] and perhaps it is language and tone that render Beardsley's vision of the Venusberg, despite the novel's pornographic elements, almost innocent.

So much for the work Beardsley wrote, for the fragment that he never completed. The novel he would have written had it been completed and true to his legend might have been another matter. At that point at which Tannhäuser begins to compare his fantasy existence with life outside the Venusberg, any writer dealing with the story must also measure his own dreams against the reality to which he is once more committing his hero. It befits the facetious perversity of *Venus and Tannhäuser* that Beardsley dedicated it to a fictitious Cardinal Giulio Poldo Pezzoli, assuring the cleric that since

> the book will be found to contain matter of deeper import than mere venery, inasmuch as it treats of the great contrition of its chiefest character, and of canonical things in its chapters, I am not without hopes that your Eminence will pardon my writing of the Hill of Venus, for which exposition let my youth excuse me. [VT 13]

Had Beardsley been faithful to the Tannhäuser legend, his joke would have lost its edge, or, rather, his mock apology would have taken on substance. Tannhäuser's contrition *is* a judgment of life in the Venusberg. What kind of language Beardsley would have used to express his hero's conflicts (for at this point the story would of necessity take on conflict) cannot be guessed at. An illustration he made for the book, one which depicts Tannhäuser's return to the Venusberg after his rejection by the Pope, suggests darkness and despair very different from the frothy prose of the manuscript, which ends with the sentence: "The salle a manger at De La Pine's was quite the prettiest that ever was" (VT 88).

Beardsley's published letters indicate that this illustration was extremely important to him. Both it and the *Story of Venus and Tannhäuser* were created during a period in which he was becoming increasingly aware of the seriousness of his illness. On November 1894 he wrote to F. H. Evans: "I have been suffering terribly from haemorrhage of the lung which of course left me horribly weak. For the time all work has stopped and I sit about all day moping and worrying about my beloved Venusberg. I can think of nothing else." [41] The letter is a pitiful one, evocative of Keats's equally realistic fears that he will die before fulfilling himself as artist. Particularly significant, however, is Beardsley's reference to the Venusberg, for it appears in his context to be more than a reference to the subject of his novel. It also seems to be a symbolic representation of art itself, a realm about which another letter reveals some uncharacteristic ambivalence. [42]

Sometime in November 1897 Beardsley wrote to André Raffalovich, who was influential in his conversion to Catholicism, that "Heine certainly cuts a poor figure beside Pascal. If Heine is the great warning, Pascal is the great example to all artists and thinkers. He understood that, to become a Christian, the man of letters must sacrifice his gifts, just as Magdalen must sacrifice her beauty." [43] There is irony in his contrast. Heine, who also wrote of the Venusberg, vacillated between religious values and aesthetic commitment; Beardsley's very expression of the dichotomy between Christianity and art, in this letter at least, allies him more closely with Heine than Pascal.

During the three years between the letter to Evans which reveals Beardsley's fascination with the Venusberg and the one to Raffalovich which suggests his attempt, at least, to reject whatever it is that he thinks Heine stands for, he apparently began to think of the Tannhäuser legend in very different terms from the *Story of Venus and Tannhäuser*. He wrote to Leonard Smithers in April 1896 about an album of drawings being prepared for publication and speaks of a recent one he would like to have included: "I took for my subject *The Return of Tannhäuser to the Venusberg. . . .* If the Tannhäuser can be got it will make a strong *last* page." The emphasis is Beardsley's, and he continues to implore, "Please use *all your influence* to get the Tannhäuser put into the forthcoming album." [44] Obviously the illustration meant a great deal to him, enough for him to conceive of it as a conclusion to the work then in preparation.

The drawing is a compelling one, fraught with emotion inherent in the Tannhäuser legend but absent in *The Story of Venus and Tannhäuser*. The background is somber, and dark are the fields that the knight must cross to reach the Venusberg, the trees that almost but not quite block his way, and even the mountain of Venus seen in the distance. Venus's lover, in contrast, is illuminated, white amidst the briars that seem to tear at him, signs of his emotional torture. His arms outstretched to the mountain, Tannhäuser in his expression reveals, however, not longing but frantic despair. Beardsley's illustration, in fact, seems perfectly to depict the paradox in Swinburne's explanation of his own *Laus Veneris*: that the knight who has renounced Christ believes in him, while the lover who has embraced Venus disbelieves in her. "Vainly, and in despair would he make the best of that which is the worst—vainly remonstrate with God, and argue on the side he would fain desert."

Although Beardsley's picture sheds light on his mock plea for understanding from the nonexistent Cardinal Pezzoli, clearly more is involved than a parody of Tannhäuser's supplication at Rome. For if the joke was not dulled in the unfinished novel itself, it was in Beardsley's life. Several months after he wrote *Venus and Tannhäuser*, Beardsley was converted to Catholicism. Even though his rejection of the Venusberg was not perfect, as the editors of his letters note, in his deathbed renunciation Beardsley can be compared to Chaucer and Donne. Writing to Leonard Smithers in March 1898, he begins, "Jesus is our Lord and Judge," and then goes on to implore that his friend destroy all copies of *Lysistrata* and what he calls "bad drawings." He adds, emphatically, "By all that is holy *all* obscene drawings." [45]

Beardsley's fantasies had been expressed in his art, and the prospect of death as for Keats intensified his devotion to the aesthetic realm. But toward the end of his life, art obviously failed to be self-sustaining, and his conversion may perhaps be read as a reaction against decadence. His novel, had he finished it, might have proven more than decadent or pornographic, thus rendering both terms irrelevant to its understanding. The question that remains, however, is how would he have reconciled his artificial prose with the emotion revealed in the illustration?

Beardsley's novel actually points to the ironic futility of trying to turn the Venusberg story into a pornographic work, however suited the two seem. Tannhäuser's dissatisfaction with Venus has to turn the work into a critique of itself. Moreover, the unavoidable element of conflict lends the tale a social dimension not generally associated with either pornography or decadence. It is thus difficult to agree with Peter Michelson that Beardsley's treatment of the Venusberg legend "denies the artistic potency of moral conflict by simply dismissing it, and thereby he exorcises morality and celebrates style." [46] Morality cannot be exorcised from the story of Tannhäuser (which is perhaps why Beardsley did not finish it). Any work true to the legend has its ethical significance built into it, inseparable from the form in which it is expressed.

10
THE NEW SOCIETY

In these days of proliferating criticism, *The Earthly Paradise* surprisingly has received little attention, perhaps because it has become caught in the midst of William Morris's unusual (and one would think unlikely) reputation as both an aesthete and Marxist socialist.[1] Readers have generally been content to take the poet at his word when he apologizes for being an idle singer of an idle day, the kind whose mood is conveyed by Henry James's enthusiastic appreciation: "To sit in the open shade, inhaling the heated air, and, while you read these perfect fairy tales, these rich and pathetic human traditions[,] to glance up from your page at the clouds and the trees, is to do as pleasant a thing as the heart of man can desire." [2] The early reviews of the work, however, were scornful of its remoteness from contemporary life,[3] a view that in more benign form can be found in Douglas Bush's pronouncement that in Morris "the attenuation of romanticism is complete," although he goes on to add that "the divorce between poetry and life [is] especially paradoxical, for he was not, like Rossetti, a secluded high-priest of estheticism." [4]

This mild bewilderment is probably all the literary critic need feel when trying to adjust his reading of *The Earthly Paradise* to his knowledge of Morris's political beliefs; but for the Marxist, the poem is an embarrassment. The need to defend it can be inferred from what is to date the most elaborate published analysis of the work. As both a literary critic and, apparently, a Marxist, Jessie Kocmanová must redeem *The Earthly Paradise* as art without diminishing Morris's political stature. The result is a mixture of insight and problematic critical maneuvering.[5] She correctly points out that in Morris's famous Apology the poet is self-critical, but her main thesis, that the work is a summation of the romance tradition that allows Morris to leave it behind, is questionable. It is true that in the Epilogue Morris bids his work adieu and asks it to "let us go our ways, / And live awhile amid these latter days!" (WM 6:329). But to make such a plea grounds for defending Morris would be ironic and reveal mainly that his dilemma as artist has been inherited by his interpreters. Kocmanová's critique says, in effect, that Morris had to get this kind of writing out of his system so he could go beyond it. Hardly a starting point for a profound analysis of the work![6]

The approach that Kocmanová uses may reveal the dangers of a Marxist approach to *The Earthly Paradise*, but one that proceeds from the assumption that Morris is an aesthete is probably fraught with even more dangers, since it could encourage an almost purely formal analysis, one already *dis*couraged by a very long (and, alas, frequently tedious) work that is a priori assumed to lack enough substantive content to make the task worthwhile. This may be why Morris's most perceptive critics, recognizing in the dichotomy between the artist and man of action a crucial dialectic rather than a puzzlement, have not taken pains to analyze *The Earthly Paradise* in any detail. But there is a way of looking at his most famous writing without being forced to decide between the aesthete and the political being: consider that on the whole the poem's content is not escapist so much as it is about escape, a view, of course, that forms the basis for this entire book. In Morris's case, such a view, which, indeed, a close reading of the Prologue encourages, is rewarding on more than one count. It reveals, first, that the subject of *The Earthly Paradise* is related to a major concern of the Victorian writers, the perils of dwelling in a palace of art. Second, and relatedly, the famous Apology would take on a more descriptive function: an introduction by way of explanation to the whole book.

Some of the tales probably do exist for their own sake and in no way gloss the themes of the Apology and Prologue. The last of the narratives, however, seems to deserve special attention. We now realize that the Tannhäuser legend, of which *The Hill of Venus* is a little-known version, epitomizes the theme of the earthly paradise, not just Morris's conception of it but in general. It is, therefore, appropriate that Morris, although he had not originally intended to do so, placed it at the end. It virtually summarizes and climaxes the concern introduced in the Prologue about the dangers of searching for an earthly paradise and at the same time, perhaps even more crucially, dramatizes and thus makes more vivid the central dilemma of the famous Apology:

> Dreamer of dreams, born out of my due time,
> Why *should* I strive to set the crooked straight?
> [WM 3:1; my italics]

A brief recapitulation of the Tannhäuser legend and its history will indicate why Morris's question in particular can be dramatized by it. A knight dwelling as paramour of the Goddess of Love decides to leave the Venusberg and seek in Rome absolution for his sins. The Pope, horrified by Tannhäuser's experience, scornfully responds that only when his own wooden staff bears flowers shall the knight be forgiven. Hopelessly, Tannhäuser returns to Venus, and when the miracle occurs and the staff blossoms, he cannot be found. With the exception of Swinburne's *Laus Veneris*, which picks up the story after Tannhäuser's return to the Venusberg from Rome, most well-known versions of the legend begin at the point where the knight decides to leave his goddess and return to the world. Originally, the motive for the return was purely religious: the knight fears for his immortal soul. It was Heine who with brilliant psychological insight and caustic wit introduced the theme of ennui: his Tannhäuser is sated with the pleasures of the Venusberg. Wagner tripled the motive, which at once involves religion, boredom, and a longing for the natural world as relief from the artificial splendor of Venus's realm. The need to supply a motive at the crucial point where the story usually begins is the emphatic point. Why should Tannhäuser, living in an earthly paradise of unending pleasures, long for a more painful existence? In a cancelled passage, Morris's Venus asks her restless lover why he wants to leave her:

> I am the thing that thou didst cry to have,
> That rest and refuge from dull common pain
> For which within the world thou didst so crave.
> [WM 6:xxii]

And why, indeed, should Morris, independently wealthy and thus able to indulge himself as an idle singer of an idle day, emerge from his palace of art, his Venusberg? That his question, "Why should I strive to set the crooked straight?" can be found echoed in what he writes when his own Tannhäuser decides to leave Venus is striking. Although memories of his love "Blinded his eyes, and wrung his heart full sore,"

> Yet grew his purpose among men to dwell,
> He scarce knew why.
>
> [WM 6:307]

The question of the knight's motivation, or lack of it, dominates the tale.

The Prologue to *The Earthly Paradise* helps us understand *The Hill of Venus*, because it focuses on Morris's (and his Tannhäuser's) predicament, contrasting the quest for paradise with the virtues of common life. We meet the Wanderers, old men who have spent their lives fleeing death and trying to locate the fabled land of immortality. Having come to a place of rest after years of fruitless travel, they spend their remaining lives there, alternating with the Elders of that place in telling stories. But at the outset, Morris confronts us with the futility of their search:

> Masters, I have to tell a tale of woe,
> A tale of folly and of wasted life,
> Hope against hope, the bitter dregs of strife,
> Ending, where all things end, in death at last.
>
> [WM 3:6]

The Wanderers provide self-judgment by admitting they sacrificed what was worthwhile to chase illusions:

> We are as men, who cast aside a feast
> Amidst their lowly fellows, that they may
> Eat with the king, and who at end of day,
> Bearing sore stripes, with great humility

Must pray the bedesmen of those men to be,
They scorned that day while yet the sun was high.
[WM 3:39]

Although Morris at the end of *The Earthly Paradise* insists the reader cannot fail to understand what drove the wanderers to search for the perfect life, there is little question but that the Prologue is a warning for those who turn their eyes away from the real world.

It is a world, however, in which Walter (the name of Morris's Tannhäuser) can find little joy and less meaning. Like the existentialist hero confronted with an absurd universe, he is overwhelmed by a general malaise resulting from his inability to find significance in what he does. Therefore, why he travels to the Venusberg is hardly more comprehensible than why he finally leaves it. His uncertainty is reflected by the narrator, who says that "why he journeyed there / Nought tells the tale, but Walter doth him name, / And saith that from the Kaiser's court he came" (WM 6:282). The knight, having heard of both the wonders of the Hill of Venus and the torments later faced by those who venture there, is ready to risk such pain for a "little taste / Of the king's banquet" (WM 6:283), thus echoing the Wanderers' metaphor but not their realization that those who wished to dine with the king would eventually long for readmission to the company of ordinary folk. Walter, also thirsting for the ideal, despises the ordinary world and the women in it who fail to satisfy his need to discover some purpose in everyday life:

Yet, as he told them over one by one,
But dimly might he see their forms, and still
Some lack, some coldness, cursed them all, and none
The void within his straining heart might fill;
For evermore, as if against his will,
Words of old stories, turned to images
Of lovelier things, would blur the sight of these.
[WM 6:284]

Like the Wanderers, he pursues these images, lost to the world, but believing it a "world made to be lost— / A bitter life 'twixt pain and

nothing tossed!" (WM 6:285). It is not he who is deluded at the
threshold of Venus's realm but those who have turned away from the
hill, afraid to venture inside

> because within their souls yet lay
> Some hope, some thought of making peace at last
> With the false world.
>
> [WM 6:285]

Or so he thinks. But once within the Venusberg, Walter
remains frustrated. And here one can be grateful to May Morris for
providing passages her father wrote but later excluded from *The Hill
of Venus*, as clues to his intentions. In an earlier version he gave
Venus a more active role and assigned to her some speeches, one of
which, significantly, concerns her indifference to the questions that
plague her lover:

> Whence came I, where I wend, what things shall save
> My beauty from the swift decay of earth
> I know not; but my heart is full of mirth.
>
> [WM 6:xxii]

In the final version, Venus never speaks and almost seems a projection
of Walter's imagination, a phantom who cannot answer his queries.
Her silence creates a vacuum that cannot be filled by her caresses, and
thus the reason for Walter's departure is prepared:

> Then a great longing would there stir in him,
> That all those kisses might not satisfy;
> Dreams never dreamed before would gather dim
> About his eyes, and trembling would he cry
> To tell him how it was he should not die;
> To tell him how it was that he alone
> Should have a love all perfect and his own.
>
> [WM 6:297]

Just such matters, as we have seen, leave Venus unperturbed. For a time physical bliss leads to quietude; but soon unhappy thoughts cause joy to diminish. And Morris can no more answer his own question than he can explain why the knight is restless. Two of the three reasons he provides are trivial. First, Walter wonders about Venus's past lovers and their eventual fate. In Keats's *La Belle Dame sans Merci* the question of the fairy's past victims, if indeed these are more than a projection of the knight's fears, provides the poem with its central ambiguity. But in *The Hill of Venus* Walter seems merely jealous and his curiosity can hardly be taken too seriously. Second, and true to the legend, he worries about his immortal soul; but, again, religion plays no significant role in the tale and, once more, this motivation for leaving the Venusberg is not convincing. Finally, without clear reason, he is seized with a strong longing for the real world and asks himself, "Is there no love amid earth's sorrowing folk?" The narrator adds, "So glared the dreadful dawn—and thus it broke" (WM 6:299).

Walter's return to the world involves him in a hope for another kind of earthly paradise, this one created by a change in social conditions. Although the world is as bad as he had left it, he muses about a prophecy he has heard,

> That now so far did wrong and misery reach,
> That soon belike earth would be visited
> At last with that supreme day of all dread;
> When right and wrong, and weal and woe of earth,
> Should change amid its fiery second birth.
> [WM 6:310]

Morris's Judgment Day concerns not the harrowing of hell but the rebirth of man into a new era of justice and material well-being for all. But within the framework of the poem, that revolution which would justify Walter's departure from the Venusberg does not seem at hand, and the "hopeless" beauty of Venus is only countered by the hopeless misery of human life. Because he is looking for the earthly paradise, otherworldly religion does not provide him with satisfactory alternatives to what he perceives as reality. Thus, in Morris's treatment of the Tannhäuser legend, it is the knight who rejects the church, "Therefore what help in them" (WM 6:316), and not the Pope who spurns him. The world from which he had initially fled has not changed after all, and he concludes that he belongs to Venus and returns to her hill.

The narrator ends the story with the complete despair of the knight:

> And what more would ye hear of him? Meseems
> It passes mind of man to picture well
> His second sojourn in that land; yet gleams
> There might be thence, if one had heart to tell,
> In sleepless nights, of horrors passing hell,
> Of joys by which our joys are misery;
> But hopeless both, if such a thing may be.
>
> [WM 6:323]

Both human and supernatural joys are hopeless, because alone neither can satisfy man nor can they be reconciled. Thus, this final tale of *The Earthly Paradise* both justifies the quest of the Wanderers and points to the emptiness of their goals, for even if in their flight from bleak reality they had found their longed-for land, as Walter did the Hill of Venus, it could not answer their needs. Man must do more than achieve immortality and everlasting bliss, or find an antidote for human misery; he must achieve some understanding of that which from within or without governs his destiny. He must, in short, know why he should "strive to set the crooked right," or he will remain, like Walter, trapped in hopeless misery.

This reading of *The Hill of Venus* would remain highly abstract were it not for the role consciousness plays in Morris's utopian vision of a world in which improved social conditions inspire a rebirth of arts both popular and of the highest quality. A brief glance at that archetypal earthly paradise, Eden, will be helpful in understanding this socialist-aesthetic dream and Morris's conception of the false quest that leads his own time away from its realization. The loss of the garden resulted in, among other things, the necessity for man to earn his bread by the sweat of his brow. This "curse of labor," as Morris knows it is generally held to be, is not the consequence of the fall but rather of a competitive society in which men are divided into servants and masters. And thus the quest for the overwhelming majority is an existence in which leisure replaces work. Morris muses in *Hopes and Fears for Art* about the assumption—taken to be a "self-evident truth" [7]—suggested by a speech lately delivered to a group of working men that "no man would work if it were not that he hoped by working to earn leisure."

Morris believes that a world of pure leisure, could it be achieved, would be analogous to Walter's Venusberg, in which the workingmen-turned-Tannhäusers of England would lack a fundamental *raison d'être* that would rescue their lives from meaninglessness; for him, the ideal society would not be one in which the necessity for work withered away, but one in which the nature of labor would be transformed. What will happen, he asks, when "the blare of the heralds' trumpets . . . have proclaimed the new order of things, what shall we turn to then, what *must* we turn to then?"

> To what else, save to our work, our daily labour? With what, then, shall we adorn it when we have become wholly free and reasonable? It is necessary toil, but shall it be toil only? Shall all we can do with it be to shorten the hours of that toil to the utmost, that the hours of leisure may be long beyond what men used to hope for? and what then shall we do with the leisure, if we say that all toil is irksome? Shall we sleep it all away?—Yes, and never wake up again, I should hope, in that case. [8]

Morris is rousing his audience to that same consciousness which finally plagues Walter and makes it impossible for him to rest content in the Hill of Venus. This emphasis on consciousness can be found throughout these lectures given by Morris scarcely more than a decade after publishing *The Earthly Paradise*, the last tale foreshadowing these very talks. He is sure that if cultivated people began to consider the arts in their present condition, and "were ever to think seriously of them, they would be startled into discomfort by the thought that civilization as it now is brings inevitable ugliness with it." [9] His world emphasizes cheap luxuries (cheap in the qualitative sense), and either denigrates the arts or ignores them as the exclusive province of a very few, and, he claims, "both wronged and wrongers have been wholly unconscious of what they were doing. Wholly unconscious—yes, but we are no longer so: there lies the sting of it, and there also the hope." [10]

Hope characterizes the tenor of these essays, although the world Morris describes seems as hopeless as the one that drives Walter back to the Venusberg, and although Morris himself admits that he does not quite know how those few aroused to consciousness will rouse the masses and convince them to turn away from the false values that will be found in the deceptive earthly paradise they seek. What then stirs his optimism? Ultimately, its source is identical with the metaphor he uses to express it, and, strikingly, the metaphor itself can be traced back to the Tannhäuser legend. The legend concludes on a less pessimistic note than Morris's final comments on Walter's second sojourn in the Hill of Venus, for the Pope's bare staff does blossom, promising the eventual redemption of the erring knight. Morris has employed the imagery of this miracle to prevent *The Earthly Paradise* from ending with the total futility otherwise expressed by *The Hill of Venus* with its ghastly vision of Walter's fate.

Each pair of the twenty-four stories in *The Earthly Paradise* is narrated in a month about which a lyric poem is written. February provides the frame for *The Hill of Venus*, and in this bleak winter month the Pope's bare staff has its counterpart in the image of "leafless elms" (WM 6:175). But a "change has come at last" (WM 6:176), and in the very winds that blow is a bidding to "turn away / From this chill thaw to dream of *blossomed* May" (WM 6:176; my italics). The image is continued in another lyric passage, not itself part of the February poem but placed just before *The Hill of Venus*:

> The happy birds were hurrying here and there,
> As something soon would happen. Reddened now
> The hedges, and in gardens *many a bough*
> *Was overbold of buds.*
>
> [WM 6:279; my italics]

And right after the tale is completed, the old men, leaving the younger folk to discuss the implications of the Venusberg legend, walk outdoors "to watch the blossoms budding on the wall" (WM 6:326).

The Pope's flowering staff is reflected in these intimations of coming spring. And in the story itself, when Walter first wonders if love might be found on earth as well as in the Venusberg, the narrator comments that this thought "bloomed, a weak flower of hope within his heart" (WM 6:299). Hope, however weak, is symbolized by the Pope's staff, hope not only for the knight trapped in the Venusberg but also for all who pray that the world might be a better place. For the old Wanderers it is too late, but some of the young folk who hear Walter's story hold in their hands the "first starred yellow blossoms of the spring (WM 6:279).

In Morris's lectures on art, the cyclical metaphor merges with Marxist dialectics so that the very ills of society become the source of hope, just as the winds of February bring signs of spring, and he speaks of "a system which is drawing near now I hope to its perfection, and therefore to its death and change." [11] In the dialectical process, however, what is summer for the privileged class is winter for the masses and those like Morris, who in this February of his times must look for signs of spring: "That faith [that man will wake up to his condition] comforts me, and I can say calmly if the blank space must happen, it must, and amidst its darkness the new seed must sprout." [12] In true cyclical fashion, the society he looks forward to actually revives an earlier time when there was no split between art and life, the artist and the common man:

> Time was when the mystery and wonder of handicrafts were well acknowledged by the world, when imagination and fancy mingled with all things made by man; and in those days all handicraftsmen were *artists*, as we should now call them. . . . This was the growth of art: like all fruitful growth, it grew into decay: like all decay of what was once fruitful, it will grow into something new.[13]

It was because of this expectation, perhaps as illogical as the miracle of the staff, that Morris directed his efforts to the amelioration of the world about him, hoping that in the socialist future the arts would again flourish.

The juxtaposition of the hopeless tale of *The Hill of Venus* and the hopeful frame Morris places around it returns us to the dichotomy between Morris the aesthete and Morris the socialist. The hopelessness of a sustained aestheticism can be found in some lines from the *Life and Death of Jason,* a work originally intended for inclusion in *The Earthly Paradise*:

> Minstrel shall we die,
> Because thou hast forgotten utterly
> What things she taught thee that men call divine?
> Or will thy measures but lead folk to wine
> And scented beds, and not to noble deeds?
>
> [WM 2:193]

Would Morris's poetry be but a lure to the Venusberg? The need to stand in relation to the world as did spring to men wearied by a long winter spared Morris the paralysis of will that characterizes his hero, who, because he could not find an unequivocal reason for dwelling with men, turned his eyes back to the Hill of Venus. It is not that Morris had to get the romance tradition out of his system, but that the romance tradition itself allowed him to explore and describe the earthly paradise and to discover the illusory hopes with which it attracts those who would escape the real world. Thus, his supposed aestheticism paradoxically leads back to reality, uniting the artist and man of action in a common vision of a regenerated world.

John Davidson in contrast to William Morris was plagued by poverty all his life and worked at unpleasant tasks just to survive. But Davidson did not willingly turn from the real toward a dream world as an escape from stark reality. Instead he stubbornly viewed the world in harshly realistic terms, and, as a result, the illusions of romanticism were frequently the object of his bitter denunciation. A typical attack on those poets who would obscure the unpleasant truth can be found in his *Fleet Street Eclogues*:

> It is you,
> With mellow purple mists
> That shade the dreary view
> Of life, a naked precipice
> Overhanging death's deep sea.[14]

Signs of romanticism are nevertheless omnipresent in Davidson's verse. A speaker in the *Eclogues* describes his own hack
journalism in such a way that memories of a very different art are
awakened:

Newspapers flap o'er the land,
And darken the face of the sky;
A covey of dragons, wide-vanned,
Circle-wise clanging, they fly.
No nightingale sings; overhead
The lark never mounts to the sun;
Beauty and truth are dead,
And the end of the world begun.[15]

The dragon as metaphor for the dreary sheets produced by London
presses is borrowed from the very romance they supposedly obliterate.
"No nightingale sings" simultaneously announces the death of
romanticism and celebrates memories of Keats, not only the *Ode to a
Nightingale* but also the stark landscape of *La Belle Dame sans
Merci.* Romance and realism conflict in Keats's ballad, and in a
similar fashion they vie for position in Davidson's poems, which
frequently expose repressed longing. But because of his avowed
anti-romanticism, Davidson must treat such longing as deplorable
weakness, and in his use of the Belle Dame sans Merci theme he
frequently emphasizes the loathly lady, the ugliness beneath the
beautiful fairy's exterior charm.

In a similarly contradictory fashion, Davidson's realism
conflicts with his emphatic materialism, with his reiterated insistence
that the sensible world alone exists, that there is no spiritual realm.
Because of this belief, he attempts, like Heine, to "redeem" the
natural world, and claims in his *New Ballad of Tannhäuser* to
celebrate the joys of physical love in such a way as "once more to bear
a hand in laying the ghost of an unwholesome idea that still haunts
the world—the idea of the inherent impurity of nature." For him the
flowering of the Pope's staff clearly sanctifies Tannhäuser's sexual love
for Venus; because he believes his poem is true to the spirit of this
symbolic blossoming, he asserts that it is "not only the most modern,

but the most humane interpretation of the world-legend with which it deals" (NB 111).

Yet there are few poets for whom Arnold's warning that the religion of pleasure could work only so long as man was never sick nor sorry is as applicable as to Davidson. For there are few poets whose work conveys so many images of sick and sorry mankind. Even his depiction of the pleasures of the working class is bleak:

> The working-men with heavy iron tread,
> The thin-shod clerks, the shopmen neat and plump
> Home from the city came. On muddy beer
> The melancholy mean suburban street
> Grew maudlin for an hour; pianos waked
> In dissonance from dreams of rusty peace,
> And unpitched voices quavered tedious songs
> Of sentiment infirm or nerveless mirth.
> [NB 23–24]

Hence there is an unadmitted disparity between Davidson's materialism, which exalts the pleasures of the physical world, and his realism, which focuses on its dreariness for the majority. Only in theory could a reconciliation take place. Davidson borrows from Nietzsche an idealized superman who will face earthly reality without flinching, and, still more important, without seeking an imaginary world which would embody fantasies about an easier existence.

> It is ours to make
> This farce of fate a splendid tragedy:
> Since we must be the sport of circumstance,
> We should be sportsmen, and produce a breed
> Of gallant creatures, conscious of their doom,
> Marching with lofty brows, game to the last.
> Oh good and evil, heaven and hell are lies!
> But strength is great: there is no other truth:
> This is the yea-and-nay that makes men hard.
> [NB 32–33]

But these heroes of Davidson, as J. B. Townsend has pointed out, "are no more than abstract symbols of an as yet unattained ideal, unrelated to ordinary human needs or those of practical politics." [16]

This is the crucial irony: to the extent that Davidson's realism pushes him toward such abstraction, it involves him in the same romantic otherworldliness that he ruthlessly abjures to the end of his career. In the introduction to a late poem, *The Testament of John Davidson*, he is emphatic about the position he has maintained: "Briefly then, and without more preamble . . . there is no Other World; there never was anything that man has meant by Other World; neither spirit, nor mystical behind-the-veil; nothing not-ourselves that makes for righteousness, no metaphysical abstraction." [17] He acknowledges, however, that man has traditionally yearned for such a realm, and goes on to describe this "aphrodisian force" of the "Other World." [18] In the poem, his variation on the Endymion motif, the poet imagines himself encountering Diana, whom he must conquer, since she represents the otherworld and man's weakness in yearning for it (in addition, she is a virgin and hence stands for the denial of physical pleasure). There is something comical about the fervor with which the poet sets out to reduce spirit to matter. Killing Diana's dragon, which she had set upon him, he listens to her anguished cry: "One man is like / Another . . . The world is full / Of men! This was the only dragon left." [19] It is difficult not to share her regret, ludicrous as its expression may appear. It echoes the sentiment of the journalist who, in the *Fleet Street Eclogues*, describes newspapers as dragons that blot out a sky once filled with Shelley's larks and Keats's nightingales.

Davidson's subject world of romance, mythology, and fairies seems then to demonstrate a repressed revolt against the destructive realism of his philosophy. Yet he is adamant about what happens when the world of fairy is exposed to the light of day.

> But could you capture the elfin queen
> Who once was Caesar's prize,
> Daunt and gyve her with glances keen
> Of unimpassioned eyes,
> And hear unstirred her magic word,
> And scorn her tears and sighs,

Lean would she seem at once, and old;
Her rosy mouth decayed;
Her heavy tresses of living gold,
All withered in the braid;
In your very sight the dew and the light
Of her eyes would parch and fade.[20]

This loathly lady reappears in the *Testament of John Davidson* when, finally possessing Diana to the point of satiety, the poet sees that

as I drained my life in one resolved
Embrace, her fire went out, her deity
Decayed; and by the sullen clouded dawn
That dredged the sky with dim, diffusive dust,
There vanished from my sight a carrion shape,
With shrivelled dugs, wry mouth and posture foul
As of a naked hag on lewdness bent.[21]

Such a view of Diana, which Davidson may have adapted from Spenser's portrait of Duessa or from the depiction of the Elf Queen in *Thomas of Erceldoune*, lacks the ambiguity of *Undine* or *Lamia*, where the hero's perception is questionable. There is no suggestion that Davidson's heroes are mistaken in what they observe. To the realist who can look with "unimpassioned eyes," the fairy will be exposed for what she is, a hideous being.

But if the otherworld did not exist, why did the fairy not merely vanish, as did Lamia when exposed to the light of reason? Probably because only her metamorphosis could adequately convey the extent of Davidson's recoil from idealism. To expose her essential ugliness was to express his conviction that although life might be hideous, more hideous still was the attempt to spread a haze of illusions over it. Not only did the romantic poets deceive their audience but they also weakened them and impeded the natural evolutionary process toward the superman who would unflinchingly face his lot without the need for fantasy. Those men in the *Fleet Street Eclogues* who once sought—like Morris's Wanderers—the land of spells, finally accept reality:

We know, we know, we spinners of sand!
In the heart of the world is that gracious land;
And it never can fade while the sap returns,
While the sun gives light, and the red blood burns.[22]

But while Davidson too resisted the allure of the otherworld by his persistent demand for an unwavering confrontation with the harsh material world, even if this demand ironically led him to an immaterial world of theoretical abstraction, there was an otherworld that he could not escape so long as he wrote poetry—the world of art itself. He considered art a luxury unrelated to the everyday needs of his family, and he recognized a sharp delineation between the palace of art and the hut which was the probable dwelling of a poet who must depend for his living on poetry. Davidson thus provides a poignantly clear example for Robert Graves's conception of how the White Goddess is opposed to domesticity. The matter is exacerbated when the artist must struggle for sheer economic survival. Townsend relates how Davidson told his wife before he committed suicide, "If I were rich . . . I would buy three houses—one for you, and one for me, and one for the boys." [23]

That this statement does more than reflect ordinary household dissension can be seen in the subjects of Davidson's early verse. *A Ballad of an Artist's Wife* shows the bride willing to share her husband's aesthetic retreat from worldly care:

> Sweet wife, this heavy-hearted age
> Is nought to us; we two shall look
> To Art, and fill a perfect page
> In Life's ill-written doomsday book.
> [NB 8]

Robert Graves has noted, however, that to play the White Goddess involves a woman of sensibility in a role that she cannot stand for more than a few years because of the "temptation to commit suicide in simple domesticity." [24] The artist's wife here is forced by economic necessity to cease her play acting.

> After a time her days with sighs
>   And tears o'erflowed; for blighting need
> Bedimmed the lustre of her eyes,
>   And there were little mouths to feed.
>   [NB 9]

The artist is reluctant to join her in this other, more harshly real existence:

> My bride shall ne'er be common-place,
>   He thought, and glanced; and glanced again:
> At length he looked her in the face;
>   And lo, a woman old and plain!
>   [NB 9]

Her transformation is reminiscent of the fairies, who wither beneath the realistic gaze of Davidson's heroes. And while the artist's wife is not a fairy, the principle remains the same. By living exclusively in his own world, the artist has no conception of reality until he looks it directly "in the face." Here is Morris's dilemma adapted to Davidson's needs: if for Morris both the Venusberg and the earth were "hopeless," for Davidson both the non-existent otherworld and this life were ugly.

This vision seemingly justifies any sacrifice made for a third world of art in which beauty can be preserved. The artist leaves his wife and family:

> Wife, children, duty, household fires
>   For victims of the good and true!
> For me my infinite desires,
>   Freedom and things untried and new!
>   [NB 10]

This uneasy admission that beauty and truth dwell in separate realms is given even harsher voice in *A Ballad of a Poet Born*. Here the poet is urged to go out into the world to sing, but he feels constrained by responsibility to his family:

"My father's dead; my mother's eyes
  Are overcast with woe;
I hear my sisters' hungry cries;
  I dare not rise and go."

They jeered him for a craven lout:
  "What care is this of thine?
Thou speakest now, without a doubt,
  Like some false Philistine!

No poet can to others give:
  Leave folk to starve alone."
He said, "I dare not while I live
  She has no other son."
                    [NB 61–62]

In *A Ballad of an Artist's Wife*, the poet does desert his family, which
is reduced to misery: the children meet a "wretched fate" (NB 13)
when their mother dies, asserting with her last words that she fed
them while she could. The pain evoked by this tragedy inspires the
artist's greatest works. Later, when he dies, he finds that the most
beautiful woman in heaven, who sits on a diamond throne and
possesses "ineffable beatitude" (NB 16), is his wife.

He said, "I pray
Thee, Lord, despatch me now to Hell."
But God said, "No; here shall you stay,
And in her peace for ever dwell."
                    [NB 17]

Miraculous endings are common to many of Davidson's
works, a noteworthy phenomenon in one who claimed to believe only
in the material world. His most famous and infamous poem, *A Ballad
of a Nun*, depicts a woman whose sexual desires drive her out of the
convent into the world, returning as an old woman to find peace. She
discovers that no one knew she was gone, for in her absence the Virgin
Mary had taken her place. The public considered this poem blasphemous, but Davidson implies that God approves the nun's behavior,

just as the blossoming of the Pope's staff would point to the sanctification of Tannhäuser's passions. Similarly, the artist who abandons his family for the sake of his work is rewarded with greater artistic powers and heaven as well. But *A Ballad of an Artist's Wife* ends where it begins; the couple can only know happiness outside of the real world, in a realm of pure art or in heaven. It is just such an otherworldly solution that belies in Davidson's *New Ballad of Tannhäuser* the triumph of materialism he imputes to the work.

Tannhäuser is an adventurous youth who sets out from his father's home in search of fame, only to be lured into the Venusberg. The poem is obviously influenced by Keats's *La Belle Dame sans Merci*:

> She took me to a place apart
> Where eglantine and roses wove
> A bower, and gave me all her heart—
> A woman wonderful to love.
>
> As I lay worshipping my bride,
> While rose leaves in her bosom fell,
> And dreams came sailing on a tide
> Of sleep, I heard a matin bell.
> [NB 99–100]

Davidson is distinctively himself in those parts of the ballad that reflect his avowed purpose: to redeem nature from taints of impurity. Sexual joy is presented not only in those scenes in which the knight enjoys the embraces of Venus but also in the rapture he experiences from his contact with nature. Tannhäuser is almost literally seduced by the universe, for it is the sensual melody of the earth that leads him to the Queen of Love:

> I heard the wayward earth express
> In one long-drawn melodious sigh
> The rapture of the sun's caress,
> The passion of the brooding sky.
> [NB 97]

The sexual symbolism involved in locating the otherworld in a cave within the earth becomes explicit after Tannhäuser leaves Rome, having witnessed the flowering of the Pope's staff. He understands that God had indicated to him that there "was no need to be forgiven" (NB 103), and he returns, full of desire, to Venus. Once more his ardor is expressed through his ecstatic reaction to nature:

> All day, he sang— I feel all day
> The earth dilate beneath my feet;
> I hear in fancy far away
> The tidal heart of ocean beat.
>
> My heart amasses as I run
> The depth of heaven's sapphire flower;
> The resolute, enduring sun
> Fulfils my soul with splendid power.
>
> I quiver with divine desire;
> I clasp the stars; my thoughts immerse
> Themselves in space; like fire in fire
> I melt into the universe.
> [NB 105]

But to get through the earth to Venus, Tannhäuser must pass through a region in which wild winds, cold hands, and serpents threaten his way—a journey reminiscent of that taken by the Little Mermaid to attain human legs. Davidson, however, is less clear in his intentions than Andersen, for whom the perils of the mermaid's quest are revealed by passage through an evil realm. Since no sin is associated with Venus, the frightening stretch that lies between Tannhäuser and his love probably embodies the negative judgment of the world hostile to his passions. Only when he gets beyond its influences can Tannhäuser dwell with Venus, secure in her purity:

> But once again the magic note,
> Transformed to light, a glittering brand,
> Out of the storm and darkness smote
> A peaceful sky, a dewy land.
> [NB 107]

But even nature in the *New Ballad of Tannhäuser* is "otherworldly," for it remains detached from history. At the end of the poem Tannhäuser, his thoughts returning once more to the world, not because of a sense of sin but because of an awakening social conscience, asks Venus to accompany him to earth:

> "Hark! Let us leave the magic hill,"
> He said, "And live on earth with men."
> "No; here," she said, "we stay, until
> The Golden Age shall come again."
>
> And so they wait, while empires sprung
> Of hatred thunder past above,
> Deep in the earth for ever young
> Tannhäuser and the Queen of Love.
>
> [NB 108]

The ambiguously placed "for ever young," modifying as it does both the lovers and the earth, suggests that in Davidson's poem nature itself is akin to the Celtic otherworld, the Land of the Living.[25] Evolution would prove circular and bring a return of the Golden Age. In the meantime, Tannhäuser and Venus remain aloof from the concerns of the world, just as Davidson remained aloof from the social movements of his own day. Unlike Morris, whose commitment to the workingmen of England distinguishes him from Tannhäuser, Davidson celebrates the Venusberg in defiance of worldly care and, like his Tannhäuser, dwells with the goddess despite misgivings and a contrary ideology.

Davidson's later use of the Endymion motif makes possible the comparisons which focus on the irony of his work in relation to his theories about society. Keats had recognized that a longing for pure essence would destroy the bonds between humans. Morris, influenced by Keats's *Endymion*, had presented his Wanderers in much the same light: their quest for the earthly paradise had driven them far from common men. Morris understood their motives but spared himself their fate by involvement in social action, acting out in his life what Keats only managed to express through his poetry. Davidson also repudiated the quest for the ideal, and did so in a more ruthless

222

fashion. But between Keats's gentle hero, longing for the Queen of the Moon, and the brutally egotistic persona of *The Testament of John Davidson*, who must destroy her, there is really little difference in their relation to the world. Because Davidson's materialism was never linked to any social program, its abstractness actually led him away from the world. His tendency toward romantic aestheticism, moreover, was intensified by his inability to reconcile art and life on the practical level. As a consequence, his reworking of the Tannhäuser legend was hardly new at all. Rather, it was old and traditional, placing Davidson among other poets who, in treating the knight's journey to the Venusberg, had failed to reconcile opposites in the real world.

11

ARTIST and PHILISTINE

Harold Bloom, in his recent book on Yeats, has convincingly argued three points useful for interpreting *The Wanderings of Oisin* and understanding the themes which relate to the romantic dilemmas of the nineteenth century.[1] He claims, first, that Yeats's early poem is better than commonly believed. (Most of the negative criticism leveled against it has been based on its supposed aestheticism, its expression of Yeats's desire to flee reality as his hero does the world.) It is true that in *The Circus Animals' Desertion*, written in the last year of his life, Yeats admits that in his youth he had been starved for the bosom of Oisin's fairy bride (YCP 336). Nevertheless, escapism is more the theme of *Oisin* than its prevailing characteristic. Second, Bloom considers that all of Yeats can already be found in *Oisin*. This would also mean that the early work points ahead to the later poems, so much in repute among critics, and that it is possible to move about in Yeats's poems and prose without concern for chronology despite the fifty-year span covered by his writing. Admittedly, Yeats's position about almost everything that interested him changed frequently, but change itself is one of his major themes and a theme which remained constant. Finally, throughout his book Bloom demonstrates the profound influence of the romantic tradition on Yeats, but while he is chiefly concerned to study the effects of Blake and Shelley, one could argue that just as important as major influences on *Oisin* are Keats and Swinburne.

The Wanderings of Oisin was published in 1889, more than twenty years after Swinburne's first *Poems and Ballads* and more than sixty after Keats's 1821 volume. The earlier poets had not only influenced Yeats's narrative poem but provided for him a means of distinguishing between two kinds of poetry: that with imagery rooted in earth and living bodies, and that which he considered mere rhetoric, full of sound but too little sense. Hence, examining the way in which Keats and Swinburne affected *Oisin* is a way of arriving at the aesthetic theme in *Oisin* and understanding how it draws together the motifs that had occupied romantic poets for longer than the previous half century. Book 1 treats of escape and evokes memories of early nineteenth-century writers uneasily contemplating their retreat from social concerns. Book 3 tells of Oisin's return to the world;[2] in Yeats's depiction of the conflict between pagan and Christian can be found clear echoes of the mid– and late–century dichotomy between Hebraism and Hellenism (in its Celtic variation). The relation of Yeats to his predecessors is, however, reciprocal. They influenced him, but he in turn gave new vitality to their themes by demonstrating in *Oisin* the manner in which the dilemmas of Keats and Swinburne modified each other.

In an early letter on *The Wanderings of Oisin* Yeats conveys his uneasiness about the escapism of his early poems:

> I have noticed some things about my poetry I did not know before . . . for instance, that it is almost all a flight into fairyland from the real world, and a summons to that flight. The Chorus to the "Stolen Child" sums it up—that it is not the poetry of insight and knowledge, but of longing and complaint—the cry of the heart against necessity. I hope some day to alter that and write poetry of insight and knowledge.[3]

Yeats's implicit pledge to write someday a more mature poetry is reminiscent of Keats's early promise in *Sleep and Poetry* to devote himself to the agony and strife of the human heart if he can first indulge himself in the realm of Flora and Pan. Like Keats, Yeats felt keenly the division between life and art, between the claims of the social and political, on one side, and the seductive lure of the imagination, on the other.[4] These contrasts formed the conflict that pursued him to the end of his life, and they were there from the beginning, even in the poems about fairyland.

The Stolen Child is not just a summons to the otherworld. In the last stanza the fairies themselves cast a longing glance back at the homeliness and warmth of the human world left behind by the child who follows them. That they require this human presence in their realm betrays its inadequacy. This point about the fairies' longing, while not a critical commonplace, has been made before and, indeed, provides a useful consideration for all stories involving the union between mortals and supernatural creatures.[5] Beyond that point, however, is another that should qualify the insight that both mortals and immortals yearn for a completion that would result only from union. Humans are unique in that they feel the conflict between the two realms, each representing seemingly irreconcilable elements in their own being. The fairies, apparently, are not torn in this fashion and are more likely to be rejected by the human realm than to return to their own under an impetus like that which eventually draws the Tannhäusers and Oisins back to where they belong.

Precisely this absence of conflict makes fairyland very attractive for Yeats, since that realm is free of the contraries that plague humans:

> It is one of the greatest troubles of life that we cannot have any unmixed emotions. There is always something in our enemy that we like, and something in our sweetheart that we dislike. It is this entanglement of moods which makes us old, and puckers our brows and deepens the furrows about our eyes. If we could love and hate with as good heart as the faeries do, we might grow to be long-lived like them . . . for they have known untrammelled hate and unmixed love, and have never wearied themselves with "yes" and "no," or entangled their feet with the sorry net of "maybe" and "perhaps." [6]

But this longing for unity itself makes up only one side of a contrary impulse in Yeats. On the other is his attraction to theories and systems of thought that emphasize dichotomy. Perhaps he is making virtue of necessity, for in a world of contraries, a philosophy based on dialectical opposition is decidedly pragmatic. Yeats's very poetic theory reveals a happy contradiction: "We make out of the quarrel with others, rhetoric, but of the quarrel with ourselves, poetry." [7] He believes that the "desire that is satisfied is not a great desire," [8] and that the artist's creativity is born of the perpetual confrontation between his transcendent yearnings and his earthly limitations. The wholeness that is art is woven from fragments the poet finds within and without, and Crazy Jane's assertion to the Bishop that "nothing can be sole or whole / That has not been rent" (YCP 255) corresponds to Yeats's aesthetics. It is because nothing has been rent for his fairies that they can never be artists.

Yeats's quarrel with society concerns the artist's familiar loathing of Philistine values:

> The Arts have failed; fewer people are interested in them every generation. The mere business of living, of making money, of amusing oneself, occupies people more and more, and makes them less and less capable of the difficult art of appreciation.[9]

His early interest in Irish peasantry and Celtic folklore was based on his belief that those not part of the middle class lived in a less "shrunken world" and "knew of no less ample circumstances than did Homer himself." [10] He would later come to think that it was the Irish aristocracy rather than the peasants who guarded and preserved the Celtic heroic tradition, but the enemy remained the middle-class Philistine.

Heine's comparable tendency to romanticize the folk because they possessed more imagination reveals how such primitive beliefs are particularly satisfactory for the artist torn between reality and the yearning for a transcendent ideal. Folk tales are compounded of both a belief in the unseen world of supernatural beings and an acceptance of the material world, since such beings inhabit or invade in one way or another the world of men. The modern age, by rejecting the supernatural, has confined the scope of the imagination to stark realism. The reaction to this is often a more extreme otherworldliness, which is usually expressed in the lyric mode, and the "lyrical temper," as Yeats explains, "is always athirst for an emotion, a beauty which cannot be found in its perfection upon earth, or only for a moment." [11] But the lyric, unlike the folk temper, usually conveys the poet's alienation, and Yeats distrusted this feature of romanticism, maintaining that people who cut themselves off from "heavy mortal hopes that toil and pass" will only "learn to chaunt a tongue men do not know" (YCP 31).

Thus, despite his revulsion from Philistinism and his frequent desire to retreat from the world into a fairyland symbolic of the imagination, Yeats's understanding that "meditations upon unknown thought / Make human intercourse grow less and less" (YCP 226) leads to a reaction against solipsistic romantic longing. This was true, he writes, even during his youth, when he was steeped in the romantic tradition.

> I read nothing but romantic literature; hated that dry eighteenth-century rhetoric; but they had one quality I admired and admire: they were not separated, individual men; they spoke or tried to speak out of a people to a people; behind them stretched the generations. I knew, though but now and then as young men know things, that I must turn from that modern literature Jonathan Swift compared to the web a spider draws out of its bowels; I hated and still hate with an ever growing hatred the literature of the point of view. I wanted, if my ignorance permitted, to get back to Homer, to those that fed at his table.[12]

The substance of this passage is comparable to that in the letter concerning *Oisin*, in which he said he must turn from poetry that was a call to fairyland and write literature of insight and knowledge. In both pieces of writing a strong social impulse makes itself felt. The heroic age of Homer reflects the communal ties that contrast with romantic isolation.

The conflict in Yeats between his anti-Philistinism and his anti-aestheticism can be traced in the two strains in the nineteenth-century tradition he inherited. Like Keats, he understood the penalties of escapism; like Swinburne, he recognized the threat to the artist of a utilitarian culture. It is in this double dilemma that Oisin is caught.

In *Oisin*, book 1, can be found echoes of Keats's *La Belle Dame sans Merci*. In both, the hero accompanies a fairy on horseback to her land; and in both, songs from the otherworld leave him oblivious to all but her enchantment:

> I set her on my pacing steed,
> And nothing else saw all day long,

For sidelong would she bend, and sing
A faery's song.

She found me roots of relish sweet,
And honey wild, and manna dew,
And sure in language strange she said—
"I love thee true."
[KP 442]

Oisin. We galloped over the glossy sea:
I know not if days passed or hours,
For [Niamh] sang continually
Danaan songs, and their dewy showers
Of pensive laughter, unhuman sound,
Lulled weariness, and softly round
My human sorrows her white arms wound.
[YP 11][13]

The unhuman sound of the Danaan songs parallels the obscure language in which Keats's fairy expresses her love.

While the seduction of Oisin recalls *La Belle Dame sans Merci*, his later resistance to the fairy can be compared with *Lamia*. In both *Oisin* and *Lamia* the hero's awakening consciousness of reality after a period of bliss evokes a pitiful response from his fairy mistress. When confronted with what she knows is an impossibility, marriage as a way of reconciling pleasure and reality, Lamia

Trembled; she nothing said, but, pale and meek,
Arose and knelt before him, wept a rain
Of sorrows at his words; at last with pain
Beseeching him, the while his hand she wrung,
To change his purpose.
[KP 2:65–69]

Oisin's adventures in book 2 also seem like a reaction against too much inactivity in fairyland, and Niamh is as fearful as Lamia that she will lose her lover:

Thereon young [Niamh] softly came
And caught my hands, but spake no word
Save only many times my name,
In murmurs, like a frighted bird.
[YP 22]

But the heroes are obdurate in their response to the fairies' pleas:

[Lycius] thereat was stung,
Perverse, with stronger fancy to reclaim
Her wild and timid nature to his aim.
[KP 2:69–71]

And Oisin is determined to battle monsters despite Niamh's entreaty, which "moved not, / Nor shook his firm and spacious soul one jot" (YP 31).

Such harshness on the part of Lycius and Oisin grows out of the poets' understanding that fairyland, however beautiful, symbolizes an impulse contrary to their ambitions to do the world some good. Although Keats and Yeats both felt that their early art was self-indulgent and wished to write poetry of knowledge and sympathy for the human plight, they differed in their attitudes toward the fairies. Keats thought of them as ambiguous creatures, demonic in that they retarded the poet's development toward a mature art, while Yeats has Niamh seemingly untainted by evil, demonic only in the eyes of a hostile world—he originally entitled his poem "Oisin, and How a Demon Trapped Him." [14] The title failed to do justice to his complex theme.

The poignant sorrow that hovers about Niamh suggests the plight of Undine, whose wooing of a mortal lover betrays the insufficiency of her own immortal existence. Yeats may have known the German novella, which had numerous English translations; in any event, its Celtic analogues provided him with the basic conception that lies behind *Undine*: the soul can only be formed in this world. Fairyland, while offering bliss, denies salvation:

Sometimes a new-wed bride or a new-born baby goes with [the fairies] into their mountains; the door swings to behind, and the new-born or new-wed moves henceforth in the bloodless land of Faery; happy enough, but doomed to melt out at the last judgment like bright vapour, for the soul cannot live without sorrow.[15]

A parallel can be drawn between the theology behind this folklore and the poet's quest for artistic integrity, which comes only from uniting the world of action (and, hence, suffering) with the realm of art. In *Oisin*, the parallel leads to an understanding of the relation Yeats establishes between sorrow and creativity.

That Oisin was a poet as well as a warrior Yeats carefully emphasized when he revised the poem after its first publication in 1889. Originally, Niamh explained her attraction to Oisin in rather vague terms: "I ne'er loved any till song brought me / To peak and pine o'er Oisin's fame." Such songs seem to be about Oisin, not by him. In revision, Niamh's attraction has a more concrete basis; she has come to fetch him because

> Of battles broken by his hands,
> Of stories builded by his word.
> [YP 8]

In fairyland, however, the warrior is inactive; and, more important, the poet is silenced; for just as the soul cannot live without sorrow, so the artist is unable to create in the earthly paradise. When Oisin sings for the fairies at their request, they destroy his harp.

> But when I sang of human joy
> A sorrow wrapped each merry face,
> And, Patrick! by your beard, they wept,
> Until one came, a tearful boy;
> "A sadder creature never stept
> "Than this strange human bard," he cried;
> And caught the silver harp away,
> And, weeping over the white strings, hurled
> It down in a leaf-hid, hollow place
> That kept dim waters from the sky;

And each one said with a long, long sigh,
"O saddest harp in all the world,
"Sleep there till the moon and the stars die!"
[YP 16]

No explanation is given for their paradoxical reaction to Oisin's song of human joy. But it is not difficult to construct the reason from Yeats's dialectical process of thought and his semi-whimsical musings in *The Celtic Twilight* that fairies, unlike humans, are never wearied out by contrary emotions. There is a vast difference between the fairies' song and songs that tell of human joy; for in the mutable world, joy is inextricably bound to its opposite emotion. The fairies cannot tolerate sorrow.

Here again Yeats may have learned from Keats. In the *Ode on Melancholy* the human condition is depicted in such a way that "in the very temple of Delight / Veil'd Melancholy has her sovran shrine" (KP 275), a conception that has two striking parallels in Yeats's verse:

What can they know of love that do not know
She builds her nest upon a narrow ledge
Above a windy precipice?
[YCP 436]

But Love has pitched his mansion in
The place of excrement.
[YCP 255][16]

For both poets delight and sorrow are bound together and fulfillment comes only when they are accepted together.

Yeats exposes the sterility of fairyland, that realm of pleasure unmixed with sorrow, although on the surface, the immortals seem fortunate to have been spared the source of human despair, mutability:

And here there is nor Change nor Death,
But only kind and merry breath,
For joy is God and God is joy.
                                    [YP 18]

Angus's song, however, also reveals the limitations of the land over
which he rules. For joy, which is a creative force in the universe, is
elsewhere in his song associated with change; and he boasts that there
is no change in his world:

And if joy were not on earth,
There were an end of change and birth,
And earth and heaven and hell would die,
And in some gloomy barrow lie
Folded like a frozen fly;
Then mock at Death and Time with glances
And wavering arms and wandering dances.
                                    [YP 17][17]

Angus's lyric is a confusing one, but its meaning seems linked to an
important theme in Yeats's poetry. Change in *Oisin* has been related
to both death and birth. If death is absent in fairyland, implicitly then
so is birth. In Yeats's source for the poem children are born to Oisin
and Niamh. No mention of such fruitfulness is to be met with in his
own poem.

Yeats frequently deals with the relation of art to a world of
process. In *Sailing to Byzantium* the whole cycle of what is "begotten,
born, and dies" is condensed into the double entendre of "dying
generations." In contrast is the work of art, the "artifice of eternity,"
which defies change (YCP 191). That such artifice may, paradoxically,
owe its very existence to mutability is an idea conveyed in *Meditations in Time of Civil War*, when the poet writes that

if no change appears
No moon; only an aching heart
Conceives a changeless work of art.
                                    [YCP 200]

233

"Conceives" like "generation" provides a key word, because it expresses the processes of life absent from the static fairy realm. Human sorrow, which finds its source in mutability and leads to an aching heart, is the ultimate source of Oisin's poetic power. The destruction of his harp by the fairies symbolizes the impossibility of art in that otherworld poets frequently and mistakenly long for.

By asserting a positive connection between mutability and earthly sorrow on the one hand, and the timeless realm of art on the other, Yeats's poetics go beyond Keats, who usually forces a choice between the deceitful elf of the imagination or a world in which is found

> The weariness, the fever and the fret
> . . . where men sit and hear each other groan;
> Where palsy shakes a few, sad, last gray hairs,
> Where youth grows pale, and spectre-thin, and dies.
> [KP 258]

Keats's lines may have an echo in book 1 of *Oisin*, in the fairies' picture of the human world:

> An old man stirs the fire to a blaze,
> In the house of a child, of a friend, of a brother;
> He has over-lingered his welcome; the days
> Grown desolate, whisper and sigh to each other;
> He hears the storm in the chimney above,
> And bends to the fire and shakes with the cold,
> While his heart still dreams of battle and love,
> And the cry of the hounds on the hills of old.
> [YP 23]

Keats's old men shaken with palsy resemble Yeats's shaken with cold, and those in the ode who sit and listen to each other groan have a counterpart in Yeats's image of days which have grown desolate and "whisper and sigh to each other." But Yeats has added to his picture of reality what Keats omitted—the blazing fire, the child, the friend and brother, as well as the memories which sustain the aged man. This was his technique in *The Stolen Child*, when in the last stanza he depicted a world which, though more "full of weeping" than the mortal child can understand, also contains lowing "calves on the warm hillside," and a "kettle on the hob" (YCP 19). These, as well as sorrow, the child leaves behind. As Yeats knew from Blake's *Marriage of Heaven and Hell*, "Eternity is in love with the productions of time." [18] In both *Oisin* and *The Stolen Child* paradoxically it is the fairies who long for contact with humans and sing of the hearth away from which they seek to lure mortals yearning for a beauty that will not die.

Yeats provides, then, at least the theoretical solution to the poet's dilemma, to his inability to reconcile the miseries of life with the beauty of art. Nevertheless, what Keats had failed to achieve theoretically, he achieved poetically. Yeats frequently compares the concreteness of Keats's poetic imagery with the abstract qualities of Swinburne's verse. In short, although Keats's view of reality may frequently have been as desolate as the town depicted on the Grecian urn, and his poems often a flight to fairyland (equally forlorn), his verse remains, nonetheless, earthbound. Swinburne, in contrast, writes poems whose abstract music sunders sound from a rhythm that would imply "a living body, a breast to rise and fall, or limbs that dance," poems that never suggest "a voice shaken with joy or sorrow." [19]

The most explicit comparison between Keats and Swinburne is made when Yeats writes to his father that "I think Keats perhaps greater than Shelley and beyond words greater than Swinburne because he makes pictures one cannot forget and sees them as full of rhythm as a Chinese painting. Swinburne's poetry, all but some early poems, is as abstract as a cubist picture." [20] At one time Yeats had responded to Swinburne's music, but he writes Lady Gregory from the British Museum, where he had been re-reading Swinburne, "I suppose that one tires of all abundant things." [21] How ironic it is then that book 3 of *Oisin* seems to be modeled on the *Hymn to Proserpine* (in which, moreover, Swinburne indicates that man is bored by sensuous pleasure alone) and that Yeats's hero turns away from the fairy world for the same reason that Yeats criticizes the poet he imitates: both Oisin and Yeats are weary of too much indulgence in pure sense.

In book 3, Niamh and Oisin travel to the Isle of Forgetfulness, where the inhabitants sleep because they are weary of pleasure:

And my gaze was thronged with the sleepers—no,
    neither in house of a cann
In a realm where the handsome are many, or in glamours
    by demons flung,
Are faces alive with such beauty made known to the
    soft eye of man,
Yet weary with passions that faded when the seven-fold
    seas were young.

                     [YP 45–46]

Swinburne's pagan is equally wearied by faded passions: "I am sick of singing; the bays burn deep and chafe. I am fain / To rest a little from praise and grievous pleasure and pain" (SP 1:200). Because Oisin does achieve this respite in the Isle of Forgetfulness, he succumbs to its spell:

Wrapt in the wave of the music, with weariness more
    than of earth,
The moil of my centuries filled me; and gone like
    a sea-covered stone
Were the memories of the whole of my sorrow and the
    memories of the whole of my mirth,
And a softness came from the starlight and filled
    me full to the bone.

                     [YP 47]

The isle functions like the realm of Proserpine, that land for which Swinburne's pagan can only long.

    The reader is also wrapped in a wave of music—in both the *Hymn* and *Oisin*. The poems are written in anapestic hexameters, a meter in which the counterpoint of energy and languor—so much a part of their themes—is suggested by the swift moving anapests that are held back by a long line which would produce weariness if not for a pronounced caesura. The anapest, in its slow but forward thrust, creates a hypnotic inertia, intensified by the marked use of alliteration. Lines such as Yeats's "Wrapt in the wave of the music, with weariness more than of earth," and "softness came from the starlight

236

and filled me full to the bone" are somewhat reminiscent of Swinburne's self-parody in *Nephelidia*. In *Oisin* Yeats is guilty—perhaps consciously so—of that for which he later censures Swinburne: an abstract use of melody that obscures or excludes concrete, earthly images—in short, of the blurring of sense by sound.[22]

But if a trancelike effect is produced by the verse form, the reader is experiencing the effect of the isle on Oisin. When Yeats's hero finally tires of the Isle of Forgetfulness and is aroused by his horse to memories of earth, they are appropriately described in concrete, visual images. Oisin remembers

That the spear-shaft is made out of ashwood, the
     shield out of ozier and hide;
How the hammers spring on the anvil, on the spearhead's
     burning spot;
How the slow, blue-eyed oxen of Finn low sadly at
     evening tide.

[YP 48–49]

It is not merely that Oisin is reminded of his duties to the Fenian warriors, but that he has become aware of the substantial quality of what he left behind when he sojourned to fairyland. Niamh attaches to his return to the world, presumably for a short visit, the condition that if any part of his body should touch ground, he can never again return to her. Through the poem's mythology, the common expression "down to earth" is given metaphorical treatment.

There is, beyond the theme of ennui and similarity in verse form, still another, perhaps even more important, analogy between the *Hymn to Proserpine* and *The Wanderings of Oisin*. The main subject of Swinburne's poem is the deposition of the old gods. His pagan speaker knows that all things pass, and in his knowledge lies his triumph over the disastrous change: "Though these that were Gods are dead, and thou being dead art a God, / Though before thee the throned Cytherean be fallen, and hidden her head, / Yet thy kingdom shall pass, Galilean, thy dead shall go down to thee dead" (SP 1:204). Similarly, when Oisin returns to earth after three hundred years in the otherworld, he is told by an old man that his Fenian companions are

237

dead and that the old order no longer exists. And he, too, realizes that all things sooner or later pass.

And the dreams of the islands were gone, and I knew
how men sorrow and pass,
And their hounds, and their steeds, and their loves,
and their eyes that glimmer like silk.

And wrapping my face in my hair, I murmured, "In old
age they ceased";
And my tears were larger than berries, and I murmured,
"Where white clouds lie spread
On Crevroe or broad Knockfefin, with many of old they
feast
On the floors of the gods." He cried, "No, the gods
a long time are dead."
[YP 57–58]

The gods are dead: this is the sorrowful cry of both the *Hymn to Proserpine* and book 3 of *Oisin*. In *Oisin* what had been up to now merely a structural device, the dialogue between Oisin and St. Patrick, has moved to the center of the work. St. Patrick is no longer merely the audience to whom Oisin relates his experiences in the otherworld, but the exponent of the new order. The poem, as a result, takes on the outlines of the Tannhäuser legend. Oisin is comparable to Tannhäuser not only because he has dwelt with a supernatural woman but also because he is forced to view his experience from the alien perspective of Christianity. There now exists a direct conflict of attitudes. For the hero, Niamh is the beautiful, sad mistress he loved and lost when he returned to earth; for St. Patrick, the warrior has "known three centuries . . . / Of dalliance with a demon thing" (YP 5).

In this analogy between *Oisin* and *Tannhäuser*, Yeats can also be compared to Heine.[23] He depicts in an essay on the Rhymers' Club the dialectical interaction between aestheticism and Philistinism when he speaks of

the reaction from the super-refinement of much recent life and poetry. The cultivated man has begun a somewhat hectic search for the common pleasures of common men and for the rough accidents of life. The typical young poet of our day is an aesthete with a surfeit, searching sadly for his lost Philistinism, his heart full of an unsatisfied hunger for the commonplace. He is an Alastor tired of his woods and longing for beer and skittles.[24]

To substitute Tannhäuser for Alastor and the Venusberg for woods is to find Heine's hero, who tells Venus

> O Venus, mistress fond and fair,
> Of your wine so sweet in flavour,
> Of your kisses warm, my soul is sick—
> Some sourness I would savour.[25]

But once confronted with the Pope, Heine's Tannhäuser needs to defend the life of the senses, and finds his passion for the goddess renewed. Similarly, although Oisin had longed to return to the world, he there finds himself unable to cope with the new order of things. Thus,

> lonely and longing for [Niamh], I shivered and
>   turned me about,
> The heart in me longing to leap like a grasshopper
>   into her heart;
> I turned and rode to the westward, and followed the
>   sea's old shout
> Till I saw where Maive lies sleeping till starlight
>   and midnight part.
>   [YP 58]

The aesthete who rediscovers his Philistinism is also likely to find himself once more defensively asserting the value of a less ordinary existence.

Heine's Heinrich Kitzler burned his treatise on Christianity when the beauty of the dead pagan gods awakened sorrow over their demise. *Tannhäuser* dramatized his predicament. Similarly, *The*

Wanderings of Oisin reveals how a hostile world can force one to positions preferably abandoned. Philistinism helped create the aesthete, although Yeats, in his dialectical reaction against aestheticism, can speak of the search for a lost Philistinism. *The Wanderings of Oisin* is in effect a summary of the nineteenth century and the paradoxical position in which the poet found himself. The romantic artist would freely give up a life of pure, asocial beauty to serve the world; but his misgivings about the nature of reality are confirmed when he confronts the society that—failing to appreciate his service to beauty—forces him to choose between art and life.

Early in the nineteenth century, Heine had described such a world when he wrote that although Fouqué's Undine was beautiful, the age demanded living beings and not nixies in love with noble knights. A century later, Philistinism was still further entrenched, not unexpectedly, and an increasingly mechanized world had less and less use for creatures of the imagination. In Jean Giraudoux's play *Intermezzo*, a town haunted by a ghost is inhabited by citizens anxious to exorcise its influence. The ghost has chosen a likely object for its attentions, a young teacher more concerned to train the imaginations of her students than their intellects. The inspector who heads the committee to expel spirits from the community warns that this kind of education aims at "nothing less than freeing these young minds from the net of truth that our wonderful nineteenth century spread over our country" (JG 116; 1:268). He has the self-appointed task to destroy the supernatural wherever it is to be found; the hint in the play that among his victims are the mermaids was developed by Maurice Valency when he adapted the play. Valency in his version had the inspector investigate a report that water nymphs were seen in the neighborhood. "After three weeks of fact-finding, he decided to pave over the brook where they lived. The army engineers did the job. Nobody's seen any water nymphs since." [26]

The sea fairies have their own way of retaliating against an age that has no use for them. Eliot's Prufrock hears the mermaids singing to each other, but thinks that they will not sing to him. Is there any worse commentary on modern man—that he no longer requires protection against the sirens?

Despite Heine's warnings about Undine and the valid observations upon which such warnings were founded, the water sprite has survived. But today she is probably known best as Ondine, the creation of Jean Giraudoux who, understanding well that his time was hostile to mermaids, wrote his play to show how the fairies are persecuted.

While Giraudoux was a student of German literature at the Sorbonne,[27] he had composed an essay on Fouqué's novella which was essentially a negative critique, attacking Fouqué for the lack of coherence and unity in his work, and expressing little of the appreciation that must have made Undine a living force over the years, until Giraudoux finally made her the heroine of his own drama. Ironically enough, Giraudoux betrays in his essay a literal-minded attitude characteristic of those in his plays who seek to destroy the spontaneous and imaginative where they are to be found and to substitute the mundane and ordinary. He complains that Fouqué's mermaid is too much like any troublesome, spoiled German adolescent and behaves not at all like a water nymph, adding, apparently without a shred of anything but seriousness, that this may be explained by her having left the water when she was so young. Here is Giraudoux examining a nineteenth-century fairy tale with the eye of a twentieth-century environmentalist. But then, how does one portray a mermaid? At the opening of the French play we are told that Ondine washes her linen on top of the rocks and says her prayers under water. Later, married to Hans (an easier name than Huldbrand) and living at court, she lacks any ladylike accomplishments, and all her husband can boast of besides her beauty is that she swims well! It is almost as if Giraudoux's earlier literalness had totally reversed itself. Having at one time viewed Fouqué's heroine too seriously, he can now, for all the beauty and tenderness in his play, hardly take her seriously at all. While it is true that she acts as the vantage point from which one can criticize the world she comes to dwell in, Ondine is less important in the play as an emanation of another world more beautiful than the real one than she is as an annoyance to those whose ordinary lives she disrupts.

The last part of Giraudoux's three-act play is given over largely to Ondine's trial by a circuit court of Imperial and Episcopal Judges empowered to decide on supernatural cases. Having left her husband to return to the sea, she has been caught by fishermen and will be tried and condemned to death for being a mermaid. The secondary charge, that she has been unfaithful to her husband, is dismissed when her love for him becomes so obvious that she must be deemed innocent. Thus her execution will be for one thing only, that she is a supernatural being whose presence cannot be tolerated in the world.

What is it that Ondine seeks in this world that has no room for her, that condemns her to death for her very nature? Fouqué, adapting the themes he found in Paracelsus and *Mélusine*, based his story on the mermaid's quest for a soul. Her marriage to a mortal is the means to her salvation. True, this motive tends to confuse the novella, as Giraudoux also recognized in his analysis of Fouqué, because there is no reason for Undine to have failed in her quest. Despite this failure, however, her motivation remains clear. But when Hans Christian Andersen wrote *The Little Mermaid* and retained the motif of the soul-quest, he added an aesthetic dimension to the ethical one: the mermaid falls in love with the beautiful statue of a young man that she tends in her undersea garden. Although Andersen explains why she loses her mortal Prince—since she surrendered her voice to obtain human legs and hence cannot communicate her love—he has obscured her reasons for coming to earth by doubling the motivation. Does she seek man for love or for salvation? Giraudoux, in contrast to both Fouqué and Andersen, drops from his story the quest for a soul. His Ondine marries for love alone, attracted like the Little Mermaid to the beauty of mortal man.

What emerges from this brief survey of the mermaid's progress through literature is a development that can perhaps be best recognized by diagraming it:

Fouqué: Undine's quest for a soul (single, unambiguous motive)
Andersen: the mermaid's quest for a soul and attraction to the world
of men (double, ambiguous motive)
Giraudoux: Ondine's attraction to the world of men (single, unambiguous motive)

Giraudoux's structure, although it provides the story with unity and singularity of purpose, paradoxically both simplifies the tale and raises the most perplexing question of all. If Ondine does not wed Hans in order to gain a soul and is attracted only by his human qualities, why then did she come to earth in the first place? If she is not seeking the redemption of her nature in the mortal realm, is she succeeding there only in annihilating it?

To ask these questions we may seem to be guilty of the same error Giraudoux has been charged with in his analysis of Fouqué: asking logical questions about a fantasy whose significance transcends the literal level of the story. But the query can be justified, for it is explicitly or implicitly raised by Giraudoux in other plays. In *Amphitryon 38*, for example, the matter is central to the theme, for there is a correlation between Alkmena's attachment to her mortal husband and Jupiter's desire for her. Whatever has first attracted the god to earthly mistresses is intensified in this one woman who more than any of the others (Leda, Europa, etc.) is herself earthbound. Alkmena's self-description is crucial:

> Of all the people I know, I'm the least disposed to quarrel with my destiny. I gladly accept all the ups and downs of human life, from birth to death, I even accept family meals. My senses are moderate and well-controlled. I'm sure I'm the only woman alive who sees fruits and spiders in their true proportions, and tastes her pleasures for what they are. It's the same with my intelligence, too. It seems to lack that element of sport or delusion which only needs a little wine, or love, or fine scenery, to kindle a desire for eternity. [JG 38; 1:129]

This unromantic acceptance of human life, including its most prosaic aspects, lends to Alkmena's character an ethical dimension of purely human qualities that the gods lack and that Jupiter finds himself drawn to. His motives therefore are comparable to those that bring mermaids to earth in quest of souls. The otherworld is amoral and only on earth is the vital moral element to be found. This theme in *Ondine* is given a bitter, satiric twist: in the ethical realm there also exists human perfidy. Ondine tells how her relatives in the sea

> knew it at once—the moment they saw him. There'd never been any question of unfaithfulness up to then, never till Hans arrived. And then they saw this beautiful man on horseback, with loyalty in his face and truth in his mouth, and suddenly the word "deceive" went humming through the waves. [JG 235; 2:250]

Giraudoux's view of the mortal world to which the mermaid commits herself is as cynical as Heine's analysis of the critical reception of Fouqué's *Undine*. And in its cynicism, Giraudoux's view is particularly modern.

Despite the distinction between the ethical realm of *Amphytrion 38* and the unethical world of *Ondine*, a real correspondence exists between Alkmena and Ondine, between the mortal interested only in her own world and the immortal who wants to dwell in that world. When Ondine leaves her husband for her final return to the sea, she promises that she will continue habits under the water that she had learned on earth: "So you see, there'll always be one little bourgeoise among all those crazy ondines" (JG 271; 2:280). Both Alkmena and Ondine are bourgeoise, both lacking the romantic imagination. Jupiter only confirms Alkmena's view of herself when he says that "she isn't susceptible to brightness or appearances. She has no imagination, and possibly not much intelligence either" (JG 42; 1:132). Similarly, Ondine is charged by the King of the Ondines with never having "had much imagination" (JG 267; 2:277). And when she is accused in court of being demoniac, he protests,

> Demoniac! On the contrary, that ondine has disowned her race, disowned and betrayed them. If she had wanted, she could have kept all their power and knowledge; she could have worked what you call miracles twenty times a day, made her husband's horse grow a trunk, or his dogs grow wings. At a word from her, the Rhine and the very vault of heaven would have answered and brought forth wonders. But what did she do? She gave it all up in favour of twisted ankles, hay fever, and greasy cooking! [JG 258; 2:270]

By giving a peculiar twist to the story, Giraudoux has succeeded in reversing the usual significance of the mermaid motif. No longer does the sea maid represent a romantic ideal; instead, she stands for a firmly entrenched reality principle. Wagner, in his comments on Lohengrin (his own version of Jupiter or Ondine or any immortal seeking union with a mortal), recognized that man's very ability to conceive of such myths, to understand that gods could burn with desire for earthly beings, demonstrates the human's essential attachment to his own element. In Giraudoux's version of the mermaid's story, this truth is most forcefully revealed. Ondine's impulse toward the human world is the very same impulse that makes the world itself condemn her to death. Such an impulse represents the triumph of the reality principle and the death of imagination.

Giraudoux's Alkmena and Ondine are prelapsarian Eves, Eves who will never cause the fall, however, because in the words of Keats's rejection of the romantic, "they seek no wonder but the human face" (KP 513). In contrast, Isabel of *Intermezzo* yearns beyond her limited mortal existence and is thus the potential victim of supernatural forces that would spirit her away. She tells the ghost who loves her that "ever since I was a child I've dreamed of one great enterprise. It's the only thing that makes me worthy of your visit" (JG 122–23; 1:274). The superintendent who wants to marry her warns against this seductive force of the otherworld, which would take her "from the herd which takes pleasure in ties and dresses, bread and wine" (JG 137; 1:286). When, at the end of the play, she renounces the spiritual world and marries her human suitor, it is said of her that she is both lost and saved.

Giraudoux's ambiguity reflects the peculiar bind in which the modern age finds itself. Man's intelligence, yearning beyond its proper limits, is a speculative and imaginative intelligence; dull indeed are those whose reach never exceeds their grasp. And yet, both mentalities are in the end hostile to the imagination, to the world from which the undines come. The speculative mind, which began by lusting after the apple, ended by producing the scientific world inimical to immaterial beings. The non-speculative mind, the Philistine, just cannot be bothered with them. Why, asks Ondine's husband Hans, do the temptresses always make a mistake? Instead of picking out extraordinary men who have time for romance, they "have to pounce on a poor soldier called Antony, a poor knight called Hans, a wretched average man; and he's doomed from that moment on" (JG 269; 2:279).

But if Ondine's visit to earth suggests a profound attraction of the imagination to a reality principle—even if this attraction results in self-annihilation—a certain dialectic persists. Reality itself finds it difficult to negate the romantic. What of the average man that Hans speaks of? Where in the prosaic twentieth-century world is his romanticism to be found? Thomas Mann takes up this question in one of the most important literary works of the modern age, *The Magic Mountain*, in which coincidentally his hero, very much an average man, is also named Hans.[28]

12
RECAPITULATION
The Magic Mountain

Thomas Mann's *The Magic Mountain* tells of young Hans Castorp, who visits his cousin Joachim at the Berghof, a tuberculosis sanatorium, only to learn that he too is ill. Thus, an intended three-week visit stretches to seven years, when the outbreak of World War I returns the hero to the flatlands. While at the Berghof, Hans falls under the spell of the Russian Clavdia Chauchat, as well as under the joint though conflicting tutelage of the Italian humanist Settembrini and the Jesuit Naphta. The seven years mark the transformation of the slightly dull Philistine, Castorp, into a man increasingly drawn toward philosophical contemplation. He realizes that "man is the lord of counter-positions, they can be only through him, and thus he is more aristocratic than they" (MM 496; 3:685). Indeed, the dialectical forces through which Castorp steers his way, while they in turn become progressively more complex, are as important to the novel as he, because through them Mann has a chance to survey the romantic thought of the nineteenth century and evaluate its impact on Europe at the time of World War I.

Mann said he loved the nineteenth century. His essay on Wagner describes the unique quality of its greatness: "a turbid, suffering kind; disillusioned, yet bitterly, fanatically aware of truth; conscious too of the brief, incredulous bliss to be snatched from beauty as she flies—such greatness as this was the meaning and mark of the nineteenth century." [1] At the same time, Mann, like Heine, was repelled by the fatal seductiveness of the romantic, and *The Magic Mountain* reflects a struggle against spirit by enlightened reason. Reason, however, poses a threat to art, which Mann will not reject in the name of social progress.

In an interpretive essay written for his English-speaking

readers, Mann offers a perhaps too neat but still interesting identification of himself with Castorp. He tells how he visited his wife in a sanatorium, where she was recovering from a lung ailment. A physical examination revealed that Mann had a similar condition.

> If I had been Hans Castorp, the discovery might have changed the whole course of my life. The physician assured me that I should be acting wisely to remain there for six months and take the cure. If I had followed his advice, who knows, I might still be there! I wrote *The Magic Mountain* instead. In *it* I made use of the impressions gathered during my three weeks' stay. They were enough to convince me of the dangers of such a milieu for young people—and tuberculosis is a disease of the young. You will have got from my book an idea of the narrowness of this charmed circle of isolation and invalidism. It is a sort of substitute existence, and it can, in a relatively short time, wholly wean a young person from actual and active life. Everything there, including the conception of time, is thought of on a luxurious scale. The cure is always a matter of several months, often of several years. But after the first six months the young person has not a single idea left save flirtation and the thermometer under his tongue. After the second six months in many cases he has even lost the capacity for any other ideas. He will become completely incapable of life in the flatland. [MM 721]

The tradition behind this preoccupation with sickness, the German romantic belief that disease is a distinguishing mark of genius, is described by Hermann J. Weigand in his early but still valuable study of the novel.[2] Mann ironically pushes the tradition still farther, because it is part of his book's theme that a marked symptom of spiritual disease *is* the belief that illness enhances the human spirit. *The Magic Mountain* literally works out Goethe's famous distinction between classicism and health on the one hand, and romanticism and disease on the other, when Mann transforms the otherworld of romantic fairy tales into a sanatorium. Symbolically, tuberculosis *is* romanticism, a disease from which to some degree all suffer. Dr. Krokowski, the psychiatrist at the Berghof, claims that he had never "come across a perfectly healthy human being" (MM 16; 3:29–30).

This German romantic tradition prevents the reader from accepting at face value Mann's explanation of how he came to write *The Magic Mountain*. Personal experience doubtlessly merged with his literary heritage; but his contention that he found it preferable to write about the magic mountain than to succumb to its allure is of more general interest. It sustains the assertion made throughout this book that the literature which takes the otherworld for its setting is often about escape and not itself escapist. It is possible to claim, furthermore, that such literature has itself had a hand in the way Mann interpreted his personal experiences. It would be surprising if he did not see a connection between Tieck's Christian, whose life in the mountains makes him unfit for life in the plains, and tubercular patients who feel no desire to return to the flatland. Perhaps he saw the patients as he did because he knew stories like Tieck's. The very title of Mann's novel may owe something to that passage in Eichendorff's *The Marble Statue* where Fortunato cautions Florio about "the marvelous minstrel who by his notes lures youth into a magic mountain, out of which no one has ever come back." It is true that in the Tannhäuser stories the knight does emerge from the Venusberg; but it is equally true that he cannot find a place in the world and so returns. Similarly, in *The Magic Mountain* patients who leave the Berghof almost invariably come back.

It could well be said that Mann's version of the Tannhäuser legend is *The Magic Mountain*. Critics have not failed to note the connection, but they evidence a tacit or explicit reluctance to make too much of the point.[3] Still, to overlook or de-emphasize the fairy-tale tradition behind *The Magic Mountain* is to miss much in the work. For it is after the reader has become acquainted with Tieck's Christian, Fouqué's Huldbrand, and Eichendorff's Florio that he more fully appreciates what Mann has done in his novel. This is not to say that the Belle Dame sans Merci theme entirely dominates the book so much as to claim that almost all of the motifs in Mann's novel can be found in earlier stories concerning the fairy. Perhaps it would be more accurate to say that virtually all of the thematic patterns that emerge from nineteenth-century stories of La Belle Dame sans Merci find a place in Mann's brilliant depiction of romanticism.

Hans Castorp is first met on a train carrying him to the Berghof and the visit with his cousin Joachim. Separated from the duties and cares of his world, he is in that precarious situation that can make a "vagabond of the pedant and Philistine" (MM 4; *3:12*). But this is hardly Tieck's Christian overcome with romantic *Sehnsucht* and fleeing the narrow confines of home. Unlike Tieck's hero, who abandons his father's house for the mysterious mountains, Castorp is sent *by* his family to the Berghof, not only to visit a relative (the destination of his voyage hence involves him *in* the family circle) but also to recover the strength he lost pursuing engineering studies. He is comfortable in his Philistinism and has no thoughts of staying away for more than the planned three weeks.

Yet Castorp is not totally lacking in those qualities of the romantic hero whose obverse he initially appears to be. For while he considers work the most estimable attribute of life and is committed to duty, he regrets, for example, that his labors stand in the way of his "unclouded enjoyment of his Maria Mancini" (MM 34; *3:53*). Maria, the first love of Louis XIV, whose marriage to her was blocked because he as monarch could not indulge his personal preferences, supplies an appropriate contrast to Hans Castorp's sense of obligation. From her name also reverberates the illicit intrigues and sexual licentiousness for which the exterior refinement and propriety at Versailles were only masks. And, finally, Maria Mancini once again evokes the traditional and symbolic contrast between Germany and Italy. But, in the end, her name signifies only Castorp's favorite cigar, as Mann effectively undercuts the romantic tendencies his hero evidences early in the novel.

Where Castorp's latent romanticism leads him to glorify death, however, the matter is treated without a trace of bathos:

> Reduced to order and put into words, [his thoughts] would have been something like the following. In one aspect death was a holy, a pensive, a spiritual state, possessed of a certain mournful beauty. In another it was quite different. It was precisely the opposite, it was very physical, it was material, it could not possibly be called either holy, or pensive, or beautiful—not even mournful. [MM 27; *3:43*]

Castorp's fascination with death would ordinarily be balanced by his skeptical reason, but at the Berghof his childhood morbidity has emerged unchecked. It is not merely that he confronts death there; indeed, death is so handled at the sanatorium that the patients are protected from conscious awareness. No, it is that the air at the mountain retreat, as the doctor who examines him claims, is good for the disease. That is, implicitly, it both cures it and feeds it, or, theoretically, feeds it to cure it, bringing to the surface what previously remained merely latent. At the Berghof, Castorp's incipient romanticism has a chance to flourish, but that a cure will result is doubtful. Meanwhile, the mystification with which he surrounds death is itself a symptom of his illness.

It can now be seen that whereas in the nineteenth-century fairy tale the romantic hero reaches the otherworld and casts a longing eye back at his lost Philistinism, Hans Castorp is a Philistine who arrives at the otherworld and accidentally becomes a romantic hero. The Berghof as "otherworld" of the novel can perhaps best be appreciated in the context of Hoffmann and Tieck. The role of the sanatorium as both realistic health resort and Venusberg is analogous to the double function of Hoffmann's mines at Falun, which were both the source of Elis's earthly sustenance and a trap for his highly introverted nature. Just as Elis descended into the mines to earn enough money to support Ulla, but found that his encounter with the Queen of the Mines rendered him unfit for ordinary life, so does Hans Castorp hope to acquire enough strength at the Berghof to undertake his job as engineer, only to discover that instead he has lost interest in the life below. In Tieck's *Runenberg*, the antithesis between the mountains and the flatlands had pointed to the difference between the classical and romantic modes of existence. The confusion of Tieck's Christian concerning his dreamworld, which he conceives of as "real," and the natural world, which he considered merely illusory, seems echoed in Castorp's feeling that "when, from the point of view of 'those up here,' he considered life as lived down in the flat-land, it seemed somehow queer and unnatural" (MM 148; 3:208).

Outside of these specific comparisons, there are general similarities between the Berghof and the otherworld. At the sanatorium disease leads to an emphasis on the physical side of life. Mann stresses in his explanation of the novel that only the taking of temperatures and flirtation occupy the inhabitants of the place. The patients frenetically pursue one another, while the married couple whose room adjoins Castorp's never seem to cease their lovemaking, much to his discomfort. In addition, the psychiatrist Krokowski delivers to the patients lectures on the connection between disease and love, suggesting that tuberculosis itself might be the surfacing of repressed desire. Finally, the sumptuous meals that are served at the establishment are not only reminiscent of the fabulous repasts in fairyland but, again, intensify the Berghof's sensuous aura.

Once more, a familiarity with the romantic conception of fairyland illuminates Mann's conception of the Berghof-as-Venusberg. It was the otherworld's timelessness that had appealed to romantic artists questing for eternal beauty. The hero who dwelt with the supernatural people often returned to discover that what he thought was a short stay had actually covered many years. In fairyland nothing changes, so that one is unaware of the passage of time; or, depending upon how you look at it, time stands still and so nothing changes. For a Keats or Yeats this changelessness signified the ultimate sterility of the immortal realm. At the Berghof time is similarly contracted as patients find that what promised to be a short stay has been extended, while, at the same time, they are almost oblivious to this extension, since life at the sanatorium hardly varies. Only Castorp's cousin, Joachim, anxious to return to a military life, expresses annoyance at the cavalier treatment which time receives at the sanatorium, indignant although resigned to the way three weeks are treated as if no more than a single day. But whereas fairyland is often referred to as the Land of the Living, the Berghof is, despite the apparent changelessness it feigns, the Land of the Dying. And here, just as he had inverted the usual notions of the romantic hero, Mann adds a macabre reversal to the ordinary picture of the otherworld. For one of the "unchanging" characteristics of the Berghof is, paradoxically, the *progression* of the disease, which—in *The Magic Mountain*—more often than not claims the life of the patient. The seeming timelessness of the Berghof is, then, only one more illusion perpetrated on its unwary visitors.

Whether the timelessness of the otherworld is illusory or not, it is linked with another common motif: the hero's boredom there. At the end of the novel, Hans Castorp is overcome with the ennui that usually sends Tannhäuser back to the real world. Most writers, while ready to grant this feature of their story a major thematic role, seem unable fully to account for it. Morris offers a particularly clear example of the difficulty in explaining why Tannhäuser becomes weary of the Venusberg. He evokes the work ethic, maintaining in his essays on art that man needs more than pleasure to strive for if his life is to have meaning. Mann, in contrast, undertakes a more abstract analysis of the subject.

Many false conceptions are held concerning the nature of tedium. In general it is thought that the interestingness and novelty of the time-content are what "make the time pass"; that is to say, shorten it; whereas monotony and emptiness check and restrain its flow. This is only true with reservations. Vacuity, monotony, have, indeed, the property of lingering out the moment and the hour and of making them tiresome. But they are capable of contracting and dissipating the larger, the very large time-units, to the point of reducing them to nothing at all. And conversely, a full and interesting content can put wings to the hour and the day; yet it will lend to the general passage of time a weightiness, a breadth and solidity which cause the eventful years to flow far more slowly than those poor, bare, empty ones over which the wind passes and they are gone. Thus what we call tedium is rather an abnormal shortening of the time consequent upon monotony. Great spaces of time passed in unbroken uniformity tend to shrink together in a way to make the heart stop beating for fear; when one day is like all the others, then they are all like one; complete uniformity would make the longest life seem short, and as though it had stolen away from us unawares. [MM 104; 3:147–48]

Mann's insight about the apparent contradiction between the hero's boredom and that what he thought was a brief stay in the otherworld was actually a very long one shows how his novel is different from those other works whose themes he too explores. While other authors give mythical expression to human experience, Mann searches for and sometimes supplies the philosophical understanding that makes the myth itself coherent.

Not only philosophizing but philosophy itself plays a major role in *The Magic Mountain*, and in this the novel bears comparison with Keats's *Lamia*.[4] Part of Keats's theme concerned "cold Philosophy," which will clip an angel's wings and unweave the rainbow. Like Apollonius, Mann's Settembrini makes it his responsibility to dispel for his pupil that "conception of moonshine and cobwebs" (MM 249; 3:348) which is responsible for Castorp's spirituality. In both works, the hero is guided by a philosopher, and in both he reacts ambivalently toward his instructor:

> 'Tis Apollonius sage, my trusty guide
> And good instructor; but to-night he seems
> The ghost of folly haunting my sweet dreams.
> [KP 1:375–76]

We know how often, in his dreams, he had sought to drive away the organ-grinder as an element offensive to his peace; but the waking man is more moral than the sleeping, and, as before, the sight of that smile not only had a sobering effect upon Hans Castorp, but gave him a sense of gratitude, as though it had responded to his need. [MM 240; 3:336]

In both *Lamia* and *The Magic Mountain* the philosophers caution the heroes about their propensity to be attracted to demonic fairies. Settembrini warns Castorp to beware of Clavdia Chauchat, whom he calls Lilith, a figure associated with Lamia in mythology.[5] When Castorp asks him who Lilith is, a dialogue ensues that, if Keats had known of it, might have seemed to him a reflection of his own theme:

> "According to the Hebraic mythus, Lilith became a night-tripping fairy . . . dangerous to young men especially, on account of her beautiful tresses." "What the deuce! A hobgoblin with beautiful tresses! You couldn't stand that, could you? You would come along and turn on the electric light and bring the young man back to the path of virtue—that's what you'd do, isn't it?" [MM 327–28; 3:456]

But here some extra-textual knowledge provides an obstacle to understanding Settembrini in his self-appointed role. His cautionary advice in the "Walpurgisnacht" chapter of *The Magic Mountain* is taken from an analogous section of Goethe's *Faust*, where Mephistopheles makes the speech. Is the philosopher's reason an instrument of the devil? Or is Mann inverting the temptation motif as he later does in *Doctor Faustus*? Not that Keats's poem is less ambiguous. Apollonius's "truth" destroys his pupil, and under his merciless stare, the serpentine temptress arouses a protective pity in the reader. Philosopher and devil are finally one, for each "tempts" the hero to deny half his nature.

Settembrini, like Apollonius, stands for the "electric light" of reason, as he never fails to remind Castorp:

> I represent the world, the interest of this life, against a sentimental withdrawal and negation, classicism against romanticism. I think my position is unequivocal . . . there is one power, one principle, which commands my deepest assent, my highest and fullest allegiance and love; and this power, this principle, is the intellect. [MM 249; 3:348]

Geist is an ambiguous word, as the translated *intellect* is not, and Settembrini's position will prove nowhere as unequivocal as he insists. He claims, however, to represent the Enlightenment, a force against which so much romantic thought was directed. His avowed purpose is to cure Hans Castorp of his romanticism, which is evidenced primarily by his desire for Clavdia Chauchat.

Clavdia is a reluctant Belle Dame sans Merci, and, in fact, Castorp's infatuation can be understood in quite naturalistic terms. His youth and her exotic attractiveness make his emotions quite understandable and no recourse is needed to the Lilith motif. Nevertheless Clavdia, Castorp's tie to the Berghof, assumes the symbolic role usually played by the otherworld mistress. Castorp admits, "I have forgotten, broken with, everything, my relatives, my calling, all my ideas of life. When Clavdia went away, I waited here for her return, so that now I am wholly lost to life down below, and dead in the eyes of my friends" (MM 610; 3:848). That they have had almost no real contact with each other does not matter, for both Hoffmann and Tieck supply precedents for Mann's conception of her effect on his hero. Neither the Queen of the Mines at Falun nor the goddess of the Runenberg makes more than a brief appearance to Elis and Christian, but the momentary glimpses are sufficient to subvert instincts toward more conventional relationships.

Mann is more complex than even these earlier writers. Clavdia takes pains to deny her role as temptress in the brief but important encounter with Castorp in the "Walpurgisnacht" chapter. She is no Venus of Eichendorff, who recognizes that she is but a customary projection of the young hero's sexual fantasies but still accepts her position as his Belle Dame sans Merci. Clavdia, knowing that like Castorp's fever she is a mere passing incident in his life, refuses the position he has placed her in. "Adieu, mon prince Carnaval! Vous aurez une mauvaise ligne de fièvre ce soir, je vous le prédis" (MM 343; 3:478). The "vous" provides the conclusive seriousness to her teasing farewell and nullifies Castorp's attempt to *tutoyer*, thereby implicating her in his plight. Thus, while Settembrini, her supposed opponent, appears to *tempt* Castorp with his illusively unequivocal claims for the intellect, the supposed temptress, Clavdia, becomes a spokesman for reason by abdicating her role as Belle Dame sans Merci. Mann, however, is only playing games if he means ironically to reverse their parts, for such reversal in no way clarifies Hans's position.

Peter Heller describes Mann's technique when he says that Mann "affirms and doubts the affirmation, and doubts the doubt in the affirmation, and proceeds to subject the affirmation regained to some doubt. He never quite breaks the circle of doubt. He never resolves the 'yes-and-no.' " [6] A comparison can be made here with Yeats, who envied the fairies for never being wearied out by contraries. Just as Yeats recognized at those times when he was not trying to evade the human condition that the dialectical process is essential to creativity, so Mann found it crucial to Hans Castorp's education that he come to see that categories are rarely distinct.

In *The Magic Mountain* many contraries can be subsumed under the larger categories of romanticism and classicism. For Settembrini disease and death are objects for the darker forces of mind that stand opposed to reason and enlightenment, which, in turn, are allied with health and life. Consequently, he vehemently rejects all romantic death-longing and tells Castorp that to feel drawn to death is a ghastly aberration. Worship of the sick and the fatal is a remnant of ancient superstition which remains in the way of human progress. Like Heine, who sees beneath Germanic folklore seething and dangerously anti-human passions, Mann feared the political effects of irrationalism. In an address called "An Appeal to Reason," delivered in Berlin in the 1930s, he warned that the mystique surrounding the worship of primitive instincts would lead Germany to disaster. The political and the irrational are treated in the novel through the contrast between words and music, a contrast that also occupied Hoffmann and Wagner, and, indeed, most important aestheticians of the nineteenth century. Hans Castorp's romanticism is expressed through his attachment to music, for he loved it "from his heart; it worked upon him in much the same way as did his breakfast porter, with deeply soothing, narcotic effect, tempting him to doze" (MM 38; 3:57–58). Clearly, Mann's hero cannot be taken seriously as a defender of music. Nevertheless, Settembrini takes up the challenge to acquaint his pupil with the true significance of the "word": "Speech is civilization itself. The word, even the most contradictious word, preserves contact—it is silence which isolates" (MM 518; 3:715). The social qualities of words bind them to politics, "for the beautiful word begets the beautiful deed" (MM 159; 3:224). He finds music politically suspect, although he is willing to grant this expression of pure emotion a place in the progressive development of mankind.

> Music? It is the half-articulate art, the dubious, the irresponsible, the insensible. Perhaps you will object that she can be clear when she likes. . . . Let music play her loftiest rôle, she will thereby but kindle the emotions, whereas what concerns us is to awaken the reason. . . . Music, as a final incitement to the spirit of men, is invaluable—as a force which draws onward and upward the spirit she finds prepared for her ministrations. But literature must precede her. By music alone the world would get no further forward. Alone, she is a danger. For you, personally, Engineer, she is beyond all doubt dangerous. [MM 113; 3:160–61]

Settembrini's classical aesthetics can easily be recognized in the context of Thomas Love Peacock's belief that the province of art is "to awaken the mind, not to enchain it. Poetry precedes philosophy, but true poetry prepares its path." For Settembrini, doctrine must precede art; for Peacock, art can precede doctrine; but for both, the two must travel in each other's company. And since the function of art is to teach as well as delight, music, like "pure" poetry, is at best trivial and at worst dangerous for Settembrini.

But the Horatian ideal could never satisfy the modern artist seeking a less utilitarian means of reconciling art to life. Nevertheless, synthesis remains the goal wherever opposites are perceived: this is, of course, the point of the Belle Dame sans Merci story, in which mortals and immortals yearn for each other's existence. But Settembrini's solution is unacceptable, since it means the virtual abandonment of beauty in favor of truth whenever the two conflict. And to the extent that he is "unequivocal" in his stance, as he himself insists, Settembrini differs from the author of *The Magic Mountain* and can in no complete sense be considered Mann's spokesman. Mann's thinking is almost always dialectical; and as Weigand notes, the "pedagogical point of the novel . . . consists in the fact that the hero steers his course between" Settembrini and Naphta, "without committing himself to the orthodoxy of either." [7] More recent critics, like Peter Heller, have shown that the matter is more complicated than even this explanation would suggest; it remains the case, nevertheless, that through the disputation between Settembrini and Naphta, Mann's dialectical thought most obviously reveals itself.

The quarrels between the Enlightenment humanist and the Jesuit priest embody the Hellenic-Hebraic dichotomy of the nineteenth century. And here the overlapping qualities of what at first appear to be contrary entities become important. Heine's materialistic Hellenism had differed from Arnold's conception of Hellenism, the latter signifying man's spiritual quest for perfection. Materialism was common to both Hellenism, which celebrated the physical joys of this earth, and Hebraism insofar as it considered worldly prosperity a sign of grace. On the other side, Hellenism was romantic when it emphasized the value of art in the face of Philistine utilitarianism, while Hebraism was equally romantic when allied with a mystical yearning for ideal perfection, a yearning that culminated in asceticism.

Similar crosscurrents in *The Magic Mountain* make it difficult for Castorp to determine just what Settembrini and Naphta actually stand for:

> Ah, this Settembrini—it was not for nothing he was a man of letters, son of a politician and grandson of a humanist! He had lofty ideas about emancipation and criticism—and

chirruped to the girls in the street. On the other hand, knife-edged little Naphta was bound by the strictest sort of vows; yet in thought he was almost a libertine, whereas the other was a very fool of virtue, in a manner of speaking. Herr Settembrini was afraid of "Absolute Spirit," and would like to see it everywhere wedded to democratic progress; he was simply outraged at the religious licence of his militant opponent, which would jumble up together God and the Devil, sanctification and bad behavior, genius and disease, and which knew no standards of value, no rational judgment, no exercise of the will. But who then was the orthodox, who the free-thinker? [MM 468; 3:646]

These differences between Settembrini and Naphta are comparable, on one hand, to Heine's attack on German romanticism, and, on the other, to Eichendorff's defense. Their works reflect the position each took in the quarrel between Hebraism and Hellenism. Neither really believed that what was involved was a simplistic opposition between Venus and the church, but each, to make his point, tended to approach his subject as though he did. Mann, however, would hold that such an approach could only lead away from the truth.

It would be difficult for a reader of *The Magic Mountain* subsequently to read Eichendorff's *The Marble Statue* without being struck by certain parallels. First, there is the arresting passage in which Florio is warned not to enter the *Zauberberg* from which unwary youths rarely emerge to resume their normal lives. Second, the hero of each work is caught between two opposing male influences. Fortunato's warning about the magic mountain has as its counterpart Settembrini's frequent urging that Castorp return to the flatlands. Fortunato also warned about Donati, Venus's emissary. Settembrini feels similarly constrained to caution Castorp about Naphta: "It is my duty to point out to your tender years the intellectual perils of intercourse with this man, and to beg you to keep your acquaintance with him within safe limits. His form is logic, but his essence is confusion" (MM 407; 3:563–64). On the surface, Donati, in league with the devil, appears to have little in common with the priest, Naphta, who, in any event, deals in logic and not in appeal to the senses. But again, Mann does not allow the matter to rest with this difference. Naphta feeds his guests fancy chocolate cakes in an opulent surrounding and Settembrini asserts, "I will characterize this man for you with a single word. He is a voluptuary" (MM 411; 3:569). The antagonism between Settembrini and Naphta can recall Heine's *Für die Mouche* in which the poet imagined the forces of Hebraism and Hellenism engaged in increasingly hostile debate. Like Heine, who claimed in *The Romantic School* that he did not contrast matter and spirit so much as he spiritualized matter, Settembrini tells Naphta that "nature . . . needs no importations of yours. She is Spirit herself" (MM 374; 3:519). Naphta's sarcastic reply, "Doesn't your monism rather bore you?" is the beginning of an argument which finally culminates in a duel. But unlike the disputants in Heine's poem, who represent beauty versus truth, there are no simply defined issues in the struggle between Mann's contestants.

Settembrini is not, in fact, a strict monist, because he reluctantly concedes that wherever the body and mind stand for opposing values, the body represents an evil principle. Heine's physical torments would justify such a belief, for he would have been forced to agree with Matthew Arnold's contention that to exalt man's body presupposes that man never be sick or sorry. For similar reasons, Settembrini must qualify his materialism. So long as the body drew man away from the path to Enlightenment, so long as it represented disease, death, decay, sensuality, and shame, the body must be despised. Settembrini's ideas, then, progress from an initial, Hellenic affirmation of the material world, through a qualification, to—finally—a suspiciously Hebraic moralizing. And it is Naphta who points out the suspect forces that lie behind Settembrini's Hellenism:

> That which [Settembrini] took for granted was precisely that which was being called in question: namely, whether the Mediterranean, classic, humanistic tradition was bound up with humanity and so coexistent with it, or whether it was but the intellectual garb and appurtenance of a bourgeois liberal age, with which it would perish. [MM 521; 3:719–20]

Insofar as Settembrini's materialism is linked to Western capitalism, it is also, according to Naphta, intricately bound up with utilitarianism: "Its end and aim was to make men grow old and happy, rich and comfortable—and that was all there was to it. And this Philistine philosophy, this gospel of work and reason, served Herr Settembrini as an ethical system" (MM 464; 3:641). Although his own combination of Christian asceticism and Marxist philosophy is no less contradictory at times, Naphta is not mistaken in attributing bourgeois Philistinism to the supposed representative of the Enlightenment.

In Heine's *Tannhäuser* the transformation of Venus from enchantress to *hausfrau* was very likely the poet's way of showing how the classical tradition would be destroyed if assimilated by practical, middle-class existence. When Settembrini presses his humanism into the service of social progress, he is effectively achieving the same destruction of aesthetic values. This can be seen in the way he interprets Dante's *Divine Comedy*: "It was not the sickly and mystagogic figure of Beatrice which the poet had celebrated under the name of '*donna gentile e pietosa*'; rather it had been his wife, who represented in the poem the principle of worldly knowledge and practical workaday life" (MM 158; 3:223). Ironically, Heine's Venus and Dante's Beatrice, ostensibly representing different values, experience the same debasement when everyday life is invoked.

Settembrini's Philistinism could have been inferred from his attack on music and defense of "the word." His aesthetic reveals a mixture of classicism and utilitarianism that tends to undermine the autonomy of art. He is scornful of a patient at the Berghof, a brewer, who first reduces literature to the depiction of beautiful characters and then dismisses art because in his own practical existence he meets few such estimable persons. Settembrini is shocked: "That is the idea he has of literature—beautiful characters! Mother of God!" (MM 96; 3:137). But he too denies art an independence based on the self-sufficient value of beauty, and he succeeds only in substituting one form of practicality for another. Informing Castorp that he is preparing a work on the sociology of suffering, he assures the young man that he will not ignore literature: "This great work will not neglect the belletrist in so far as he deals with human suffering: a volume is projected which shall contain a compilation and brief analysis of such masterpieces of the world's literature as come into question by depicting one or other kind of conflict—for the consolation and instruction of the suffering" (MM 246; 3:344). It is difficult not to applaud the compassion behind his intention. Keats's reputation comes in no small part from his sympathy for suffering mankind, from his distinction between the poet who is physician to all men and the mere dreamer. But Keats, unlike Settembrini, would never have sacrificed beauty to his social conscience, transforming art into sociology.

In short, unlike Heine's Hellenism, which expresses love for ancient art and pity for its demise at the hands of Hebraic moralism, Settembrini's classicism achieves Hebraic ends by defeating art on its own grounds. And yet, in Mann's complicated dialectics, Settembrini cannot be viewed in simple contrast to the German poet, who himself is too ambiguous a figure to be neatly categorized. Insofar as Heine's Hellenism led to his love of beauty for its own sake, he differs from Settembrini. But insofar as such Hellenism reflects the principle of reason and stands opposed to the spiritual asceticism of the Hebraists, Heine and Settembrini are as one. This can be seen in the exchange between Settembrini and Naphta concerning a religious painting that the former considers both ugly and formless. Naphta explains that what

> we had here was conscious emancipation from the natural, a contempt for nature manifested by a pious refusal to pay her any homage whatever. Whereupon Settembrini declared that disregard of nature and neglect of her study only led men into error. He characterized as absurd the formlessness to which the Middle Ages and all periods like them had been a prey, and began, in sounding words, to exalt the Graeco-Roman heritage, classicism, form, and beauty, reason, the pagan joy of life. To these things and these alone, he said, was it given to ameliorate man's lot on earth. [MM 395; 3:548]

If Settembrini here sounds like Heine, he can also be compared to Eichendorff—which, again, reveals the difficulty of, first, simply categorizing Mann's humanist, and, second, making clear-cut distinctions between two poets, Heine and Eichendorff, who are usually treated as antagonists. In any event, the formlessness of Naphta's Pieta can be likened to the undisciplined romantic lyric Eichendorff criticizes, partially because it expresses the self-absorption of the artist and thus his extreme individualism. A close attention to form would indicate a turning away from the subjective life toward the external world. Thus the Catholic Eichendorff would not share the Jesuit's disregard for nature. Only through attention to God's creation, while remembering its proper role in man's life, could the artist hope to influence his audience. Naphta's otherworldliness, so far as it was contemptuous of form, was too remote from that positive ethic which paradoxically drew on the earth's beauty as a means of leading man to God.

The disputes between Naphta and Settembrini are useful to understand the complex web of contraries that make up the Hebraic-Hellenic controversy. In turn, the controversy provides an illuminating background for recognizing and then untangling the snarl of forces that characterize Mann's disputants, who more than any others in the book illustrate the author's complex dialectics. Another area in which Mann is able to summarize the contradictory romantic thought of the nineteenth century is the opposition between linear and cyclical theories of time and progress.

In its treatment of time, *The Magic Mountain* proves to be a novel about decadence as well as romanticism. At the Berghof there paradoxically coexists a seeming changelessness resulting from its monotonous routine and from an actual deterioration as the disease saps the life of its victims. Castorp's cousin Joachim, as we have seen, is bitter about the disregard for time that he finds at the health resort: "A year is so important at our age. Down below, one goes through so many changes, and makes so much progress, in a single year of life. And I have to stagnate up here—yes, just stagnate like a filthy puddle; it isn't too crass a comparison" (MM 15; 3:28). Perhaps because of his youth, Joachim associates change with progress, with growth instead of decay. As a result of this unphilosophical optimism, he too falls victim to the illusion of permanence at the Berghof, although his angry use of terms like "stagnation" and "filthy puddle" does signify a subconscious understanding that decadence and hence process, not permanence, characterize life at the sanatorium. His choice of words brings to mind Swinburne's image in the *Hymn to Proserpine* of waste water back of the sea, to which float all of life's poisonous matter.

That no change meant decadence seems clear in Swinburne; but that change necessarily meant progress was nowhere as certain. This accounts for the fear that seems to lurk behind the closing lines of *Songs before Sunrise*, that if *no* "morning must behold / Man, other than were they now cold, / And other deeds than past deeds done," then let the earth itself perish and be lost in a worldless sea. Swinburne acquired his political optimism from Mazzini, whom some critics have taken to be the model for Mann's Settembrini. According to the latter, time and change point to human betterment, although only after a struggle, because the forces of reaction will not surrender their positions so easily. Hans Castorp through his instructor learns to associate time and progress, seeing "how if there was no time there could be no human progress, and the world would be only a standing drain and stagnant puddle—what should I have known of all that if it weren't for you?" (MM 328–29; 3:458). His words echo Swinburne's defense of time in *Genesis*:

> For if death were not, then should growth not be,
> Change, nor the life of good nor evil things;
> Nor were there night at all nor light to see,
> Nor water of sweet nor water of bitter springs.
> [SP 2:182]

Swinburne, however, looks at change here in terms of both positive and negative forces, and his cyclical theory of time contrasts with Settembrini's linear approach.

In this context, a still further analogy can be made between the Mazzini / Swinburne and Settembrini / Castorp relationships. Despite his apocalyptic vision, the cyclical metaphor employed by Swinburne in *Songs before Sunrise* undermines his revolutionary optimism, since sunset is as much a part of the recurring day as is dawn. It would be interesting to know if Swinburne recognized this. Similarly, Hans Castorp's natural tendency to view time in cycles contradicts what he has learned from Settembrini.

At the Berghof, Castorp's childhood view of time, in which he had perceived change in the midst of duration, of recurrence in continuity, assumes a philosophical form:

> The days lengthen in the winter-time, and when the longest comes, the twenty-first of June, the beginning of summer, they begin to go downhill again, toward winter. You call that "of course"; but if one once loses hold of the fact that it *is* of course, it is quite frightening, you feel like hanging on to something. It seems like a practical joke—that spring begins at the beginning of winter, and autumn at the beginning of

summer. You feel you're being fooled, led about in a circle, with your eye fixed on something that turns out to be a moving point. A moving point in a circle. For the circle consists of nothing but such transitional points without any extent whatever; the curvature is incommensurable, there is no duration of motion, and eternity turns out to be not "straight ahead" but "merry-go-round"! [MM 370–71; 3:515]

His speculation took only a different form when Undine noted that smiles break forth out of tears, and tears out of eyes that are in the very act of smiling, and when the priest who marries her to Huldbrand reminded them that there really was no difference between wedding and weeping. It found expression when Keats placed the shrine of melancholy in the temple of delight, and when Yeats wrote that love pitches its mansion in the place of excrement. What all this signifies depends on the individual point of view. For Swinburne, who concluded most of the poems in *Songs before Sunrise* with images of night ending or of dawn breaking, it meant that tyranny would yield before freedom. It had the same significance for Morris, who brought *The Earthly Paradise* to a close by describing signs of spring that could be found at the very height of winter. But for the morbid Tieck, who admitted that as a youngster he saw decay in the midst of growth, spring would only be a mournful reminder that happiness could not persist. Keats, who achieved some stoicism about the world of process and learned to find beauty in autumn, stands somewhere between these two points of view. Closest to Mann, perhaps, is Yeats, whose model of the gyres also describes Castorp's conception of the seasons.[8] Just as this model signifies for Yeats the perpetual confrontation of opposites,[9] so dialectical thought would mean for Mann, as Peter Heller noted, that the affirmation would always contain the seeds of doubt, and those seeds the beginning of reaffirmation. What was permanent was the cycle itself. And if this meant that progress could not be taken for granted, since progress is conceived of in linear terms, so does it more hopefully promise that corruption, where it exists, will not endure.

    Much of Mann's concern with time, change, art, and Philistinism stands outside of the Belle Dame sans Merci theme in *The Magic Mountain*, although Castorp's dilemmas are focused upon his infatuation for his Lilith, Clavdia Chauchat. Indeed, Mann's use of the pattern which places the gullible hero between two conflicting mentors points out some inadequacy on the part of La Belle Dame sans Merci to bear alone the weight of meaning that her love affair with a mortal infers. Perhaps Mann understood this and for this reason both altered and subordinated Clavdia's role in the novel, while sustaining her symbolic value. In some works the temptress makes only a brief appearance for the same reason. Nevertheless, almost all of the themes in *The Magic Mountain* can be found intrinsically bound up with the fairy tales and myths that comprised the subject of so much romantic fiction and poetry, some known by Mann, some not. Even when he did not, it is noteworthy that his novel bears a striking resemblance to the unfamiliar analogues.

In the Belle Dame sans Merci stories, Mann was able to discover the concern he shared with the nineteenth century: the relationship of beauty to a troubled world. The world was on the brink of disaster when he made what was chiefly a political speech, "An Appeal to Reason." And even then he could not assign to art a utilitarian role.

> I do not hold with the remorselessly social point of view which looks upon art—the beautiful and the useless—as a private pastime of the individual, which in times like these may almost be relegated to the category of the criminal. There was a day—the epoch of aesthetic idealism—when Schiller could extoll "pure play" as the highest state of man. But even though that day be past, yet we need not quite subscribe to the school of action which would put idealism on the level of frivolity. For form, be it never so playful, is akin to the spirit, to that which leads man on to social betterment; and art is the sphere wherein is resolved the conflict between the social and the ideal.[10]

There is some bravado in this last clause, bravado akin to Heine's boast that he had spiritualized matter. Hans Castorp leaves the magic mountain without Clavdia; indeed he had never possessed her. And his end is uncertain. Mann claims it makes little difference. But that La Belle Dame sans Merci and her mortal lover usually fail in any attempt at union suggests that the "conflict between the social and the ideal" is less easily reconciled than Mann's simple assertion would have it. That the dialectical opposites he presented could be resolved through form alone is on the surface too easy, for it is only a deceptively clear idea. This kind of abstract simplicity is what Mann attacks throughout *The Magic Mountain*.[11]

CONCLUSION:
The Lorelei and the Mermaid

Romantic writers not only drew on legendary stories of fairy mistresses for their poetry and fiction but they also created their own legend. Heine made it famous, telling about a story that "haunts me and will not leave my thoughts." He sees a "maiden of surpassing beauty" seated atop a rock in the Rhine, "decked in shining gold and combing her golden tresses." At the same time she sings a song "with a strange, compelling melody."

> It grips the boatman in his little boat, filling him with a wild anguish. He does not look at the rocky reef, he looks at naught but the heights above him. In the end, methinks, the waves devour both boatman and boat: that has the Lorelei done by her singing![1]

Perhaps Heine's reference to the fatal powers of her song inspired Thomas Mann to use this quasi-legend[2] as a symbol in *Felix Krull*. Krull's father bottles champagne with a label which depicts the Lorelei adorning her rock. Like the beautiful but dangerous sea maiden who lures her victims to a watery grave, Krull's Lorelei champagne, on whose outward appearance is lavished such care, is of such poor quality that it has a deleterious effect on the consumer's health. Similarly the son Felix, absorbed in his own handsome looks, is a self-confessed fraud. The Krull family belongs to the Rhine region, and their decadent sensuality is like that associated with the region's deadly siren. "The artist as fraud" could very well be the subtitle of Mann's novel, for one of its early scenes presents the beautiful child, Felix, pretending to play a violin that in reality has been greased and so emits no sound. What sends his audience into paroxysms of delight and admiration is all gesture and no substance—an art emptied of all meaning, in short, an art like that which the romantics feared they would produce while under the influence of their Lorelei muse.

The beautiful siren of the Rhineland was the creation of Clemens Brentano, who told a different story from Heine's. Brentano's Lore Lay is a penitent who asks to be converted so she can die a Christian. Her motives seem less related to religious aspiration, however, than to her sorrow at having lost a mortal lover. He, the ballad suggests, has deserted her. But her contrition is to no avail. En route to a convent, she thinks she sees her beloved and plunges into the water, trapping the knights who were accompanying her on the rock from whence she derives her name. This Lore Lay is an ambiguous, pathetic–evil creature, who, in her betrayal by the mortal world and in her search for a soul, seems more like Andersen's Littte Mermaid reacting to her alienation from man by transforming herself into a fatal siren.[3]

The Little Mermaid as temptress appears in Mann's *Doctor Faustus* to help the author depict the "inverse temptation" that provides his novel with its central paradox. This theme makes comprehensible the presence of Andersen's heroine in a novel based on the Faust legend. Both the fairy tale and the legend are concerned with the human soul. In *Doctor Faustus* the soul is relinquished as a price for artistic greatness, or regained at the expense of art. These two motifs interact to dramatize not only Leverkühn's plight but that of the artist in the modern world as well.

Adrian Leverkühn understands why he is an object for the devil's attention: his artist's solitude, his remoteness from the concerns of the ordinary world mark him for damnation. But at times he hopes to save himself, and because of such hopes, decidedly dangerous to his art, the mermaid with whom he identifies himself in his despair appears to be his temptress. As such, she must be distinguished from Helen of Troy, for example, who is summoned for Marlowe's Faust to prevent him from recanting and thus preserving his soul. The Little Mermaid only seems to be analogously offered to Leverkühn by the devil—"She would be a sweetheart for you! Just say the word and I will bring her to your couch" (DF 230; 6:308)—but she could never be a partner in their pact. To the contrary, by following her example, Leverkühn is tempted to break his agreement. The condition of his contract with the devil is that he may not enjoy human love, but it is a condition that he tries to evade. And what happens to him is almost identical with what happens to the Little Mermaid: dumb, unable to express her love for her prince, the mermaid loses him to another. Similarly, Leverkühn finds it impossible by either direct speech or letter to confess his feelings to Marie Godeau, and because of his speechlessness is thwarted in his attempts to wed her. Thus, the mermaid offered him should be contrasted with Helen of Troy. Helen is a symbol of that for which Faust imperils his soul. The Little Mermaid represents the peril Leverkühn faces in being *tempted to save* his.

The irony is that Leverkühn loses Marie to a friend, Rudolph Schwerdtfeger, whom he has asked to be his John Alden. Schwerdt-feger, in turn, is the friend responsible for the thaw that initially tempts Leverkühn into the sphere of human love. And, finally, he is the same friend who points out to Leverkühn how dangerous this sphere is for the composer: "Has your music been inhuman up till now? Then it owes its greatness to its inhumanity. Forgive the simplicity of the remark, but I would not want to hear any humanly inspired work from you." Leverkühn's reply is a cry of pain: "But don't you think it's cruel to let me know that only out of inhumanity I am what I am and that humanity is not becoming to me?" (DF 436; 6:579). He is bitterly aware that he is being rejected by the very person in whom for the first time he had found human warmth.

Perhaps this is the betrayal that turns the Leverkühns into the Felix Krulls, as it had turned a mermaid into the deadly Lorelei, although, of course, the matter is far from simple. Mann was clearly aware of the distinction between the fairies he used as symbols in his two late novels. In his essay on Wagner, he describes Kundry (in *Parsifal*) as a "tortured and distracted duality, now as *instrumentum diaboli*, now as salvation-seeking penitent." [4] Kundry reappears in *Doctor Faustus* as a symbol for music: "she . . . wills not what she does and flings soft arms of lust round the neck of the fool . . . she was the penitent in the garb of the seductress" (DF 61; 6:85). Music, like art in general, longs to free itself from the mundane world but is yet bound to the senses. So does art feel allied with a world which too often has no place for it, or, perhaps worse, absorbs it into the mundane as had happened to Fouqué's Undine or Heine's Venus, only to destroy what is most beautiful in it. These are the world's terms for the artist's salvation, and the muse's only recourse is to retreat from men and hope that they will come to her. It is in this role that she is deemed a seductress.

For shall the artist follow the mermaid into her exile and dwell with her on that remote rock where she is known as the Lorelei? This was the dilemma facing the romantic, who could not quite fathom the process through which he had lost his place in society, and who frequently courted the world with a fervent desire to re-establish his ties. Of one thing, however, he was certain: art like the mermaid was innocent, but because each was rejected by the practical life and could find no role to play in everyday concerns, both had become transformed. This metamorphosis of the sea maiden from innocent to temptress is the theme of *Two Sonnets of the Sirens* by Andrew Lang, in which he metaphorically depicts the introverted art of the romantics, their alientaion from society, and thus their threat.

> The Sirens once were maidens innocent
>   That through the water-meads with Proserpine
> Plucked no fire-hearted flowers, but were content
>   Cool fritillaries and flag-flowers to twine,
>   With lilies woven and with wet woodbine;
> Till once they sought the bright Aetnaean flowers,
> And their bright mistress fled from summer hours
>   With Hades, down the irremeable [*sic*] decline.
> And they have sought her all the wide world through
>   Till many years, and wisdom, and much wrong
> Have filled and changed their song, and o'er the blue
>   Rings deadly sweet the magic of the song,
> And whoso hears must listen till he die
> Far on the flowery shores of Sicily.

> So is it with this singing art of ours,
>   That once with maids went maidenlike, and played
>   With woven dances in the poplar-shade,
> And all her song was but of lady's bowers
> And the returning swallows, and spring-flowers,
>   Till forth to seek a shadow-queen she strayed,
>   A shadowy land; and now hath overweighed

Her singing chaplet with the snow and showers.
Yea, fair well-water for the bitter brine
She left, and by the margin of life's sea
Sings, and her song is full of the sea's moan,
And wild with dread, and love of Proserpine;
And whoso once has listened to her, he
His whole life long is slave to her alone.[5]

The artist has a unique opportunity to regain the earthly paradise, because he may imaginatively create it through his art. But to live in his imagination is to dwell in a "shadowy land," usually with a demon, as his art becomes more and more remote from the common life. The question then becomes whether he can redeem his penitent, La Belle Dame sans Merci, and dwell in the world. That he almost invariably cannot, despite her usual willingness to venture into the human realm, suggests that the fate of the modern world is more dire than what happens to the artist and his fairy muse. In banishing the fairy to her distant sphere, the world has defined the common life in terms that have become more and more remote from art.

 *Notes*

INTRODUCTION

1. Andrew Lang, *Fairyland,* in *Ballads and Lyrics of Old France: with Other Poems* (London: Longmans, Green, 1872), p. 153.

2. *Tannhäuser and the Mountain of Venus: A Study in the Legend of the Germanic Paradise* (New York: Oxford Univ. Press, 1916), p. vii.

3. Recent scholarly interest in both Aubrey Beardsley and Swinburne has resulted in renewed attention to the Tannhäuser legend [chap. 9, notes] and more writing on the subject will undoubtedly be forthcoming.

4. See Rose Frances Egan, *The Genesis of the Theory of "Art for Art's Sake" in Germany and England,* Smith College Studies in Modern Languages, vols. 2,5 (Northampton, Mass., 1921, 1924); John Wilcox, "The Beginnings of L'Art pour L'Art," *The Journal of Aesthetics and Art Criticism* 11 (1953): 360–77.

5. *Hoffmann: Author of the Tales* (Princeton: Princeton Univ. Press, 1948), p. 116.

6. Charles Baudelaire, *The Painter of Modern Life and Other Essays,* trans. and ed. Jonathan Mayne (London: Phaidon, 1964), p. 125.

7. Quoted in George H. Ford, *Keats and the Victorians: A Study of His Influence and Rise to Fame, 1821–1895* (New Haven: Yale Univ. Press, 1944), p. 152.

8. See, for example, Clarice Short, "William Morris and Keats," *PMLA* 59 (1944): 513–23.

9. Nerval was famous as a translator of Goethe's *Faust,* and later translated the poems of Heine, whose good friend he was. See Charles Dédéyan, *Gérard de Nerval et l'Allemagne.* 3 vols. (Paris: Société d'edition d'enseignement supérieur, 1957–59), for a full history of Nerval's association with German literature. Jean Giraudoux was a student in Germany, and the influence on him of German literature is discussed by Laurent Le Sage, *Jean Giraudoux: His Life and Works* (University Park: Pennsylvania State Univ. Press, 1959).

10. *Mélusine* is one of the two major sources discussed by Wilhelm Pfeiffer, *Über Fouqué's Undine* (Heidelberg: C. Winter, 1903).

11. Norma Rinsler, "Gérard de Nerval: The Goddess and the Siren," *PQ* 43 (1964): 109. French scholars prefer to think that Nerval acquired his knowledge of French legend on home ground. Jean Gaulmier, *Gérard de Nerval et Les Filles du Feu* (Paris: Nizet, 1956), p. 119, n. 10, points out that material on the Mélusine legend was

published during Nerval's lifetime and was almost certainly read by him, but this assertion is not supported by direct evidence.

12. There are variants in the spelling of Chartier's work.

13. *The Romantic Agony*, trans. Angus Davidson, 2d ed. (London: Oxford Univ. Press, 1970), p. 197; first published, 1933.

14. For a scholarly edition with an extensive bibliography, consult Marie de France, *Lais*, ed. Alfred Ewert (Oxford: Basil Blackwell, 1960). For studies of the Celtic fairies in these stories, two articles by Tom Peete Cross are particularly interesting: "The Celtic Fée in Launfal," *Anniversary Papers: By Colleagues and Pupils of George Lyman Kittredge* (Boston: Ginn and Co., 1913), pp. 377–87; "The Celtic Elements in the Lays of *Lanval* and *Graelent*," *MP* 12 (1915): 1–60.

15. *Der Percevalroman (Li Contes del Graal)*, ed. Alfons Hilka (Halle: M. Niemeyer, 1932), p. 375.

16. See Arthur C. L. Brown, *The Origin of the Grail Legend* (Cambridge, Mass.: Harvard Univ. Press, 1943), pp. 151–52, for a discussion of Orguelleuse's fairy origins.

17. *Arthurian Tradition and Chrétien de Troyes* (New York: Columbia Univ. Press, 1949), p. 53.

18. Ibid., p. 182.

19. For a significant examination of the fairy mistress and her counterparts in the Renaissance, see A. Bartlett Giamatti, *The Earthly Paradise and the Renaissance Epic* (Princeton: Princeton Univ. Press, 1966).

20. For a discussion of Chartier's poem and its history in its own time, see Edward Joseph Hoffman, *Alain Chartier: His Work and Reputation* (New York: Wittes Press, 1942).

21. For a comparison of the fairy and the heroine of courtly love romance, see Alfred Nutt, *Studies on the Legend of the Holy Grail* (1888; reprint ed., New York: Cooper Square, 1965), p. 232.

22. Quotations from this poem of doubtful authorship and the following one are in *The Works of Geoffrey Chaucer*, ed. F. N. Robinson, 2d ed. (Boston: Houghton Mifflin, 1957), p. 542.

23. Ibid., p. 540.

24. As a gypsy, Carmen can claim a less exalted birth than the aristocratic or middle class ladies of the courtly love tradition. Prosper Mérimée has added romantic primitivism to the *femme fatale* motif.

25. Angel Flores, ed., *An Anthology of French Poetry from Nerval to Valéry in English Translation with French Originals*, trans. Stephen Stepanchev, rev. ed. (Garden City, N.Y.: Doubleday, 1962), p. 42.

26. The traditions are, of course, related. I note shortly that *Ligeia* should be compared to *Undine*, about which Edgar Allan Poe wrote a critical review.

27. *Japanese Fairy Tales*, trans. Mildred Marmur (New York: Golden Press, 1960). The story of Urashima more closely resembles Oisin's than Tannhäuser's. Both the Irish and Japanese heroes, absent from earth for long periods of time, are young when they return from the otherworld. Upon breaking a tabu imposed upon them there, each is immediately transformed into an old man.

28. "The 'Fatal Woman' Symbol in Tennyson," *PMLA* 74 (1959): 438–44.

This article does not distinguish, as I do, between the *femme fatale* and La Belle Dame sans Merci.

29. *The Poetical Works* (London: Oxford Univ. Press, 1954), p. 402.

30. *Miracles of Rare Device: The Poet's Sense of Self in Nineteenth-Century Poetry* (Detroit: Wayne State Univ. Press, 1972).

31. *Elsie Venner: A Romance of Destiny, The Works of Oliver Wendell Holmes*, vol. 5 (Boston: Houghton Mifflin, 1891), pp. ix–x.

32. *Hawthorne: A Critical Study* (Cambridge, Mass.: Belknap Press, Harvard Univ. Press, 1955), p. 113.

33. I have in mind an extension of E. Dubedout, "Romantisme et Protestantisme," *MP* 1 (1904): 117–33.

34. *Mosses from an Old Manse, The Works of Nathaniel Hawthorne*, vol. 1 (Boston: Houghton Mifflin, 1900), p. 126.

35. Ibid., p. 2.

36. Ibid., p. 3.

37. Edmund Wilson attempted to defend and revive interest in him in "The James Branch Cabell Case Reopened," *The New Yorker*, April 21, 1956, pp. 140–68.

38. *Biography of Manuel*, about the medieval province of Poictesme.

CHAPTER 1: SEDUCTRESS OR PENITENT

1. The text as well as a scholarly study of the tale can be found in Werner Söderhjelm, "Antoine de la Sale et la légende de Tannhäuser," *Mémoires de la Société Néo-Philologique a Helsingfors* 2 (1897): 101–68.

2. For further discussions, see Gaston Paris, *Légendes du Moyen Age* (Paris: Hachette, 1904); and the dispute between Arthur F. J. Remy, "The Origin of the Tannhäuser-Legend," *JEGP* 12 (1913): 32–77, and Philip S. Barto, "The German Venusberg," *JEGP* 12 (1913), 295–303.

3. *Des Knaben Wunderhorn: alte deutsche Lieder* (Munich: Winkler, 1957), pp. 60–63.

4. For discussions of the Tannhäuser legend, see Adolf N. Ammann, *Tannhäuser im Venusberg: Der Mythos im Volkslied* (Zurich: Origo, 1964); Philip S. Barto, "Studies in the Tannhäuserlegend," *JEGP* 9 (1910): 293–320, and his full-length study [intro., n. 2]; Ernst Elster, *Tannhäuser in Geschichte, Sage und Dichtung* (Bromberg: Mittler, 1908); Victor Junk, *Tannhäuser in Sage und Dichtung* (Munich: C. H. Beck, 1911); Alexander H. Krappe, "Die Sage vom Tannhäuser," *Mitteilungen der Schlesischen Gesellschaft für Volkskunde* 36 (1937): 106–32; Jessie L. Weston, *The Legends of the Wagner Drama: Studies in Mythology and Romance* (London: D. Nutt, 1896).

5. Tom Peete Cross and Clark Harris Slover, *Ancient Irish Tales* (New York: Henry Holt, 1936), p. 488.

6. Ibid., p. 490.

7. Bryan O'Looney, trans., "The Lay of Oisin in the Land of Youth: As He Related It to Saint Patrick," in *Transactions of the Ossianic Society, for the Year 1856* 4 (1859): 227–79. See also Russell K. Alspach, "Some Sources of Yeats's 'The Wanderings of Oisin,'" *PMLA* 58 (1943): 849–66.

8. Krappe compares Oisin and Tannhäuser, "Die Sage vom Tannhäuser," p. 125.

9. *The Anatomy of Melancholy*, ed. Floyd Dell and Paul Jordan-Smith (New York: Tudor, 1938), p. 648. See also Katherine Garvin, "Snakes in the Grass (with Particular Attention to Satan, Lamia, Christabel)," *REL* 2 (1961): 11–27; Eugene Edward Irwin, "The Lamia Motif in English Literature," master's thesis, University of Florida (Kentucky Microcards, Series A, Modern Language Series, 1958). Richard Monckton Milnes, Lord Houghton, compares Lamia and the Venus of the Tannhäuser legend in "The Goddess Venus in the Middle Ages," *Poems Legendary and Historical* (London: Edward Moxon, 1844), p. 21.

10. *Gesta Romanorum*, trans. and ed. Charles Swan and Wynnard Hooper (1876; reprint ed., New York: Dover, 1959), pp. 21–22.

11. For comparisons of *Lamia* and *Rappaccini's Daughter*, see Norman A. Anderson, " 'Rappaccini's Daughter': A Keatsian Analogue?," *PMLA* 83 (1968): 271–83; Julian Smith, "Keats and Hawthorne: A Romantic Bloom in Rappaccini's Garden," *Emerson Society Quarterly* 42 (1966): 8–12.

12. For extensive studies of this story and its variants, see Paull F. Baum, "The Young Man Betrothed to a Statue," *PMLA* 34 (1919): 523–79; 35 (1920): 60–62; G. Huet, "La Légende de la statue de Vénus," *Revue de l'Histoire des Religions* 68 (1913): 193–217; Robert Mühler, "Der Venusring: Zur Geschichte eines romantischen Motivs," *Aurora* 17 (1957): 50–62. Unlike *Tannhäuser*, this story is not prevalent in English literature, although William Morris included a version in *The Earthly Paradise* and Anthony Burgess used the legend in his *Eve of Saint Venus*. Burton told the story in *The Anatomy of Melancholy*; but although it immediately follows the *Lamia* episode, there is no evidence that Keats was interested in the bridegroom who pledged himself to Venus.

13. A tabu is common to the Belle Dame sans Merci stories. See John R. Reinhard, *The Survival of Geis in Mediaeval Romance* (Halle: Niemeyer, 1933), for a general study of the tabu motif.

14. A convenient text of Egenolf von Staufenberg's work is in *Zwei altdeutsche Rittermaeren: Moriz von Craon und Peter von Staufenberg*, ed. Edward Schröder (Berlin: Weidmann, 1913). For a summary, see C. William Prettyman, "Peter von Staufenberg and Marie de France," *MLN* 21 (1906): 205–06. *Peter von Staufenberg* is the second work discussed by Pfeiffer as a source for *Undine* [intro., n. 10]. The work is rarely mentioned with regard to English literature, although Francis J. Child finds in it an analogue to the ballad, *Clerk Colvill*, no. 42. See his *The English and Scottish Popular Ballads* (1884; reprint ed., New York: Dover Publications, 1964), 1: 372–74.

15. Thomas Keightley tells the story in *The Fairy Mythology: Illustrative of the Romance and Superstition of Various Countries* (1850; reprint ed., New York: AMS Press, 1968), pp. 46–50. Morris included the story in *The Earthly Paradise*.

16. The ballad, its variants, and sources can be found in Child, 2: 317–29. Child compares Thomas to Ogier, p. 319. Similar comparisons are made by Josephine M. Burnham, "A Study of Thomas of Erceldoune," *PMLA* 23 (1908): 391; and Thomas F. Henderson, *Scottish Vernacular Literature: A Succinct History* (Edinburgh: John Grand, 1910), p. 23. The more obvious parallel between Thomas and Tannhäuser was noted by Burnham, pp. 390–91; Remy, "The Origin of the Tannhäuser-Legend," pp.

53–55; John Fiske, *Myths and Myth-makers: Old Tales and Superstitions Interpreted by Comparative Mythology* (Boston: Houghton Mifflin, 1890), p. 30; and Victor Junk, *Tannhäuser in Sage und Dichtung,* p. 14.

17. Child, 37, C, p. 325.

18. The romance is a more elaborate version of the ballad. A convenient text is *The Romance and Prophecies of Thomas of Erceldoune,* ed. James A. H. Murray, Early English Text Society, no. 61 (London: N. Trübner, 1875).

19. This transformation in medieval literature is discussed in Robert P. Miller, "The Wife of Bath's Tale and Mediaeval Exempla," *ELH* 32 (1965): 442–56. Miller goes well beyond Burnham's discussion in "A Study of Thomas of Erceldoune"; she interprets the event as a trial for the hero, while he examines the motif in terms of medieval conceptions of reason and imagination. See also G. H. Maynadier, *The Wife of Bath's Tale: Its Sources and Analogues* (London: D. Nutt, 1901). The relation of La Belle Dame sans Merci (in the generic sense) and the loathly lady motif can be found in Ananda K. Coomaraswamy, "On the Loathly Bride," *Speculum* 20 (1945): 391–404.

20. The French tale *Mélusine* by Jean d'Arras was translated into Middle English by an unknown author. See A. K. Donald's edition in Early English Text Society, no. 68 (London: K. Paul, Trench, Trübner, 1895). For a facsimile of the French manuscript, see *L'Histoire de la belle Mélusine de Jean d'Arras,* ed. W. J. Meyer (Paris: E. Champion, 1924). For studies of the legend, see Auguste Coynault, *Mélusine: son histoire et sa légende* (Niort: Floralies, 1954); E. Sidney Hartland, "The Romance of Melusine," *Folk-Lore* 24 (1913): 187–200; Josef Kohler, *Der Ursprung der Melusinensage; Eine ethnologische Untersuchung* (Leipzig: Eduard Pfeiffer, 1895); François Nodot, *Histoire de Mélusine* (Niort: L. Favre, 1876); and C. de Saint-Marc, "La Légende Poitevine de Mélusine," *Mémoires de la Société Historique et Scientifique des Deux-Sèvres* 6 (1910): 151–200. The relation of the Mélusine and Tannhäuser stories is pointed out by Remy, "The Origin of the Tannhäuser-Legend," p. 75, and Houghton, "The Goddess Venus in the Middle Ages," p. 21.

21. Paracelsus (Theophrastus von Hohenheim), "A Book on Nymphs, Sylphs, Pygmies, and Salamanders, and on the Other Spirits," *Four Treatises of Theophrastus von Hohenheim: Called Paracelsus,* trans. and ed. Henry E. Sigerist (Baltimore: Johns Hopkins Press, 1941), pp. 245–46.

22. Ibid., pp. 238–39.

23. For a fascinating and comprehensive study of mermaids, see Gwen Benwell and Arthur Waugh, *Sea Enchantress: The Tale of the Mermaid and Her Kin* (New York: Citadel Press, 1965).

24. Pfeiffer provides a study of these sources and their influences in *Über Fouqué's Undine* [intro., n. 10]. See also Oswald Floeck, *Die Elementargeister bei Fouqué und anderen Dichtern der romantischen und nachromantischen Zeit* (Heidelberg: C. Winter, 1909); and Julius Haupt, *Elementargeister bei Fouqué, Immermann und Hoffmann* (Leipzig: Wolkenwanderer, 1923).

25. Houghton, in "The Goddess Venus in the Middle Ages," p. 29, compares Venus and the undines. Coomaraswamy connects the undine story to those concerning the disenchantments of other loathly ladies in "The Loathly Bride," p. 393. For Celtic analogues, see John Rhŷs, *Celtic Folklore: Welsh and Manx,* 2 vols. (Oxford: Clarendon Press, 1901), chap.: "Undine's Kymric Sisters."

26. It is not clear if Undine keeps her soul after she returns to the sea. Critics of Fouqué's work assume she does; but I have always felt that she does not. The folk belief on which her story is based demands as a price for the soul a successful union between the nature spirit and her mortal husband.

27. A convenient text is *The Bodley Version of Mandeville's Travels*, ed. M. C. Seymour, Early English Text Society, no. 253 (London: Oxford Univ. Press, 1963). Morris included the story in *The Earthly Paradise*. See Genevieve Apgar, "Morris' 'The Lady of the Land,' " *Poet Lore* 33 (1922): 274–85.

28. "Some Elements in Mediaeval Descriptions of the Otherworld," *PMLA* 33 (1918): 614.

29. Ibid., p. 609.

30. A discussion of the word's meaning can be found in Albert Gérard, "Keats and the Romantic Sehnsucht," *Univ. of Toronto Quarterly* 28 (1959): 160–75.

31. *Four Treatises*, p. 224.

32. *Curious Myths of the Middle Ages* (London: Rivingtons, 1868), 1: 212.

33. *The Mythology of All Races*, ed. Louis H. Gray (1918; reprint ed., New York: Cooper Square, 1964), 3: 181–82.

34. For a discussion of this genre, see Robert Herndon Fife, Jr., "The German Romantic 'Märchen,' " *MP* 9 (1911): 239–57.

35. *Hoffmann* [intro., n. 5], p. 215.

36. *Ludwig Tieck: The German Romanticist: A Critical Study* (Princeton: Princeton Univ. Press, 1935), p. 85.

37. *Poetry and the Criticism of Life* (1931; reprint ed., New York: Russell and Russell, 1963), p. 17.

38. Ibid.; my italics.

39. *Royal Highness*, trans. A. Cecil Curtis (New York: Alfred A. Knopf, 1939), p. viii.

40. Ibid., p. 128; *Königliche Hoheit, Gesammelte Werke*, vol. 2 (Frankfurt: S. Fischer, 1960), p. 140.

41. *Tannhäuser in Geschichte, Sage und Dichtung* [chap. 1, n. 4], p. 2; my translation.

42. See Alfred Nutt, *Studies on the Legend of the Holy Grail* [intro., n. 21], p. 232.

43. *The Complete Works in Verse and Prose*, ed. Alexander B. Grosart (1885; reprint ed., New York: Russell and Russell, 1963), 1: 272. I have used modernized spelling.

44. *The White Goddess: A Historical Grammar of Poetic Myth* (New York: Creative Age Press, 1948), p. 11.

45. *Irish Fairy and Folk Tales* (New York: Modern Library, n.d.), p. 86.

CHAPTER 2: THE ARTIST'S QUEST FOR A SOUL

1. Quoted in Zeydel, *Ludwig Tieck* [chap. 1, n. 36], p. 176.

2. Tieck wrote versions of the Tannhäuser and Mélusine legends.

3. Friedrich de la Motte Fouqué, *Undine*, retold by Gertrude C. Schwebell (New York: Simon and Schuster, 1971), p. 64.

4. See F. Scott Fitzgerald, *Tender Is the Night* (New York: Charles Scribner's, 1962), p. 57, where Dick Divers speaks of "Lewis Carroll and Jules Verne and whoever wrote Undine," indicating that the work's reputation has fared better than the author's.

5. W. J. Lillyman points to this lack of scholarship in "Fouqué's *Undine*," *Studies in Romanticism* 10 (1971): 94–105.

6. See, for example, H. A. Korff, *Geist der Goethezeit: Versuch einer ideellen Entwicklung der Klassisch-Romantischen Literaturgeschichte* (Leipzig: Koehler and Amelang, 1966), 4: 341–47.

7. *German Romantic Literature* (London: Methuen, 1955), p. 327.

8. *The Magic Ring: A Romance* (Edinburgh, 1825), 1: 3–4. *Der Zauberring: Ein Ritterroman* (Nuremberg: J. H. Schrag, 1816), 1: 2–3.

9. For a study of Undine's sources, see Pfeiffer, *Über Fouqué's Undine* [intro., n. 10].

10. *German Romantic Literature*, p. 328.

CHAPTER 3: THE SAGE AND THE TEMPTRESS

1. This passage especially demonstrates the influence of *Rhododaphne* on Keats's *La Belle Dame sans Merci*. For a comparison, see Karel Stepanik, "A Source of Keats's 'La Belle Dame sans Merci,' " *Philologica Pragensia* 1 (1958): 104–15.

2. For a study of the "death of Pan" motif, see Patricia Merivale, *Pan the Goat-God: His Myth in Modern Times* (Cambridge, Mass.: Harvard Univ. Press, 1969).

3. For another comparison, see William E. Harrold, "Keats's *Lamia* and Peacock's *Rhododaphne*," *MLR* 61 (1966): 579–84. Harrold, however, makes no mention of a significant parallel between the poems, which involves Keats's concern with cold philosophy. For earlier and briefer comparisons, see Sidney Colvin, *John Keats* (London: Macmillan, 1917), p. 405; Douglas Bush, "Notes on Keats's Reading," *PMLA* 50 (1935): 188; and his *Mythology and the Romantic Tradition in English Poetry* (Cambridge, Mass.: Harvard Univ. Press, 1937), pp. 111, 183–84.

4. *His Fine Wit: A Study of Thomas Love Peacock* (London: Routledge and Kegan Paul, 1970), pp. 46–54.

5. For a survey of the interpretations of *Lamia* (as well as *La Belle Dame sans Merci*), see Gerald Enscoe, *Eros and the Romantics: Sexual Love as a Theme in Coleridge, Shelley and Keats* (The Hague: Mouton, 1967).

6. I agree with Aileen Ward, who in her biography, *John Keats: The Making of a Poet* (New York: Viking, 1963), places more than the usual emphasis on how Keats's decision to leave medicine affected his subsequent career as a poet.

7. *Blackwood's Edinburgh Magazine*, Aug. 1818, p. 519.

8. *John Keats*, p. 185.

9. For a study of parallel passages, see David B. Green, "Keats and La Motte Fouqué's *Undine*," *Delaware Notes* 27 (1954): 33–48.

10. For a history of this discussion, see H. W. Garrod, *Keats* (Oxford: The Clarendon Press, 1926), p. 61; John Bayley, "Keats and Reality," *Proceedings of the British Academy* 48 (1962; publ. 1963): 113; and Ian Jack, *English Literature: 1815–1832, Oxford History of English Literature*, ed. F. P. Wilson and Bonamy Dobree, vol. 10 (Oxford: The Clarendon Press, 1963), p. 110.

11. Among numerous articles on the sources of *Lamia* (and *La Belle Dame sans Merci*), a comprehensive single account is Bernice Slote, *Keats and the Dramatic Principle* (Lincoln: Univ. of Nebraska Press, 1958); for Keats's sources and reading, see Claude L. Finney, *The Evolution of Keats's Poetry*, 2 vols. (Cambridge, Mass.: Harvard Univ. Press, 1936.)

12. See Werner W. Beyer, *Keats and the Demon King* (New York: Oxford Univ. Press, 1947) for Wieland's influence on Keats; Spenser's influence is obvious.

13. *Spenser's Faerie Queene*, ed. J. C. Smith (Oxford: The Clarendon Press, 1964), 2: 191.

14. William Sotheby, trans., *Oberon: A Poem from the German of Wieland* (London: W. Bulmer, 1805), 2: 175.

15. For a facsimile of Keats's markings, see Caroline F. E. Spurgeon, *Keats's Shakespeare* (London: Oxford Univ. Press, 1928).

16. *The Tragedy of Antony and Cleopatra*, ed. Peter G. Phialas (New Haven: Yale Univ. Press, 1955).

17. Cowden Clarke reports on this in an anecdote quoted by Walter J. Bate, *John Keats* (Cambridge, Mass.: Harvard Univ. Press, 1963), p. 65.

18. Most studies of Keats contain extensive discussions of *Lamia* and *La Belle Dame sans Merci*. Of particular interest are Mario D'Avanzo, *Keats's Metaphors for the Poetic Imagination* (Durham, N.C.: Duke Univ. Press, 1967); Walter H. Evert, *Aesthetic and Myth in the Poetry of Keats* (Princeton: Princeton Univ. Press, 1965); Barry E. Gross, "*The Eve of St. Agnes* and *Lamia*: Paradise Won, Paradise Lost," *Bucknell Review* 13 (1965): 47–57; Paul Haeffner, "Keats and the Faery Myth of Seduction," *REL* 3 (1962): 20–31 (although a study of *Endymion*, this article deals with Keats and the Celtic fairies); Edward T. Norris, "Hermes and the Nymph in *Lamia*," *ELH* 2 (1935): 322–26; David Perkins, *The Quest for Permanence: The Symbolism of Wordsworth, Shelley, and Keats* (Cambridge, Mass.: Harvard Univ. Press, 1959); Donald H. Reiman, "Keats and the Humanistic Paradox: Mythological History in *Lamia*," *SEL* 11 (1971): 659–71; John H. Roberts, "The Significance of *Lamia*," *PMLA* 50 (1935): 550–61; Earl R. Wasserman, *The Finer Tone: Keats's Major Poems* (Baltimore: Johns Hopkins Press, 1967).

CHAPTER 4: DEMONIC GEMS

1. *Ludwig Tieck* [chap. 1, n. 36], p. 8. For an essay on romantic self-consciousness, see Geoffrey H. Hartman, "Romanticism and Anti-self-consciousness," *Centennial Review* 6 (1962): 553–65.

2. For further discussion, see Rudolf Lieske, *Tiecks Abwendung von der Romantik* (Berlin: E. Ebering, 1933); Raimund Belgardt, "Poetic Imagination and External Reality in Tieck," *Essays on German Literature: In Honor of G. Joyce Hallamore*, ed. Michael S. Batts and Marketa G. Stankiewicz (Toronto: Univ. of Toronto Press, 1968). I am less ready than Belgardt to grant that Tieck satisfactorily reconciled opposites by a positive portrayal of "lower" reality in his fiction.

3. Zeydel says that Tieck wrote *The Runenberg* in a single night in 1802; *Ludwig Tieck*, p. 160. The letter of December 16, 1803, can be found in *Ludwig Tieck und die Brüder Schlegel: Briefe mit Einleitung und Anmerkungen*, ed. H. Lüdeke

(Frankfurt: J. Baer, 1930). The letter makes clear that he is describing to Schlegel a state of mind which has persisted for a long time; it accounts for the year-long silence which Tieck alludes to.

4. This polarization of romanticism and classicism is a simplistic reduction, as Lawrence Ryan points out in "Romanticism," *Periods in German Literature*, ed. James M. Ritchie (London: Oswald Wolff, 1966). Nevertheless, romantic artists torn by conflict were apt to depict their dilemma precisely through this kind of polarization, abstracting and pitting against each other the forces warring within them. Ryan's thesis is that the romantics, too, were concerned with form, but one might respond that no great writer is ever "purely" romantic.

5. See Theodore Gish, "*Wanderlust* and *Wanderleid*: The Motif of the Wandering Hero in German Romanticism," *Studies in Romanticism* 3 (1964): 225–39.

6. For further discussion of this opposition, see Richard W. Kimpel, "Nature, Quest, and Reality in Tieck's *Der Blonde Eckbert* and *Der Runenberg*," *Studies in Romanticism* 9 (1970): 176–92. But whereas Kimpel distinguishes between untamed and cultivated nature, I will argue that in *The Runenberg* there is also the opposition between nature and art.

7. Kimpel's essay reveals the complexity of the matter.

8. *German Romantic Literature* [chap. 2, n. 7], p. 96.

9. *Geist der Goethezeit* [chap. 2, n. 6], 3: 472.

10. *Eros and Civilization: A Philosophical Inquiry into Freud* (Boston: Beacon Press, 1966), p. 172.

11. Ibid., p. 185.

12. Ibid., p. 144.

13. Ibid., p. 179.

14. *The Runenberg*, which appeared in Thomas Carlyle's translation in 1828, has only recently received the attention it deserves from scholars. An essay devoted exclusively to it is by W. J. Lillyman, "Ludwig Tieck's 'Der Runenberg': The Dimensions of Reality," *Monatshefte* 62 (1970): 231–44. See also the discussion by Max Diez, "Metapher und Märchengestalt" (pt. IV), *PMLA* 48 (1933): 877–87.

15. Hoffmann's *Mines of Falun* has only lately been recognized as of major significance in its author's canon. The text I quote is a highly selective collection of Hoffmann's tales. Angel Flores also included the story in his collection of *Nineteenth Century German Tales* (Garden City, N.Y.: Doubleday Anchor, 1959). The legend of the mines at Falun, however, has long commanded scholarly attention. See Georg Friedman, *Die Bearbeitungen der Geschichte von dem Bergmann von Fahlun* (Berlin: L. Metzoldt, 1887); Emil Franz Lorenz, "Die Geschichte des Bergmanns von Falun," *Imago* 3 (1914): 250–301; Karl Reuschel, "Über Bearbeitungen der Geschichte des Bergmanns von Falun," *Studien zur vergleichenden Literaturgeschichte* 3 (1903): 1–28. The legend also seems to have a popular analogue to the Russian fairy tale *The Stone Flower*.

16. The brief story of the "Unverhofftes Wiedersehen" can be found in Hebel, *Poetische Werke* (Munich: Winkler, 1961), pp. 252–54. For a comparison of the legend in Hebel and Hoffmann, see Wilhelm Raabe, "Die Geschichte von dem Bergmann zu Fahlun," *Wege zur Erzählkunst: Über den Umgang mit dichterischer Prosa*, ed. Johannes Pfeiffer (Hamburg: Friedrich Wittig, 1955).

17. Arnim's poem is part of his novel, *Armuth, Reichthum, Schuld und Busse der Gräfin Dolores* (Berlin: Realschul Buchhandlung, 1810), 2: 336–42.

18. See Peter Bruning, "E.T.A. Hoffmann and the Philistine," *German Quarterly* 28 (1955): 111–21; Estelle Morgan, "E.T.A. Hoffmann and the Philistine," *Modern Languages* (London), 42 (1961): 140–44.

19. *Hoffmann* [intro., n. 5], p. 225.

20. For further discussion, see Alfred Neumann, "Musician or Author? E.T.A. Hoffmann's Decision," *JEGP* 52 (1953): 174–81.

21. *Main Currents in Nineteenth Century Literature* (New York: Boni and Liveright, 1923), 2: 3.

22. *Hoffmann* (London: Bowes and Bowes, 1963), p. 34.

23. For an excellent discussion of the German fairy tale as well as a comparison of Hoffmann and Tieck, see W. Jost, *Von Ludwig Tieck zu E.T.A. Hoffmann: Studien zu Entwicklungsgeschichte des romantischen Subjectivismus* (1921; reprint ed., Darmstadt: Wissenschaftliche Buchgesellschaft, 1969). The distinction between Hoffmann and Tieck in their treatment of the otherworld is also briefly discussed by V. C. Hubbs, "Tieck's Romantic Fairy Tales and Shakespeare," *Studies in Romanticism* 8 (1969): 230.

24. *Henry von Ofterdingen*, trans. Palmer Hilty (New York: Frederick Ungar, 1964), pp. 70–71. See also Gerhard Schulz, "Novalis und der Bergbau," *Freiberger Forschungshefte: Kultur und Technik*, series D, 11 (1955): 242–63. This issue, which stresses the theme of mining, also contains an essay by Carl Beck, "E.T.A. Hoffmanns Erzählung 'Die Bergwerke von Falun,'" pp. 264–72.

25. *Henry von Ofterdingen*, p. 93.

26. Ibid., p. 69.

27. *The Life of Richard Wagner* (New York: Alfred A. Knopf, 1933), 1: 203. Robert Gutman writes of *The Mines of Falun* that the theme of "a hero torn between a mysterious mountain queen and a faithful earthly maid, whose love goes beyond the grave [was] the very conflict the composer was to treat again in his Tannhäuser," *Richard Wagner: The Man, His Mind and His Music* (New York: Harcourt, Brace and World, 1968), p. 83.

CHAPTER 5: VENUS AND THE POPE

1. For a history of the word *Philistine*, see Estelle Morgan, "Bourgeois and Philistine," *MLR* 57 (1962): 69–72.

2. Arnold's poem contains a rare example of children being born to a mortal in the otherworld. Margaret's beautiful but cold mermaiden daughter seems, however, to be a symbolic contrast to the productive work Margaret performs in the real world.

3. *The Poetical Works of Matthew Arnold*, ed. C. B. Tinker and H. F. Lowry (London: Oxford Univ. Press, 1963), pp. 161–65.

4. *Culture and Anarchy. Complete Prose Works*, ed. R. H. Super, 7 vols. (Ann Arbor: Univ. of Michigan Press, 1960–70), 5: 163–64. All citations to Arnold's prose will be to this edition.

5. The German text of *Für die Mouche* can be found in Heine's *Werke*, ed. Martin Greiner (Cologne-Berlin: Kiepenheuer and Witsch, 1956), 1: 603–10.

6. See Milton Himmelfarb, "Hebraism and Hellenism Now," *Commentary* (July 1969), pp. 50–57. For the relation of Heine's ideas and life to English conceptions of Hebraism and Hellenism, see E. M. Butler, "Heine in England and Matthew Arnold," *German Life and Letters* 9 (1956): 157–65; John S. Harrison, "Pater, Heine, and the Old Gods of Greece," *PMLA* 39 (1924): 655–86; S. Liptzin, "Heinrich Heine, Hellenist and Cultural Pessimist: A Late Victorian Legend," *PQ* 22 (1943): 267–77; and his *English Legend of Heinrich Heine* (New York: Bloch, 1954).

7. *Culture and Anarchy*, 5: 238.

8. *Pagan and Mediaeval Religious Sentiment*, 3: 227–28.

9. Ibid., 3: 225.

10. This episode inspired numerous English poems: see Liptzin, *English Legend of Heinrich Heine*. For a discussion of Heine's illness and awakening religious consciousness, see Hermann J. Weigand, "Heine's Return to God," *MP* 18 (1920): 309–42.

11. *Pagan and Mediaeval Religious Sentiment*, 3: 222–23.

12. *Religion and the Rise of Capitalism: A Historical Study* (1926; reprint ed., Gloucester, Mass.: Peter Smith, 1962), p. 240.

13. *Culture and Anarchy*, 5: 97.

14. Ibid., 5: 255.

15. *Religion and the Rise of Capitalism*, p. 243.

16. *Culture and Anarchy*, 5: 249.

17. Ibid., 5: 95.

18. *The Alien Vision of Victorian Poetry: Sources of the Poetic Imagination in Tennyson, Browning, and Arnold* (1952; reprint ed., Hamden, Conn.: Archon Books, 1963), p. v.

19. *Art for Art's Sake* (Boston: Lothrop, Lee and Shepard, 1936), pp. 61–62.

20. "Die Sage vom Tannhäuser" [chap. 1, n. 4], p. 106.

21. *Once a Week*, Aug. 17, 1861, pp. 210–12. Clyde K. Hyder cites this issue as the source of Swinburne's conception of the Tannhäuser story: "Swinburne's *Laus Veneris* and the Tannhäuser Legend," *PMLA* 45 (1930): 1203–13.

CHAPTER 6: EXILED GODS

1. Charles Leland's translations of Heine are frequently an amalgam of the German and French texts that Heine had excised from the German version. The French text can usually be found in the notes of the German edition.

2. *Henri Heine, "romantique défroqué": héraut du symbolisme français* (New Haven: Yale Univ. Press, 1954), p. 209.

3. *The Gods of Greece* bears significant comparison to Swinburne's *Hymn to Proserpine*.

4. Margaret Armour's translation is in *Prose and Poetry by Heinrich Heine*, Everyman's Library, no. 911 (London: J. M. Dent and Sons, 1934), pp. 86–92 (HW 4:429–38). The translation in Leland's edition is frequently so ludicrous in its rendering of Heine's irony ("Your too sweet wine, fairy lady mine, / And kisses give me twitters") that in this poem I have not been able to overlook the aesthetics of the translation and have found one less jarring.

5. For the French text, see *Revue des Deux Mondes*, April 1, 1853, p. 5.

6. Trusty Eckhart plays a major role in Tieck's version of the Tannhäuser legend, *Der Getreue Eckart.*

7. Richard Monckton Milnes, Lord Houghton, *Monographs, Personal and Social* (New York: Holt and Williams, 1873), p. 300.

8. *Heinrich Heine: A Biography* (London: Hogarth, 1956), p. 264. See also her *The Tyranny of Greece over Germany: A Study of the Influence Exercised by Greek Art and Poetry over the Great German Writers of the Eighteenth, Nineteenth, and Twentieth Centuries* (Cambridge, Eng.: The University Press, 1935), for a study of the background to Heine's conflict between Hebraism and Hellenism.

9. The scholarship on Heine is enormous, but little is devoted to a detailed study of *Tannhäuser*; an important analysis is in S. S. Prawer, *Heine: The Tragic Satirist: A Study of the Later Poetry 1827–1856* (Cambridge, Eng.: The University Press, 1961). Jeffrey L. Sammons, in *Heinrich Heine, The Elusive Poet* (New Haven: Yale Univ. Press, 1969), p. 195, calls Prawer's interpretation "just about the last possible word on that poem." I disagree and my analysis has touched on material—specifically the contexts of the poem—not yet sufficiently explored.

10. For further discussion, see Otto Friedrich Bollnow, "Das romantische Weltbild bei Eichendorff," *Unruhe und Geborgenheit im Weltbild neuerer Dichter* (Stuttgart: W. Kohlhammer, 1953), p. 252.

11. See [chap. 1, n. 2].

12. For a study of Eichendorff's relation to nature, see Alexander Borman, *Natura Loquitur: Naturpoesie und emblematische Formel bei Joseph von Eichendorff* (Tübingen: Niemeyer, 1968).

13. Lawrence R. Radner, "Religious Faith in the Novels and 'Novellen' of Eichendorff" (Ph.D. diss., Princeton University, 1957), p. 12.

14. Many of Eichendorff's literary ballads could stand as analogues to Keats's *La Belle Dame sans Merci*; and the Venus statue is a motif to be found in other of his prose tales. See Rudolf Haller, *Eichendorffs Balladenwerk* (Bern: Francke, 1962); Radner's dissertation; Gillian Rodger, "Eichendorff's Conception of the Supernatural World of the Ballad," *German Life and Letters* 13 (1960): 195–206.

15. For a study of subjectivity in Eichendorff, see Oskar Seidlin, "Eichendorff und das Problem der Innerlichkeit," *Aurora* 29 (1969): 7–22.

16. For a detailed discussion of symbolism in *The Marble Statue*, see Radner's dissertation.

17. See Manfred Beller, "Narziss und Venus: klassische Mythologie und romantische Allegorie in Eichendorffs Novelle *Das Marmorbild*," *Euphorion* 62 (1968): 117–42, for a study of the narcissus theme in Eichendorff's work.

18. Most general studies of Eichendorff devote some attention to *The Marble Statue*. Among those specifically are Ernst Feise, "Eichendorffs *Marmorbild*," *The Germanic Review* 11 (1936): 75–86; Alfons Hayduk, "Der dämonisierte Eros bei Eichendorff und Hauptmann. Von der Novelle 'Das Marmorbild' 1817 zum posthumen Roman 'Winckelmann' 1954," *Aurora* 15 (1955): 25–29; Lawrence R. Radner, "Eichendorff's 'Marmorbild': 'Götterdämmerung' and Deception," *Monatshefte* 52 (1960): 183–88; Egon Schwarz, "Ein Betrag zur allegorischen Deutung von Eichendorffs Novelle 'Das Marmorbild,' " *Monatshefte* 48 (1956): 215–20; Gerhard Uhde,

"Treue dem Genius: Zu Joseph von Eichendorffs 'Das Marmorbild,'" *Schlesien* 3 (1958): 157–60; Friedrich Weschta, *Eichendorff's Novellenmärchen "Das Marmorbild"* (Prague: Koppe-Bellmann, 1916).

CHAPTER 7: MORE PAGAN RUINS

1. *Lettres à Une Inconnue* (Paris: Michel Lévy, 1874), 1:43. After Mérimée's death, a woman who chose to remain anoymous published letters he had written to her over many years.
2. Ibid., 1:15.
3. *Poems Legendary and Historical* [chap. 1, n. 9], pp. 34–35.
4. Ibid., p. 49.
5. Ibid., p. 22.
6. *The Well-Beloved: A Sketch of a Temperament* (London: Macmillan, 1952), p. 76.
7. Ibid., p. 136.
8. *The Complete Works of Percy Bysshe Shelley*, ed. Roger Ingpen and Walter E. Peck (New York: Gordian Press, 1965), 2:364.
9. Ibid., 1:173.
10. *The Collected Poems of Thomas Hardy* (London: Macmillan, 1962), pp. 121–23.
11. *The Poetry of Thomas Hardy* (New York: Columbia Univ. Press, 1947), pp. 28–29.
12. *Prosper Mérimée: Heroism, Pessimism, and Irony.* University of California Publications in Modern Philology, no. 66 (Berkeley: Univ. of California Press, 1962), p. 57.
13. *Lettres à Une Inconnue*, 1:78.
14. For discussions of *The Venus of Ille*, see Frank P. Bowman, "Narrator and Myth in Mérimée's *Venus of Ille*," *French Review* 33 (1960): 475–82; J. B. Ratermanis, "La Perspective temporelle dans La Vénus d'Ille de Prosper Mérimée," *Le Français moderne* 31 (1963): 207–18; A. W. Raitt, *Prosper Mérimée* (New York: Scribner, 1970). Raitt's footnotes and bibliography contain other references, mostly concerned with the sources of Mérimée's story.
15. For the relationship between Mérimée's and James's stories, see P. R. Grover, "Mérimée's Influence on Henry James," *MLR* 63 (1968): 810–17.
16. "The Last of the Valerii," *The Complete Tales of Henry James*, ed. Leon Edel, vol. 3 (Philadelphia: J. B. Lippincott, 1962), p. 111.
17. Ibid., p. 122.
18. *The Eve of Saint Venus* (New York: W. W. Norton, 1970), p. 2.
19. Ibid., p. 62.
20. Ibid., p. 1.
21. See Stillinger's essay in *The Hoodwinking of Madeline: And Other Essays on Keats's Poems* (Urbana: Univ. of Illinois Press, 1971).
22. *The Eve of Saint Venus*, publisher's dust jacket.
23. Ibid., p. 136.

CHAPTER 8: FAIRIES AND SAINTS

1. [Intro. n. 9].

2. "Les Poésies de Henri Heine," *Revue des Deux Mondes*, Sept. 15, 1848, pp. 914–30. The following combination of translation and paraphrase is mine.

3. Norma Rinsler, "Gérard de Nerval: The Goddess and the Siren" discusses the role of the siren in Nerval's work [intro. n. 11].

4. *Larousse Encyclopedia of Mythology*, trans. Richard Aldington and Delano Ames, from *Larousse Mythologie Générale*, ed. Felix Guirand (New York: Prometheus Press, 1959), p. 142.

5. From the first part of "Les Poésies de Henri Heine," *Revue des Deux Mondes*, July, 15, 1848, pp. 224–43. The combination of translation and paraphrase is mine.

6. Ibid., p. 224.

7. *Gérard de Nerval: Le Poète, L'Homme* (Paris: Hachette, 1914), p. 16.

8. *The Queen of the Fish* is not a folktale, but a creation of Nerval's imagination, according to Michel Olsen, "La Reine des poissons, conte populaire ou création poétique," *Revue Romane*, special no. 1 (1967): pp. 224–31.

9. The story of *The Queen of the Fish* can be found in two of Nerval's works: *Songs and Legends of Valois*, which is included in *The Daughters of Fire*, and *La Bohème Galante*.

10. Marie-Therese Goosse, " 'El Desdichado' de Gérard de Nerval," *Les Lettres Romanes* 18 (1964): 243–45, does not note this softening of Mélusine's character in an otherwise interesting article which touches on the role played by the French fairy in one of Nerval's poems. Michel Olsen, "La Reine des poissons," p. 230, discusses the ominous qualities suggested by the Queen of the Fish, but I would disagree, because the negative attributions he mentions are part of the description by the wicked uncle in the story. Although Nerval found it difficult to disengage himself from the world, there is nothing in this story to suggest any sympathetic identification with the uncle, whose views he would reject.

11. See Arthur Waugh, "The Folklore of the Merfolk," *Folk-Lore* 71 (1960): 77.

12. Geoffrey Wagner, Introduction (GN 39, 50).

13. "Les Poésies de Henri Heine," *Revue des Deux Mondes*, Sept. 15, 1848, p. 930.

14. For further discussion, see Frida F. L. Huige, "Nerval's 'Aurelia': Schizophrenia and Art," *American Imago* 22 (1965): 255–74.

15. For further discussion, consult James Villas, *Gérard de Nerval: A Critical Bibliography, 1900–1967* (Columbia: Univ. of Missouri Press, 1968).

16. For the sources of Wagner's opera, see Hedwig Guggenheimer, "E. T. A. Hoffmann und Richard Wagner," *Richard Wagner Jahrbuch* 2 (1907): 165–203; Friedrich Panzer, "Richard Wagners Tannhäuser: sein Aufbau und seine Quellen," *Die Musik* 7 (1908): 11–27: J. G. Robertson, "The Genesis of Wagner's Drama 'Tannhäuser,' " *MLR* 18 (1923): 458–70; Alexandra von Schleinitz, *Wagner's Tannhäuser und Sängerkrieg auf der Wartburg* (Meran: Ellmenreich, 1891); Rudolf Sokolowsky, "Richard Wagners Tannhäuser und seine literarischen Vorgänger," *Bayreuther Blätter* 27 (1904): 223–34.

17. *The Singer's Contest*, in *The Serapion Brethren*, trans. Major Alex Ewing, vol. 1 (London, George Bell and Sons, 1908): 296–97 (SB 277).
18. Ibid., p. 299 (SB 280).
19. Ibid., p. 339 (SB 316).
20. Ibid., p. 299 (SB 279).
21. Ibid., pp. 299–300 (SB 280).
22. Ibid., p. 301 (SB 281).
23. For a discussion of the *Gesamtkunstwerk*, see Alfred R. Neumann, "The Evolution of the Concept of the Gesamtkunstwerk in German Romanticism" (Ph.D. diss., University of Michigan, 1951); Jack M. Stein, *Richard Wagner and the Synthesis of the Arts* (Detroit: Wayne State Univ. Press, 1960).
24. *The Life of Richard Wagner* [chap. 4, n. 27], 1: 259.
25. "The Evolution of the Concept of the Gesamtkunstwerk," p. 227.
26. *The Painter of Modern Life* [intro., n. 6], p. 121.

CHAPTER 9: ART AND MORALITY

1. *The Triumph of Time: A Study of the Victorian Concept of Time, History, Progress, and Decadence* (Cambridge, Mass.; Belknap Press, Harvard Univ. Press, 1966), p. vii.
2. *Art for Art's Sake* [chap. 5, n. 19], p. 73.
3. See Clarice E. Short, "The Poetic Relationship of John Keats and William Morris" (Ph.D. diss., Cornell University, 1941).
4. For a discussion of the play's publishing history, see Margaret Jacobs, "Hugo von Hofmannsthal: *Das Bergwerk zu Falun*," *Hofmannsthal: Studies in Commemoration*, ed. F. Norman (London: Institute of Germanic Studies, 1963). For further discussion of the play, see Walther Brecht, "Über Hugo von Hofmannsthals 'Bergwerk zu Falun,' " *Corona* 3 (1932): 210–35; Gotthart Wunberg, "Bemerkungen zu Hofmannsthals Vorspiel 'Das Bergwerk zu Falun,' " *Neue Sammlung* 5 (1965): 174–91; [chap. 4, n. 15].
5. Hugo von Hofmannsthal, *Poems and Verse Plays*, ed. Michael Hamburger (New York: Pantheon, 1961).
6. For a discussion of Hofmannsthal's aestheticism, see Michael Hamburger's introduction to *Poems and Verse Plays*.
7. For a controversy surrounding the word *decadence*, see Clyde de L. Ryals, "Towards a Definition of *Decadent* as Applied to British Literature of the Nineteenth Century," and Robert L. Peters, "Toward an 'Un-Definition' of *Decadent* as Applied to British Literature of the Nineteenth Century," *Journal of Aesthetics and Art Criticism* 17 (1958): 85–92; 18 (1959): 258–64. See also Barbara Charlesworth, *Dark Passages: The Decadent Consciousness in Victorian Literature* (Madison: Univ. of Wisconsin Press, 1965); William York Tindall, *Forces in Modern British Literature: 1885–1946* (New York: Alfred A. Knopf, 1947), p. 18; *Encyclopedia of Poetry and Poetics*, ed. Alex Preminger et al. (Princeton: Princeton Univ. Press, 1965), pp. 185–86.
8. As Tindall does when he claims that the word "does not imply value." *Forces in Modern British Literature*, p. 18.
9. *The Fleshly School of Poetry and Other Phenomena of the Day* (London: Strahan and Co., 1872), p. 1.

10. *British Poetry of the Eighteen-Nineties* (Garden City, N.Y.: Doubleday, Doran, 1937), p. xxxiii.

11. C. Williamson claimed that "the foundations of 'decadence' were laid when Keats identified truth with beauty": "The Decadents," *The Search Quarterly* 3 (1933): 68. Philippe Jullian perpetuates the association of Keats with decadence by mentioning *La Belle Dame sans Merci* in a discussion of Psychopathia Sexualis, in *Dreamers of Decadence: Symbolist Painters of the 1890s*, trans. Robert Baldick (New York: Praeger, 1971), pp. 106–107. Here the influence on Jullian seems to be Mario Praz.

12. *Decadence: A Philosophical Inquiry* (London: Faber and Faber, 1948), p. 53.

13. *The Eighteen Nineties: A Review of Arts and Ideas at the Close of the Nineteenth Century*, rev. ed. (New York: Alfred A. Knopf, 1922), p. 59.

14. I am not suggesting that this is a correct reading of Pater's intentions. He made assumptions about a cultivated reader or audience for art which would eliminate the necessity to consider the relationship of quantity of experience to quality. Objectively, however, his essay on the Renaissance points to a philosophical dilemma which would be intensified as time went on.

15. The *Erotic in Literature: A Historical Survey of Pornography as Delightful as It Is Indiscreet* (New York: Julian Messner, 1961), p. 10.

16. Ibid., p. 179.

17. *The Other Victorians: A Study of Sexuality and Pornography in Mid-Nineteenth-Century England* (New York: Basic Books, 1966), pp. 277–78. Since the publication of Marcus's book many essays have appeared dealing with the same questions, some disagreeing with his conclusions. His conception of pornotopia, however, makes his study the most useful for my purposes. For more recent discussions, see Douglas A. Hughes, ed., *Perspectives on Pornography* (New York: St. Martin's Press, 1970).

18. Francis Jacques Sypher, Jr., "Swinburne and Wagner," in *VP* 9 (1971): 165–83, argues that the theme of ennui used by Swinburne in *Laus Veneris* came from Wagner's *Tannhäuser*. I believe, however, that Heine's influence on Swinburne could be profitably explored. An important link between them was Lord Houghton.

19. *The Life of Algernon Charles Swinburne* (London: Macmillan, 1917), p. 141.

20. *Contemporary Review*, Oct. 1871, p. 338. The passage was cut out of Buchanan's revised version of the essay [see n. 9 above].

21. Introduction, *VP* 9 (1971). The volume is devoted to Swinburne.

22. *The Swinburne Letters*, ed. Cecil Y. Lang (New Haven: Yale Univ. Press, 1959), 1: 51–52.

23. *The Swinburne Letters* (1960), 3: 168–69.

24. See Julian Baird, "Swinburne, Sade, and Blake: The Pleasure-Pain Paradox," *VP* 9 (1971): 63; Jerome J. McGann, " 'Ave atque Vale': An Introduction to Swinburne," ibid., p. 156. A more traditional interpretation of Swinburne's Venus and aestheticism is given by Leonard M. Findlay, "Swinburne and Tennyson," ibid., pp. 217–36.

25. "Dedicatory Epistle," *Swinburne Replies; Notes on Poems and Reviews,*

Under the Microscope, Dedicatory Epistle, ed. Clyde K. Hyder (Syracuse: Syracuse Univ. Press, 1966), p. 98.

26. "Notes on Poems and Reviews," *Swinburne Replies,* p. 26.

27. *Swinburne Letters,* 1: 99.

28. "Gosse's *Swinburne,* 'The Triumph of Time,' and the Context of 'Les Noyades,' " *VP 9 (1971):* 95–110.

29. Marvel Shmiefsky, "Swinburne's Anti-Establishment Poetics," ibid., pp. 261–76. Shmiefsky is applying to *aestheticism* the same principles applied to *decadence* by those who wished to make the latter a descriptive rather than pejorative term [see n. 7 above].

30. Quoted in Harry W. Rudman, *Italian Nationalism and English Letters: Figures of the Risorgimento and Victorian Men of Letters* (London: George Allen and Unwin, 1940), p. 145.

31. For reviews of *Songs before Sunrise,* see Clyde K. Hyder, *Swinburne: The Critical Heritage* (New York: Barnes and Noble, 1970).

32. *Aubrey Beardsley: The Clown, the Harlequin, the Pierrot of His Age* (New York: Simon and Schuster, 1927), p. 178.

33. "Aubrey Beardsley, Man of Letters," *Romantic Mythologies,* ed. Ian Fletcher (New York : Barnes and Noble, 1967), p. 245.

34. Ibid., p. 266, n. 9. That I differ with Lavers on some points in no way lessens my admiration for her essay, which is rare for being an extended discussion of *The Story of Venus and Tannhaüuser.*

35. *Under the Hill: Or the Story of Venus and Tannhäuser* (London: New English Library, 1966), p. 97.

36. *The Other Victorians,* p. 279.

37. *The Beardsley Period: An Essay in Perspective* (1925; reprint ed., New York: Cooper Square, 1969), p. 194.

38. *The Eighteen Nineties,* p. 114.

39. *The Beardsley Period,* p. 195.

40. *The Shores of Light: A Literary Chronicle of the Twenties and Thirties* (New York: Farrar, Straus and Young, 1952), p. 71.

41. *The Letters of Aubrey Beardsley,* ed. Henry Maas, J. L. Duncan, and W. G. Good (Rutherford: Fairleigh Dickinson Univ. Press, 1970), p. 79.

42. Beardsley's letters, unlike Keats's and Tieck's, for example, reveal no general ambiguity toward the worth of art or the artist's role in the world.

43. *Letters of Aubrey Beardsley,* p. 249.

44. Ibid., p. 177.

45. Ibid., p. 439.

46. *The Aesthetics of Pornography* (New York: Herder and Herder, 1971), p. 62.

CHAPTER 10: THE NEW SOCIETY

1. There is some critical argument about whether or not Morris is to be considered a Marxist. Paul Thompson notes that he read *Capital* twice and that it "should be said here that stories, such as those recorded by Bruce Glasier in his *William*

Morris and the Early Days of the Socialist Movement, which portray Morris as hostile to Marx, are not seriously credible," *The Work of William Morris* (New York: Viking, 1967), p. 230. My later discussion will focus on a dialectical view which indicates that at least in my context Morris's views are consistent with Marxism.

2. "The Poetry of William Morris," *Views and Reviews* (1908; reprint ed., Freeport, N.Y.: Books for Libraries, 1968), p. 71.

3. See Oscar Maurer, Jr., "William Morris and the Poetry of Escape," *Nineteenth-Century Studies*, ed. Herbert Davis (Ithaca: Cornell Univ. Press, 1940), for a survey of the critical reception of *The Earthly Paradise*.

4. *Mythology and the Romantic Tradition* [chap. 3, n. 3], p. 326.

5. "The Poetic Maturing of William Morris: From 'The Earthly Paradise' to 'The Pilgrims of Hope,' " *Brno Studies in English* 5 (1964): 5–212. See also her review of E. P. Thompson's *William Morris: Romantic to Revolutionary* (New York: Monthly Review, 1962): "Some Remarks on E. P. Thompson's Opinion of the Poetry of William Morris," *Philologica Pragensia* 3 (1960): 168–78; and "The Aesthetic Opinions of William Morris," *Comparative Literature Studies* 4 (1967): 409–24.

6. Although I generally admire Kocmanová's works, that she sees the theme of the "justification of love" as the main point of *The Hill of Venus* and that she regrets the return to the Venusberg motif at the end of *The Earthly Paradise* ("Poetic Maturing," p. 178) are for me evidence that marks the limitation of a Marxist approach to Morris's poetry.

7. *Hopes and Fears for Art* (Boston: Roberts Bros., 1882), p. 201.

8. Ibid., pp. 45–46.

9. Ibid., p. 173.

10. Ibid., p. 80.

11. Ibid., p. 175.

12. Ibid., p. 13.

13. Ibid., pp. 9–10.

14. *Fleet Street Eclogues* (London: Elkin Mathews and John Lane, 1893), p. 81.

15. Ibid., pp. 4–5.

16. *John Davidson: Poet of Armageddon* (New Haven: Yale Univ. Press, 1961), pp. 452–53.

17. *The Testament of John Davidson* (London: Grant Richards, 1908), pp. 28–29.

18. Ibid., p. 118.

19. Ibid., p. 67.

20. *A Second Series of Fleet Street Eclogues* (London: John Lane, 1896), pp. 7–8.

21. *Testament*, p. 133.

22. *Second Series of Fleet Street Eclogues*, pp. 9–10.

23. *John Davidson*, p. 426.

24. *The White Goddess* [chap. 1, n. 44], p. 374.

25. The phrase "forever young" may also be an echo from the *Ode on a Grecian Urn*. In Keats's poem, however, the words are in part ironic, since the price paid for immortality is infinite frustration.

CHAPTER 11: ARTIST AND PHILISTINE

1. *Yeats* (New York: Oxford Univ. Press, 1970), a book which closely analyzes *Oisin*. Others are Charles Berryman, "*W. B. Yeats: Design of Opposites*" (New York: Exposition Press, 1967); Patty Gurd, *The Early Poetry of William Butler Yeats* (Lancaster, Pa.: 1916); Amy G. Stock, *W. B. Yeats: His Poetry and Thought* (Cambridge, Eng.: The University Press, 1961); John Unterecker, *A Reader's Guide to William Butler Yeats* (New York: Noonday Press, 1959).

2. I will give book 2 only passing mention because I found it unrelated to the themes of my study, except insofar as Oisin's need for action reflects his unwillingness to exist merely as Niamh's lover in fairyland.

3. *W. B. Yeats: Letters to Katharine Tynan*, ed. R. McHugh (New York: McMullen Books, 1953), p. 47.

4. For a discussion of similarities between the poets, see Malcolm Magaw, "Yeats and Keats: The Poetics of Romanticism," *Bucknell Review* 13 (1965): 87–96.

5. See Alex Zwerdling, "W. B. Yeats: Variations on the Visionary Quest," *Univ. of Toronto Quarterly* 30 (1960): 72–85.

6. W. B. Yeats, *The Celtic Twilight* (London: Lawrence and Bullen, 1893), pp. 109, 114.

7. "Per Amica Silentia Lunae," *Mythologies* (New York: Macmillan, 1959), p. 331.

8. Ibid., p. 337.

9. "Ireland and the Arts," *Essays and Introductions* (New York: Macmillan, 1961), p. 203.

10. *Celtic Twilight*, p. 6.

11. "Cuchulain of Muirthemne," *Explorations* (New York: Macmillan, 1962), p. 8.

12. "A General Introduction for My Work," *Essays and Introductions*, pp. 510–11.

13. Yeats constantly revised his poems, even the earliest. A major revision was made in *Oisin* after its first appearance; thereafter, changes were less substantive. My text, from *Poems* (London: T. Fisher Unwin, 1895), is the earliest version after its first revision. Since my discussion focuses on Yeats's early attitudes toward aestheticism, I use an early version so that there can be no mistake about a particular passage being added in subsequent years. I use the later name, Niamh, however, for the earlier Neave, since I refer to her elsewhere in my book by the name she has in Yeats's final edition of his poetry.

14. For all changes made in *Oisin*, consult *The Variorum Edition of the Poems of W. B. Yeats*, ed. Peter Allt and Russell K. Alspach (New York: Macmillan, 1957).

15. *Celtic Twilight*, pp. 94–95.

16. A. Norman Jeffares has traced these lines to Blake's *Jerusalem*: "For I will make their places of Love and joy excrementitious." *A Commentary on the Collected Poems of W. B. Yeats* (Stanford: Stanford Univ. Press, 1968), p. 376. This does not necessarily invalidate the analogy to Keats's ode; indeed, a case could be made for the similarities between Keats and Blake, the dialectics of both appealing to Yeats.

Moreover, the lines in *Melancholy* are related both to one of Yeats's own major themes and to the source of his praise of Keats.

17. This may show some influence of Swinburne's *Genesis:*

> For if death were not, then should growth not be,
> Change, nor the life of good nor evil things;
> Nor were there night at all nor light to see,
> Nor water of sweet nor water of bitter springs. [SP 2:182]

18. *The Poetry and Prose of William Blake*, ed. David V. Erdman (New York: Doubleday, 1965), p. 35.

19. *The Letters of W. B. Yeats*, ed. A. A. Wade (London: Rupert Hart-Davis, 1954), pp. 608–609.

20. Ibid., p. 608.

21. Ibid., p. 546. Yeats is a less perceptive reader of Swinburne than of Keats.

22. Ibid., p. 220.

23. I know of no direct influence between Yeats and Heine. But Heine's works were widely translated into English and he enjoyed a lively reputation in England.

24. *Letters to the New Island*, ed. Horace Reynolds (Cambridge, Mass.: Harvard Univ. Press, 1934), p. 146.

25. *Prose and Poetry by Heinrich Heine* [chap. 6, n. 4], p. 86.

26. *The Enchanted* (New York: Samuel French, 1950), p. 8.

27. For the text and commentary on Giraudoux's essay, see Laurence Le Sage, "*Die Einheit von Fouqué's Undine*: An Unpublished Essay in German by Jean Giraudoux," *Romantic Review* 42 (1951): 122–34.

28. For a study of *Ondine*, see Antoine Fongaro, "Ambigüité d'Ondine," *Letterature moderne* 12 (1962): 32–46. To compare the undine motif in Fouqué and Giraudoux, see J. J. Anstett, "Ondine de Fouqué à Giraudoux," *Les Langues modernes* 44 (1950): 81–94; Richard Beilharz, "Ondine dans l'oeuvre de Giraudoux et de la Motte Fouqué," *Zeitschrift für französische Sprach und Literatur* 80 (1970): 323–34.

CHAPTER 12: RECAPITULATION

1. "Sufferings and Greatness of Richard Wagner," *Essays of Three Decades*, trans. H. T. Lowe-Porter (New York: Alfred A. Knopf, 1948), pp. 307–08; *Gesammelte Werke*, 9:363.

2. *Thomas Mann's Novel Der Zauberberg: A Study* (New York: D. Appleton-Century, 1933), p. 45.

3. See, for example, Weigand, *Thomas Mann's Novel Der Zauberberg*, pp. 97–98; Harry Slochower, "Bourgeois Liberalism: Thomas Mann's *Magic Mountain*," *Three Ways of Modern Man* (New York: International Publishers, 1937), p. 70; William Blissett, "Thomas Mann: The Last Wagnerite," *Germanic Review* 35 (1960): 58. On the other hand, Henry Hatfield says that the "talent in Mann for dealing with the non-rational and 'otherworldly' . . . is too often ignored." *Thomas Mann: An Introduction to His Fiction* (Norfolk, Conn.: New Directions, 1951), p. 21.

4. When Mann began to read English poetry, Keats and Blake were the

poets he favored. In *Doctor Faustus* Adrian Leverkühn composes music for Keats's odes.

5. See *The Jewish Encyclopedia*, ed. Isidore Singer et al. (New York: Funk and Wagnalls, 1912), 8: 87–88.

6. *Dialectics and Nihilism: Essays on Lessing, Nietzsche, Mann, and Kafka* (Amherst: Univ. of Massachusetts Press, 1966), p. 168.

7. *Thomas Mann's Novel Der Zauberberg*, p. 3. For a survey of the dialectical opposites in the novel, see Johannes A. Gaertner, "Dialectical Thought in Thomas Mann's *The Magic Mountain*," *German Quarterly* 38 (1965): 605–18.

8. For a comparison of Mann and Yeats, see Leonard Conversi, "Mann, Yeats and the Truth of Art," *Yale Review* 56 (1967): 506–23.

9. In "Private Thoughts," Yeats described the conception behind his gyres: "Opposites are everywhere face to face, dying each other's life, living each other's death." *Explorations* [chap. 11, n. 11], p. 430.

10. Trans. H. T. Lowe-Porter, in *The Criterion* 10 (1931): 394; *Deutsche Ansprache: Ein Appel an die Vernunft* (Berlin: S. Fischer, 1930), pp. 7–8.

11. For a list of discussions of *The Magic Mountain*, consult Klaus W. and Ilsedore B. Jonas, *Fifty Years of Thomas Mann Studies: A Bibliography of Criticism*, 2 vols. (Minneapolis: Univ. of Minnesota Press, 1955–67).

CONCLUSION

1. *Prose and Poetry by Heinrich Heine* [chap. 6, n. 4], p. 27.

2. For a study of the Lorelei "legend," see Hermann Seeliger, *Die Loreleysage in Dichtung und Musik* (Leipzig: August Hoffmann, 1898).

3. A translation of the Brentano ballad can be found in *An Anthology of German Poetry from Hölderlin to Rilke*, ed. Angel Flores (Garden City, N.Y.: Doubleday Anchor, 1960).

4. "Sufferings and Greatness of Richard Wagner" [chap. 12, n. 1], p. 313; *Gesammelte Werke*, 9: 371.

5. *Ballads and Lyrics of Old France* [intro., n. 1], pp. 146–47.

 Selected Bibliography

Abrams, M. H. *The Mirror and the Lamp: Romantic Theory and the Critical Tradition.* New York: Oxford Univ. Press, 1953.

Albérès, René Marill. *Esthétique et morale chez Jean Giraudoux.* Paris: Nizet, 1962.

Applejoy, Petronius. "A View of John Davidson against a 'Nineties Background." *The Catholic World,* Feb. 1942, pp. 552–61.

Armstrong, John. *The Paradise Myth.* London: Oxford Univ. Press, 1969.

Ayrault, Roger. *La Genèse du romantisme allemand; situation spirituelle de l'allemagne dans la deuxième moitié du XVIIIe siècle.* 2 vols. Paris: Aubier, 1961.

Béguin, Albert. *L'Âme romantique et le rêve: essai sur le romantisme allemand et la poésie française.* 2d ed. Paris: J. Corti, 1946.

———. *Gérard de Nerval.* Paris: J. Corti, 1945.

Blunt, Hugh F. "Aubrey Beardsley: A Study in Conversion." *The Catholic World,* March 1932, pp. 641–50.

Brennan, Joseph G. *Thomas Mann's World.* New York: Columbia Univ. Press, 1942.

Briggs, K. M. "The English Fairies." *Folk-Lore* 68 (1957): 270–87.

Brod, Max. *Heinrich Heine: The Artist in Revolt (1934).* Trans. Joseph Witriol. London: Vallentine Mitchell, 1956.

Brophy, Brigid. "The Perversity of Aubrey Beardsley." *The Atlantic,* Feb. 1968, pp. 61–67.

Burkhard, Arthur. "Thomas Mann's Appraisal of the Poet." *PMLA* 46 (1931): 880–916.

Chandler, Alice. "The Quarrel of the Ancients and Moderns: Peacock and the Medieval Revival." *Bucknell Review* 13 (1965): 39–50.

Chew, Samuel C. *Swinburne.* 1929. Reprint. Hamden, Conn.: Archon Books, 1966.

Connolly, Thomas E. *Swinburne's Theory of Poetry.* Albany: State Univ. of New York, 1964.

Daemmrich, Horst S. "Mann's Portrait of the Artist: Archetypal Patterns." *Bucknell Review* 14 (1966): 27–43.

Dale, Robert C. *The Poetics of Prosper Mérimée.* The Hague: Mouton, 1966.

Danton, George H. *The Nature Sense in the Writings of Ludwig Tieck.* New York: Columbia Univ. Press, 1907.

Dottin, Paul. "Swinburne et les Dieux." *Revue Anglo-Americaine* 2 (1925): 419–27.

Dubruck, Alfred. *Gérard de Nerval and the German Heritage.* The Hague: Mouton, 1965.

Selected Bibliography

Eckhoff, Lorentz. *The Aesthetic Movement in English Literature*. Oslo: Oslo Univ. Press, 1959.

Eickhorst, William. *Decadence in German Fiction*. Denver: A. Swallow, 1953.

Ellmann, Richard. *The Identity of Yeats*. London: Macmillan, 1954.

————. *Yeats: The Man and the Masks*. New York: Macmillan, 1948.

Eshleman, Lloyd W. *A Victorian Rebel: The Life of William Morris*. New York: Charles Scribner's, 1940.

Étienne, Louis. "Le Paganisme poétique en Angleterre: John Keats et Algernon Charles Swinburne." *Revue des Deux Mondes*, May 1867, pp. 291–318.

Fairley, Barker. *Heinrich Heine: An Interpretation*. Oxford: The Clarendon Press, 1954.

Farmer, Albert J. *Le Mouvement esthétique et "décadent" en Angleterre*. Paris: H. Champion, 1931.

Faulkner, Peter. *William Morris and W. B. Yeats*. Dublin: Dolmen Press, 1962.

Freeman, Alexander M. *Thomas Love Peacock: A Critical Study*. London: M. Secker, 1911.

Fries, Othmar. *Richard Wagner und die deutsche Romantik, Versuch einer Einordnung*. Zurich: Atlantis, 1952.

Fuerst, Norbert. *The Victorian Age of German Literature*. University Park: Pennsylvania State Univ. Press, 1966.

Gallas, K. R. "Mérimée et la théorie de l'art pour l'art." *Neophilologus 5 (1919–20)*: 11–21; 105–12.

Gaunt, William. *The Aesthetic Adventure*. New York: Harcourt, Brace, 1945.

Gloor, Arthur. *E. T. A. Hoffmann: Der Dichter der entwurzelten Geistigkeit*. Zurich: n. p., 1947.

Görte, Erna. *Der junge Tieck und die Aufklärung*. Berlin: E. Ebering, 1926.

Grennan, Margaret R. *William Morris: Medievalist and Revolutionary*. New York: King's Crown Press, 1945.

Grierson, H. "Fairies—from Shakespeare to Mr. Yeats." *Dublin Review* 148(1911): 271–84.

Guder, G. "Joseph von Eichendorff and Reality." *Modern Languages* (London) 39 (1958): 89–95.

Hamburger, Michael. *Contraries: Studies in German Literature*. New York: E. P. Dutton, 1970.

Hartland, E. S. *The Science of Fairy Tales: An Inquiry into Fairy Mythology*. London: Walter Scott, 1891.

Hatfield, Henry. *Aesthetic Paganism in German Literature: From Winckelmann to the Death of Goethe*. Cambridge, Mass.: Harvard Univ. Press, 1964.

Heller, Erich. *The Artist's Journey into the Interior and Other Essays*. New York: Random House, 1965.

————. *The Ironic German: A Study of Thomas Mann*. London: Secker and Warburg, 1958.

Henderson, Philip. *William Morris: His Life, Work and Friends*. New York: McGraw-Hill, 1967.

Hirschbach, Frank D. *The Arrow and the Lyre: A Study of the Role of Love in the Works of Thomas Mann*. The Hague: Nijhoff, 1955.

Selected Bibliography

Hoare, Dorothy M. *The Works of Morris and of Yeats in Relation to Early Saga Literature.* Cambridge, Eng.: The University Press, 1937.

Hough, Graham. *The Last Romantics.* London: Duckworth, 1949.

Hyde, H. Montgomery. *A History of Pornography.* New York: Farrar, Straus and Giroux, 1965.

Inskip, Donald. *Jean Giraudoux: The Making of a Dramatist.* London: Oxford Univ. Press, 1958.

Johnstone, George H. *Prosper Mérimée: A Mask and a Face.* New York: E. P. Dutton, 1927.

Kamenetsky, Christa. "'Thomas Mann's Concept of the 'Bürger.'" *College Language Assn. Journal* 5 (1962): 184–94.

Keller, Oscar. *Eichendorffs Kritik der Romantik.* Zurich: Juris, 1954.

Kiessling, Arthur. *Richard Wagner und die Romantik.* Leipzig: Xenien, 1916.

Kunz, J. *Eichendorff, Höhepunkt und Krise des Spätromantik.* Oberursel: Altkönig, 1951.

Lafourcade, Georges. *La Jeunesse de Swinburne: 1837–1867.* 2 vols. Paris: Les Belles lettres, 1928.

———. *Swinburne's Hyperion and Other Poems with an Essay on Swinburne and Keats.* London: Faber and Gwyer, 1928.

Le Gallienne, Richard. *The Romantic '90s.* Garden City, N. Y.: Doubleday, Page, 1925.

Levin, Harry. *The Broken Column: A Study in Romantic Hellenism.* Cambridge, Mass.: Harvard Univ. Press, 1931.

Lock, D. R. "John Davidson and the Poetry of the 'Nineties.'" *London Quarterly and Holborn Review* 161 (1936): 338–52.

Loose, Gerhard. "Thomas Mann and the Problem of Decadence." *University of Colorado Studies,* series B, 1 (1941): 345–75.

Lukács, György. *Essays on Thomas Mann.* Trans. Stanley Mitchell. London: Merlin Press, 1964.

Lussky, Alfred E. *Tieck's Approach to Romanticism.* Borna-Leipzig: R. Noske, 1925.

McGann, Jerome J. *Swinburne: An Experiment in Criticism.* Chicago: Univ. of Chicago Press, 1972.

Mackail, J. W. *The Life of William Morris.* 2 vols. London: Longmans, Green, 1911.

MacNeice, Louis. *The Poetry of W. B. Yeats.* London: Oxford Univ. Press, 1941.

March, George. "Thomas Mann and the Novel of Decadence." *Sewanee Review* 37 (1929): 490–503.

Martin, John S. "Circean Seduction in Three Works by Thomas Mann." *MLN* 78 (1963): 346–52.

Mayoux, Jean Jacques. *Un Épicurien anglais, Thomas Love Peacock.* Paris: Nizet, 1933.

Meyer, Kuno, trans. *Voyage of Bran, Son of Febal to the Land of the Living* (with an Essay upon the Irish Vision of the Happy Other World and the Celtic Doctrine of Rebirth, by Alfred Nutt). 2 vols. London: n. p., 1895–97.

Minder, Robert. *Un Poète romantique allemand: Ludwig Tieck.* Paris: Les Belles lettres, 1936.

Mistler, Jean. *Hoffmann le fantastique.* Paris: Michel, 1950.

Möbus, Gerhard. *Der andere Eichendorff: zur Deutung der Dichtung Joseph von Eichendorffs.* Osnabrück: A. Fromm, 1960.

Mollenauer, R. R. "Three 'Spätromantiker' on Romanticism: Hoffmann, Heine, and Eichendorff." Ph.D. dissertation, University of Indiana, 1960.

Moore, John R. "Yeats as a Last Romantic." *Virginia Quarterly Review* 37 (1961): 432–49.

Moos, Paul. *Richard Wagner als Äesthetiker: Versuch einer kritischen Darstellung.* Berlin: Schuster and Laeffler, 1906.

Natan, Alex, ed. *German Men of Letters: Twelve Literary Essays.* Philadelphia: Dufour, 1962.

Negus, Kenneth. *E. T. A. Hoffmann's Other World: The Romantic Author and His "New Mythology."* Philadelphia: Univ. of Pennsylvania Press, 1965.

Neider, Charles. "Thomas Mann: The Artist as Bourgeois." *Rocky Mountain Review* 9 (1945): 167–76.

Newman, Ernest. *The Wagner Operas.* New York: Alfred A. Knopf, 1949.

Orrick, James B. "Hebraism and Hellenism." *The New Adelphi* 2 (1928): 50–56.

Oswald, Victor A., Jr. "Thomas Mann and the Mermaid: A Note on Constructivistic Music." *MLN* 65 (1950): 171–75.

Pascal, Roy. *The German Sturm und Drang.* Manchester: Manchester Univ. Press, 1953.

Paton, Lucy A. *Studies in the Fairy Mythology of Arthurian Romance.* Boston: Ginn and Co., 1903.

Peters, Robert L. *The Crowns of Apollo: Swinburne's Principles of Literature and Art.* Detroit: Wayne State Univ. Press, 1965.

Porterfield, Allen W. *An Outline of German Romanticism: 1766–1866.* Boston: Ginn and Co., 1914.

Prawer, Siegbert, ed. *The Romantic Period in Germany: Essays by Members of the London University Institute of Germanic Studies.* New York: Schocken Books, 1970.

Priestley, J. B. *Thomas Love Peacock.* London: Macmillan, 1927.

Raymond, Agnes G. *Jean Giraudoux: The Theatre of Victory and Defeat.* Amherst: Univ. of Massachusetts Press, 1966.

Reymond, Berthe. "Le Mythe féminin dans l'oeuvre de Nerval." *Études de Lettres* (Univ. of Lausanne) 6 (1963): 246–69.

Rhodes, S. A. *Gérard de Nerval, 1808–1855: Poet, Traveler, Dreamer.* New York: Philosophical Library, 1951.

Ricci, Jean F. *E. T. A. Hoffmann, l'homme et l'oeuvre.* Paris: J. Corti, 1947.

Robertson, John G. *The Gods of Greece in German Poetry.* Oxford: The Clarendon Press, 1924.

Rosenblatt, *L'Idée de l'art pour l'art dans la litterature anglaise pendant la période victorienne.* Paris: H. Champion, 1931.

Rutland, William R. *Swinburne: A Nineteenth Century Hellene.* Oxford: B. Blackwell, 1931.

Sagave, Pierre P. *Réalité sociale et idéologie religieuse dans les romans de Thomas Mann: Les Buddenbrook, La montagne magique, Le docteur Faustus.* Paris: Les Belles lettres, 1954.

Sandor, A. I. *The Exile of Gods: Interpretation of a Theme and a Technique in the Work of Heinrich Heine.* The Hague: Mouton, 1967.

Selected Bibliography

Savage, D. S. "The Aestheticism of W. B. Yeats." *Kenyon Review* 7 (1945): 118–34.

Schmidt, Arno. *Fouqué und einige seiner Zeitgenossen: Biographischer Versuch.* Stahlberg: Karlsruhe, 1958.

Seidlin, Oskar. "Eichendorff's Symbolic Landscape." *PMLA* 72 (1957): 645–61.

Silz, Walter. *Early German Romanticism: Its Founders and Heinrich von Kleist.* Cambridge, Mass.: Harvard Univ. Press, 1929.

Spann, Meno. "Exoticism and Heinrich Heine." *SP* 30 (1933): 86–102.

Spoerri, Theophil. "Mérimée and the Short Story." *Yale French Studies,* no. 4 (1949), pp. 3–11.

Staiger, Emil. "Ludwig Tieck und der Ursprung der deutschen Romantik." *Neue Rundschau* 81 (1960): 596–622.

Stigand, William. *The Life, Work, and Opinions of Heinrich Heine.* 2 vols. New York: J. W. Bouton, 1880.

Stockley, V. *German Literature as Known in England: 1750–1830.* London: G. Routledge and Sons, 1929.

Strich, Fritz. *Klassik und Romantik: Oder Vollendung und Unendlichkeit.* Munich: Beck, 1924.

———. *Die Mythologie in der deutschen Literatur von Klopstock bis Wagner.* 2 vols. Halle: M. Niemeyer, 1910.

Symons, Arthur. *Aubrey Beardsley.* London: At the Sign of the Unicorn, 1898.

———. "The Decadent Movement in Literature," *Dramatis Personae.* Indianapolis: Bobbs-Merrill, 1923.

Thalmann, Marianne. *Probleme der Dämonie in Ludwig Tiecks Schriften.* Weimar: A. Duncker, 1919.

———. *The Romantic Fairy Tale: Seeds of Surrealism.* Trans. Mary B. Corcoran. Ann Arbor: Univ. of Michigan Press, 1964.

Thomas, R. Hinton. *Thomas Mann: The Mediation of Art.* Oxford: The Clarendon Press, 1963.

Thompson, E. P. *William Morris: Romantic to Revolutionary.* London: Lawrence and Wishart, 1955.

Thompson, Stith. *The Folktale.* New York: The Dryden Press, 1946.

Untermeyer, Louis. *Heinrich Heine, Paradox and Poet.* 2 vols. New York: Harcourt, Brace, 1937.

Van Doren, Carl. *The Life of Thomas Love Peacock.* New York: E. P. Dutton, 1911.

Vendler, Helen Hennessey. "Yeats's Changing Metaphors for the Other World." *Modern Drama* 7 (1964): 308–21.

Wehrli, René. *Eichendorffs Erlebnis und Gestaltung der Sinnenwelt.* Frauenfeld: Huber, 1938.

Weintraub, Stanley. *Beardsley: A Biography.* New York: G. Braziller, 1967.

Willoughby, L. A. *The Romantic Movement in Germany.* London: Oxford Univ. Press, 1930.

Wilson, Edmund. *Axel's Castle: A Study in the Imaginative Literature of 1870–1930.* 1931. Reprint. New York: Charles Scribner's, 1943.

Wormley, Stanton L. *Heine in England.* Chapel Hill: Univ. of North Carolina Press, 1943.

Zeydel, Edwin H. *Ludwig Tieck and England: A Study in the Literary Relations of Germany and England during the Early Nineteenth Century.* Princeton: Princeton Univ. Press, 1931.
Zwerdling, Alex. *Yeats and the Heroic Ideal.* New York: New York Univ. Press, 1965.

Index

Index

Lawrence, D. H., 94
The Legend of Urashima, 23
Leland, Charles, 119
Lessing, Gotthold Ephraim, 132
Letter on Music. See Wagner, Richard
Letters to an Unknown. See Mérimée, Prosper
Letters to the New Island. See Yeats, William Butler
The Life and Death of Jason. See Morris, William
Ligeia (Poe, Edgar Allan), 24
Lilith, 254, 255, 265
Literature and music, 40, 93, 257. *See also* *Gesamtkunstwerk*
The Little Mermaid. See Andersen, Hans Christian; Giraudoux, Jean; Mann, Thomas
Loathly lady motif: 32, 56, 277n18; in John Davidson, 213, 215–16. *See also* Mélusine legend
Lohengrin. See Wagner, Richard
Lokis. See Mérimée, Prosper
Loomis, Roger Sherman, 20
Lore Lay. See Brentano, Clemens
Lorelei. See Heine, Heinrich
Lorelei, legend of, 268–71, 293n2
Los Desdichados. See Nerval, Gérardde
Loth, David, 173
The Lovesong of J. Alfred Prufrock (Eliot, T. S.), 240
Lysistrata. See Beardsley, Aubrey Vincent

MacCulloch, John A., 38
MacFall, Haldane, 193
The Magic Ring. See Fouqué, Friedrich de la Motte
The Magic Mountain. See Mann, Thomas
Mandeville's Travels, 35
Mann, Thomas, 26, 166, 170, 245; compared to Keats, 18, 42, 253–55, 261–62, 265; influenced by Andersen, 34, 40–41, 269–70; and the Philistine, 247, 251, 260; compared to Heine, 247, 256, 259, 260, 261, 262; and the nineteenth cen-

tury, 247; compared to Tieck, 249, 250, 251, 255, 265; compared to Hoffmann, 251, 255; theme of time in, 252–53, 263–64; compared to Eichendorff, 249, 256, 259, 262; compared to Yeats, 256, 265; compared to Swinburne, 263–64, 265; dialectics in, 256, 267; romanticism vs. classicism in, 256 passim; and irrationalism, 256–57; and music, 257; the Hebraic-Hellenic dichotomy in, 258–63; and decadence, 263–64; compared to Fouqué, 265; compared to Morris, 265. Works: "An Appeal to Reason," 256–57, 266–67; *Doctor Faustus*, 34, 40–41, 53, 255, 269–70; *Felix Krull*, 268–69, 270; *The Magic Mountain*, 15, 124, 246, 247–67; *Royal Highness*, 41; "Sufferings and Greatness of Richard Wagner," 247, 270
The Marble Statue. See Eichendorff, Joseph von.
Marcus, Steven, *The Other Victorians*, 173–74, 194, 196
Marcuse, Herbert, 88, 90
Marie, Aristide, 153–54
Marlowe, Christopher, 269
The Marriage of Heaven and Hell. See Blake, William
Marxist attack on aestheticism, 39
Mazzini, Giuseppe, 191, 263–64
Meditations in Time of Civil War. See Yeats, William Butler
Mélusine, legend of: in French literature, 19, 277n20; in Nerval, 19, 150, 154–55; summarized, 32; and Tannhäuser legend, 32, 35, 39; and "quest for a soul" motif, 34, 39; as source for *Undine*, 33, 34, 50, 55, 56, 242
Merciles Beaute. See Chaucer, Geoffrey
Mérimée, Prosper: and the Venusring story, 25, 140–45; aversion to marriage, 134, 135, 141–45; Hebraic-Hellenic dichotomy in, 142, 144; and Philistinism, 142, 143, 144; compared to James, 145; compared to Burgess, 146, 147. Works: *The Blue Chamber*, 141; *The Etruscan*

Barbara Fass is assistant professor of English at Queens College, City University of New York. She received her B.A. in 1964 from Queens College, and her M.A. and Ph.D. from New York University in 1965 and 1968 respectively.

The manuscript was edited by Marguerite C. Wallace. The book was designed by Joanne Kinney. The typeface for the text is Electra designed by W. A. Dwiggins in 1935; and the display face is Palatino designed by Hermann Zapf in 1950.

The text is printed on Nashoba Text paper and the book is bound in Columbia Mills' Llamique cloth. Manufactured in the United States of America.